VEGETARIANISM:
An Annotated Bibliography

by

JUDITH C. DYER

The Scarecrow Press, Inc.
Metuchen, N.J., & London
1982

Library of Congress Cataloging in Publication Data

Dyer, Judith C., 1947-
    Vegetarianism : an annotated bibliography.

    Includes indexes.
    1. Vegetarianism--Bibliography. I. Title.
Z5776.V44D93 [TX392]   016.6132'62   82-3159
ISBN 0-8108-1532-X   AACR2

For that rascal, Dan

CONTENTS

PREFACE

Introduction

Vegetarianism is the dietary philosophy and practice of abstaining from the consumption of animal flesh, including beef, pork, poultry, fish and seafood. The term vegetarian was first used in the early 1840's, prior to which vegetarians were known as Pythagoreans or simply flesh-abstainers.

Vegetarians generally belong to one of five groups, depending upon the degree to which animal foods are excluded from the diet. Lacto-ovo-vegetarians combine dairy products and eggs with a diet of vegetables, fruits, nuts, and grains. Lacto-vegetarians consume dairy products, but not eggs. Likewise, an ovo-vegetarian would eat eggs, but exclude dairy products.

Vegans, also known as strict vegetarians or pure vegetarians, exclude both dairy products and eggs, consuming a varied diet derived entirely from the plant kingdom. The vegan diet is founded on a humane philosophy of life desiring to minimize the exploitation and suffering of non-human animals. Thus, vegans avoid not only all foods of animal origin, but also products derived from animals, such as leather, wool, furs, silk, ivory, down, pearl, honey, and certain cosmetics and household items that contain animal ingredients or that are tested on animals.

Fruitarians extend the philosophy of non-exploitation to plants as well as animals. The fruitarian diet consists of just fruits, nuts, grains, that is, those parts of the plant that are cast off or dropped from the plant, and that do not involve the destruction of the plant itself.

The Zen macrobiotic diet is sometimes mistakenly considered a type of vegetarian diet. However, the early stages of the macrobiotic diet allow the consumption of flesh foods, namely poultry and fish. In contrast to the vegetarian and vegan diets, which encourage the consumption of a wide variety of plant foods, the macrobiotic diet limits the types and amounts of foods and liquids consumed, according to numerical ratings expressed in terms of yin and yang.

People become vegetarians primarily for health or ethical reasons, or a combination of the two. Those who are vegetarians for health considerations point out the link between the consumption of meat and other animal products and an array of chronic, degenerative diseases, including cardiovascular disease, cancer of the colon and breast, and osteoporosis. The ethical issues of the vegetarian diet focus on the morality of the slaughter of animals for food; the conditions of animals raised on intensive, factory-style farms; and the ecological consequences and economic inefficiency of livestock production, especially in view of the world hunger situation.

A Roper poll conducted in 1978 estimated that there were nine to ten million American vegetarians, with another forty to fifty million people in the United States who limit their consumption of meat.

The current popularity and widespread attention given to the principles and practice of vegetarianism may produce the erroneous impression that it is a mere fad: here today with great fanfare and visibility, but surely gone tomorrow. On the contrary, there has hardly been a period in recorded history which has not had articulate advocates of the meatless diet.

Such Eastern religions as Hinduism, Brahmanism, Buddhism, and Jainism have long regarded vegetarianism as a basic tenet, consistent with belief in the transmigration of souls, a concept also held by Pythagoras in the sixth century B.C. Pythagoras is generally recognized as the founder of the vegetarian movement. Other ancient Greek and Roman philosophers, scientists, and poets who are known to have advocated the vegetarian diet were Plotinus, Porphyry, Diogenes, Virgil, Ovid, and Horace.

Vegetarian philosophers and religious leaders of the early Christian era included Clement of Alexandria and St. Francis of Assisi. The Catholic Church kept the vegetarian philosophy alive until the Renaissance period, when it had such adherents as Leonardo da Vinci and Sir Isaac Newton.

Early British and American vegetarians included Alexander Pope, John Wesley, Benjamin Franklin, Percy Bysshe Shelley, Bronson Alcott, and Clara Barton.

The modern vegetarian movement began in 1809 with the vegetarian Bible Christian Church in Manchester, England. In 1847, the church founded a separate vegetarian society. In the meantime, the Bible Christian Church had also established itself in Philadelphia under the leadership of Reverend William Metcalfe. The movement quickly spread to other Western countries.

From the middle of the 19th century to the present, vegetarianism has flourished under the leadership of such figures as breakfast cereal developers John Harvey Kellogg, C. W. Post, and Sylvester Graham, as well as writers, social reformers and religious leaders, such as Upton Sinclair, Ellen G. White, Helena Blavatsky, and Mohandas Gandhi. Contemporary vegetarians include Nobel Prize winner Isaac Bashevis Singer, political activists Dick Gregory and Cesar Chavez, and celebrities Dennis Weaver, Susan St. James, Cloris Leachman, Steve Martin, and Marty Feldman, among many others.

About the Bibliography

Whether addressing philosophical or health issues, the writings on vegetarianism represent a rich and varied tradition. The purpose of this work is to bring these publications together by date and by subject for the use of those inquiring about the subject from a historical, ethical or medical standpoint, from the most light-hearted approach to the most serious. Through the years, vegetarianism has been alternately blamed for many conditions, including stuttering and left-handedness, and credited with the prevention and cure of a wide range of diseases. The moral issues it raises provoke intense reactions on both sides.

The types of material included in the bibliography are books, periodical articles, pamphlets, government documents, letters to editors, newspaper articles, and audio-visual productions. To be included, an entry must deal in some way with the vegetarian diet, regardless of point of view, or, conversely, with the pros and cons of the meat-based diet, since a major argument for vegetarianism assumes deleterious effects on the health from the consumption of meat.

Publications from earliest times through 1980 in all languages were collected through a combination of methods. Thousands of documents were searched through the use of more than fifty online bibliographic databases and over thirty abstracting and indexing sources not covered online.

Since publications of vegetarian and animal welfare organizations are not generally indexed in standard bibliographic sources, many documents were obtained directly from the organizations themselves. Reading lists of suggested materials provided by such organizations yielded additional materials not found elsewhere.

The Vegetarian Information Service based in Washington, D. C. was particularly supportive of this project. The American Vegan Society, the North American Vegetarian Society and the Vegan Society of the United Kingdom also provided assistance. The National Livestock and Meat Board sent its publication on the vegetarian diet as well.

Contact with the Historical Society of Pennsylvania yielded a number of valuable publications related to the Bible Christian Church and early vegetarian activities in the United States.

The journal Vegetarian Times and similar publications were scanned and indexed for citations not identified through other sources.

Most entries have been briefly annotated as an aid to the user in determining publications to be read in their entirety. Those entries without annotations were not available for examination. The current availability of the publications was not a criterion for inclusion.

This bibliography is an attempt, however humble, at completeness; therefore, very few types of publications were excluded from selection. Newspaper or journal reviews of vegetarian restaurants were not included, although book-length directories or guides to vegetarian restaurants were included. Articles containing only vegetarian recipes without supporting text were excluded. A compilation of English-language cookbooks is appended to the main body.

Publications dealing with the Zen macrobiotic diet were not sought. However, since the distinction between the two types of diet is frequently blurred in the literature, en-

x

tries having to do with the Zen macrobiotic diet were included if they had been indexed as a type of vegetarian diet. Otherwise, they were excluded.

The book is divided into two major parts: Early Works (up through 1959) and Recent Works (1960-1980). The two sections of Part I, pre-twentieth-century through 1899 and from 1900 through 1959, group together all types of subject matter (from philosophical discussions to medical studies), facilitating a historical study of the early writings on vegetarianism. Before extensive medical studies had been conducted on vegetarians, writers relied upon persuasiveness of logic and eloquence of style to sway their audiences. The comparatively few medical studies prior to 1960 stand out as pioneering research.

In Part II, recent works from 1960 through 1980 are divided into various subject headings broadly categorized as general interest, philosophy, and medical aspects of vegetarian diet. Copious cross-references direct the reader to related and earlier works.

A supplement to update material published from 1981 through 1985 may be undertaken, provided sufficient reader interest and author motivation are generated and maintained.

Acknowledgments

I would like to express unending gratitude to the people without whom this project would never have gotten off the ground: first, to my husband, Dan, whose high humor, patience, and prodding sustained me during the long hours of preparation of this manuscript; to Julia Hornbeck and Beth Heim in the Information Exchange Center of the Georgia Institute of Technology Library, whose professionalism and untiring efforts made it possible to obtain many of the documents contained herein; to my parents, Elsie and Jerry Clements, and my aunt Barbara Springfield, who came to my rescue when aspects of the manuscript began to get out of control; to many friends and relatives whose interest in the project convinced me in times of despair that it was all worthwhile and should be completed; and last, to the authors themselves, who down through the ages felt strongly enough about the subject to take the time to record their thoughts.

J. C. D.

PART I:

EARLY WORKS

1 Alcott, William Andrus. Vegetable diet: as sanctioned
by medical men, and by experience in all ages. Including a system of vegetable cookery. 2nd ed. New
York, Fowlers and Wells, 1849.
   Testimonials from numerous prominent individuals
on the positive physical and mental effects of a vegetarian diet; historical account of vegetarianism; anatomical, medical, political, economic and moral arguments.

2 Anon. Was ist Vegetarianismus? Eine Beleuchtung dieses
Universal Princips. Neustadt, n.p., 1855. (In German.)

3 Aquinas, Saint Thomas. "On killing living things and the
duty to love irrational creatures." In: Regan, Tom,
and Singer, Peter. Animal rights and human obligations. Englewood Cliffs, N.J., Prentice-Hall, 1976,
p. 118-121.
   Thirteenth-century theologian addresses questions
of the taking of life and the responsibilities toward
animals.

4 Beard, Sidney Hartnoll. Is flesh-eating morally defens-
ible? 7th ed. Providence, n.p., 1895.

5 Bennett, William. A letter to a friend, in reply to the
question, What is vegetarianism? London, Horsell,
Pitman, Gilpin, 1849.
   Analysis of biblical passages; considerations based
upon enjoyment of life, economy, health, humanity,
morality, religion.

6 Clubb, H. S. Visit of the Rev. Wm. Metcalfe, minister
of the Bible-Christian Church, Philadelphia, to the

Bible-Christians and vegetarians of England. Frankford, PA, William Higgs, Jr., 1851.
Text of speeches delivered on the occasion of a visit by Rev. William Metcalfe.

7 Clubb, Henry Stephen. The illustrated vegetarian almanac for 1855. New York, Fowlers and Wells Publishers, 1855.
Brief articles, advertisements, chronology of vegetarianism, plus calendar of eclipses, moon phases, etc.

8 Clubb, Henry Stephen. Synopsis of the doctrines and principles of the Bible Christian Church.... Philadelphia, Office of the Peacemaker, 1884.
Pamphlet details the sixteen tenets of the Bible Christian Church, one of which is the abstaining from "eating flesh, fish or fowl as food."

9 Clubb, Henry Stephen. Synopsis of the vegetarian system. Philadelphia, Vegetarian Society of America, 1898.

10 Clubb, Henry Stephen. The vegetarian principle. Philadelphia, The Vegetarian Society of America, 1898.
Essay views vegetarianism as a necessary step to end war, murder, and intemperance.

11 Cocchi, Antonio. The Pythagorean diet of vegetables only: conducive to the preservation of health, and the cure of diseases; a discourse delivered at Florence, in the month of August, 1743. London, R. Dodsley, 1745.
Biographical information on Pythagoras and the history of the Pythagorean movement; description of vegetarian precepts and dietary practices, and their use in the treatment of disease.

12 Domestica (pseud.). The vegetist's dietary and manual of vegetarian cookery.... 9th ed. Manchester, England, The Vegetarian Society, 1897.

13 Forward, Charles Walter. Fifty years of food reform: a history of the vegetarian movement in England. London, Ideal Publishing Union, 1898.

14 Fowler, Harriet P. Vegetarianism, the radical cure for

intemperance. New York, M. L. Holbrook and Co.,
1879.
Elaboration of and further support for Groom-
Napier's position that the vegetarian diet is able to
reform alcoholics.

15 Gompertz, Lewis. Moral inquiries on the situation of
man and brutes. London, The author, 1824.

16 Groom-Napier, Charles Ottley. Vegetarianism, a cure
for intemperance. A paper read before ... the British Association, at Bristol, 26th August 1875. London,
William Tweedie and Co., 1875.
Twenty-seven cases of alcoholism cured through application of vegetarian diet based on macaroni, beans,
peas, rice, and bread.

17 Haig, Alexander. Diet and food: considered in relation
to strength and power of endurance, training and athletics. London, J.&A. Churchill, 1898.
Physiological studies of albumen and urea levels
lead author to advocate strict vegetarian diet for optimal endurance and athletic skill.

18 Kellogg, Ella Ervilla Eaton. Science in the kitchen: a
scientific treatise on food substances and their dietetic
properties together with a practical explanation of the
principles of healthful cookery.... Rev. ed. Battle
Creek, MI, Modern Medicine Publishing Co., 1892.
Principles and methods of the vegetarian system
employed at the Battle Creek Sanitarium.

19 Kingsford, Anna Bonus. The perfect way in diet; a
treatise advocating a return to the natural and ancient
food of our race. 2nd ed. London, Kegan Paul,
Trench and Co., 1885.
Translation of author's doctoral thesis of 1880 examines vegetarian cultural and ethnic groups; health
hazards of meat-eating; and anatomical, economic,
and ethical considerations.

20 Lambe, William. Reports of the effects of a peculiar
regimen in scirrhous tumours and cancerous ulcers.
London, J. Mawman, 1809.

21 Lambe, William. Water and vegetable diet in consumption, scrofula, cancer, asthma, and other chronic
diseases. New York, Fowlers and Wells, 1850.

22 Lane, Charles. A brief practical essay on vegetable
    diet in its material, social, personal, and spiritual
    aspects. London, Strange, 1847.
        Booklet discusses health, economy, humanity, and
    morality as motives for vegetarian diet, as well as
    an examination of vegetarian cultures around the
    world.

23 Leadsworth, Mrs. J. R. Natural food of man, and how
    to prepare it. San Francisco, Pacific Press Pub-
    lishing Co., 1899.

24 Manchester vegetarian lectures. 2nd series. Man-
    chester, England, Vegetarian Society, 1889.
        Fourteen lectures delivered in 1887 and 1888 on
    wide range of practical and philosophical issues of
    interest to vegetarians.

25 Metcalfe, William. Bible testimony on abstinence from
    the flesh of animals as food; being an address deli-
    vered in the Bible-Christian Church ... on the eighth
    of June 1840.... Philadelphia, J. Metcalfe and Co.,
    1840.
        Scriptural support and documentation of the vege-
    tarian diet.

26 Moore, John Howard. Why I am a vegetarian. An ad-
    dress delivered before the Chicago Vegetarian Soci-
    ety, Great Northern Hotel, March 3, 1895. Chicago,
    The Ward Waugh Publishing Co., 1895.

27 Newton, John Frank. The return to nature; or, a de-
    fence of the vegetable regimen; with some account of
    an experiment made during the last three or four
    years in the author's family. London, T. Cadell
    and W. Davies, 1811.
        Explores vegetarian diet from standpoints of
    mythological and classical literature, anatomy, water
    pollution from animal wastes, and the superiority of
    wild versus domestic animals.

28 Plutarch. "Beasts are rational." In: Plutarch's moralia
    in fifteen volumes with an English translation by Harold
    Cherniss and William C. Helmbold. Cambridge,
    Harvard University Press, 1968, vol. 12, p. 492-
    533.
        The efforts of Odysseus to release men from a

spell which has turned them into animals are spurned
by a pig who argues that animals possess a natural
endowment of reason and intellect; are far more
virtuous, courageous, temperate, and better able to
regulate their desires than men; do not enslave one
another; and place the female in equal position with
the male.

29 Plutarch. "The cleverness of animals, both of the sea
and of the land." In: Plutarch. Moral essays.
Translated by Rex Warner. Harmondsworth, England, Penguin Books, 1971, p. 97-158.
Dialogue considers the reasoning powers of animals.

30 Plutarch. "The eating of flesh." In: Plutarch's moralia in fifteen volumes with an English translation by
Harold Cherniss and William C. Helmbold. Cam-
bridge, Harvard University Press, 1968, vol. 12, p.
537-579.
Two fragmented discourses explore origins of
meat-eating, concluding that it arose, not from necessity, but from insolence and debauchery. Urges
abstention from meat on the grounds of physiology
and morality, noting the cruelty inflicted on animals,
the dehumanizing and spiritually coarsening influence
of slaughter, and the disregard for life inherent in
meat-eating, which transfers to relations with humans. (Also in: Regan, Tom, and Singer, Peter.
Animal rights and human obligations, p. 111-117.)

31 Porphyrius. Porphyry on abstinence from animal food.
Translated by Thomas Taylor. Edited and introduced
by Esmé Wynne-Tyson. London, Centaur Press,
1965.
Arranged in four sections, this work addresses
arguments to Porphyry's wayward disciple Firmus
Castricius who had forsaken the vegetarian habits of
his master.

32 Ritson, Joseph. An essay on abstinence from animal
food, as a moral duty. London, Wilks and Taylor,
1802.
Drawing upon classical literature and ancient and
contemporary cultures, argues eloquently that flesh-
eating is unnatural, unnecessary, leading to cruelty,
human sacrifices and cannibalism; whereas the vege-

tarian diet promotes health, well-being and compassion among individuals and nations.

33 Salt, Henry Stephens. Animals' rights considered in relation to social progress. Clarks Summit, PA, Society for Animal Rights, 1980.
    Essays by the influential 19th-century social activist, covering treatment of wild and domestic animals for food, sport, fashion, and science; extensive bibliography by C. R. Magel.

34 Salt, Henry Stephens. "The humanities of diet." In: Salt, Henry Stephens. Humanitarian essays. London, William Reeves, 1897, part 6. (Cruelties of civilization, vol. 3)
    Classic essay argues for vegetarianism on ethical grounds, concluding that vegetarianism is the "diet of the future, as flesh-food is the diet of the past."

35 Salt, Henry Stephens. A plea for vegetarianism, and other essays. Manchester, England, Vegetarian Society, 1886.

36 Shelley, Percy Bysshe. "Essay on the vegetable system of diet." In: Shelley, Percy Bysshe. Shelley's prose; or, the trumpet of a prophecy. Edited by David Lee Clark. Albuquerque, University of New Mexico Press, 1954, p. 91-96.
    Argues that the meat diet is most unnatural for man, and the root of disease of the body and mind.

37 Shelley, Percy Bysshe. On the vegetable system of diet. Folcroft, PA, Folcroft Library Editions, 1975.

38 Shelley, Percy Bysshe. "A vindication of natural diet." In: Shelley, Percy Bysshe. Shelley's prose; or, the trumpet of a prophecy. Edited by David Lee Clark. Albuquerque, University of New Mexico Press, 1954, p. 81-90.
    Eloquent statement on behalf of the vegetarian diet links physical and moral depravity to unnatural diet and lifestyle by citing mythology, literature, philosophy. Points out health, economic and political advantages to be accrued from a change to the vegetarian diet.

39 Springer, Robert. Wegweiser in der vegetarianischen Literatur. Nordhausen, Germany, n. p., 1878.

40 Stomach worship. A growl, by a vegetarian. Liverpool,
     E. Howell, 1881.

41 Tolstoy, Leo. "The first step." In: Rudd, Geoffrey
     L. Why kill for food? Madras, Indian Vegetarian
     Congress, 1973, p. 106-112.
         Moving account of the great vegetarian writer's
     visits to a local slaughterhouse.

42 Trall, Russell Thacher. The scientific basis of vege-
     tarianism. Mokelumne Hill, CA, Health Research,
     1961.
         Address to the American Vegetarian Society in
     1860 discusses the merits of vegetarianism as op-
     posed to the vices of flesh-eating, alcohol, and
     tobacco.

                    1900 THROUGH 1959

43 Abhedânanda, Swâmi. Why a Hindu is a vegetarian.
     3rd ed. New York, Vedânta Society, 1900.
         Consideration of ethical, moral, and humane fac-
     tors which figure prominently in Hindu thought and
     traditions.

44 Adolph, William H. "Vegetarian China." Scientific
     American 169 (Sept. 1938): 133-135.
         Comparison of Chinese and American diets. Also
     reprinted in China Weekly Review 87 (Dec. 24, 1938):
     124-125.

45 Agee, James. "A mother's tale." In: The best Amer-
     ican short stories, 1953. Edited by Martha Foley.
     Boston, Houghton Mifflin Co., 1953, p. 1-18.
         (See also no. 798.)

46 Albertoni, P., and Rossi, F. "The action of meat on
     vegetarians." Archiv für Experimentelle Pathologie
     und Pharmakologie. Suppl (1908): 28-38.
         Meat added to a vegetarian diet resulted in de-
     creased caloric value of food, decreased amount of
     food consumed, decreased amount of feces, and in-
     creased weight of the subjects. (In German.)

47 Albu, Albert. Die vegetarische Diät. Kritik ihrer An-
    wendung für Gesunde und Krank. Leipzig, George
    Thieme, 1902. (In German.)

48 Allaway, Gertrude E. "How it strikes a vegetarian. "
    Spectator 118 (Mar. 17, 1917): 334.
        Letter recounts economic advantages of vegetarian
    diet during war-time food shortages and rationing.

49 Allison, Bertrand P. "The case for vegetarianism on
    health grounds. " Vegetarian News 29, 268 (Summer
    1950): 53-55, 59.
        Informal observations by the writer indicate vege-
    tarians enjoy better overall physical and mental health
    than meat-eaters.

50 Allsopp, A. H. "Vegetarianism and Christianity. "
    Vegetarian Messenger and Health Review 8, 48 (Jan.
    1951): 5-6.
        Vegetarian Christians who are troubled with the
    lack of a positive prohibition against meat-eating in
    the Bible are reminded that there are no such con-
    demnations of slavery or war in the Old or the New
    Testaments.

51 Almflet, G. A.; Liebstein, A. M.; Warmbrand, M.;
    and Gould, S. "Vegetarianism and nutrition. "
    New York (State). Legislature. Legislative Docu-
    ment 1945, 49 (1945): 178-184.
        Evidence that the vegetarian diet is the original
    and natural diet of man.

52 Anderson, Hans Steele. Food and cookery. Rev. 4th
    ed. Mountain View, CA, Pacific Press Publishing
    Association, 1917.
        Vegetarian food principles, preparation, combina-
    tions, menu planning and recipes.

53 Anderson, Hans Steele. Food therapy; diet and the
    healing art. Fort Meade, FL, Anderson Publishing
    Co. , 1942.

54 Anderton, R. "Meat-eating delusions. " Vegetarian 10,
    2 (May-June 1954): 76-80.
        Author feels that meat-eaters are simply deluded,
    rather than deliberately inhumane; explores ethical
    issues involved in hunting and slaughter of animals
    for food and sport.

55 Anon. "America going vegetarian." Literary Digest
   98, 3 (July 21, 1928): 19-20.
       Bemoans the fact that since World War I, vege-
   tarianism has become increasingly popular in the
   U. S.

56 Anon. "Does meat injure athletes?" Literary Digest
   50, 8 (Feb. 13, 1915): 312-313.
       Discussion of the possible relationship between the
   prevalence of appendicitis among football players and
   the preponderance of meat in their diets.

57 Anon. "Flesh-eating and ferocity." Literary Digest
   61, 8 (May 24, 1919): 25.
       Discusses the relationship between diet and ag-
   gression, hunting, and cruelty in man and other animals.

58 Anon. "How the teeth of vegetarians give evidence
   against them." Current Literature 48 (May 1910):
   509-510.
       Discourse on the debate that cooked, not raw,
   meat is the proper food for man; discounts argument
   that meat is toxic, since serious diseases have also
   been contracted from contaminated fruits and vegetables.

59 Anon. "In quest of a cure, II; a vegetarian sanitorium."
   Blackwood's Magazine 191 (June 1912): 820-825.
       Account of a stay in a vegetarian sanitorium par-
   taking of "The Diet" as a cure for rheumatism.

60 Anon. "Investigation of vegetarianism." Scientific
   American 112 (Apr. 24, 1915): 384.
       Brief account of two experiments comparing vege-
   tarians and meat-eaters finding no significant difference in metabolic or endurance levels between the
   two groups.

61 Anon. "Meatless diet adequate." Science News Letter
   61 (Feb. 2, 1952): 70. Brief summary of study
   concluding that both vegetarian and carnivorous types
   of diets are adequate.

62 Anon. "Medical slap at the vegetarian gospel." Literary Digest 107, 8 (Nov. 22, 1930): 26.
       Review of editorial in the Journal of the American
   Medical Association promoting a high-meat diet.

63 Anon. "Murder, its use and abuse; a parable of Safed the Sage." Christian Century 47 (May 28, 1930): 681-682.
   Dialogue on the ethics of vegetarianism versus meat-eating.

64 Anon. "Notable vegetarians." Literary Digest 46, 21 (May 24, 1913): 1196-1199.
   Excerpts from article in New York Sun on famous vegetarians of the day and their reasons for adopting the vegetarian diet.

65 Anon. "Tabus and humors of a life bowed down to spinach." Literary Digest 98, 9 (Sept. 1, 1928): 43-44.
   Describes humorous and philosophical aspects of the vegetarian life.

66 Anon. "Vegetable diet and the length of life." Science 61, Suppl. (June 26, 1925): 10-12.
   Summary of early experiments in which rats fed various restricted vegetable diets failed to thrive and reproduce.

67 Anon. "Vegetarian practitioner in the East." New Yorker 22 (Oct. 5, 1946): 23-24.
   Profile of Dr. Max Warmbrand, vegetarian physiotherapist.

68 Anon. "Vegetarian suggestions." Good Housekeeping 49 (Oct. 1909): 470-471.

69 Axon, Geoffrey R. "What is a vegetarian?" Vegetarian Messenger and Health Review 45 (Mar. 1948): 64-65.
   Clarification of vegetarian diet and principles in light of popular misconceptions.

70 Axon, Geoffrey R. "What is vegetarianism?" Vegetarian Messenger and Health Review 47 (June 1950): 168-169.
   Points out misleading and incorrect statements in the entry for vegetarian diet in Chambers's Encyclopedia.

71 Bansi, H. "Stickstoffbilanz-Versuche bei rein vegetabiler Ernährung." Angewandte Chemie 70, 12 (June 21, 1958): 378. (In German.)

72 Barahal, Hyman S.   "The cruel vegetarian."   Psychiatric
    Quarterly 20 Suppl. (1946): 3-13.
        Psychiatric profile of vegetarians characterizes
    them as eccentric, idiosyncratic, with underlying
    tendencies for cruelty, sadism, and maliciousness;
    concludes that while the average vegetarian is "def-
    initely not a lunatic, he certainly fringes on it."

73 Basu, K. P.; Basak, M. N.; and Sircar, B. C. Rai.
    "Studies in human metabolism. II. Calcium and
    phosphorous metabolism in Indians on rice and wheat
    diets." Indian Journal of Medical Research 27, 2
    (1939): 471-500.
        Calcium and phosphorous metabolism experiments
    on three individuals consuming vegetarian diets based
    on rice and whole wheat.

74 Batilwalla, K. C.   "Incidence and causation of glycosuria
    in pregnancy." Indian Medical Gazette 82 (1947):
    191-193.
        Vegetarian women and those with low calcium and
    vitamin C intakes had greater incidence of glucose in
    the urine during pregnancy.

75 Baty, Thomas.   "Vegetarianism and Buddhism."   Vege-
    tarian Messenger and Health Review 48 (May 1951):
    113-114.
        Traces vegetarian concept through Hinduism and
    Buddhism.

76 Bayly, M. Beddow.   "The scientific basis of vegetarian-
    ism." Vegetarian News 34 (Dec. 1955-Feb. 1956):
    136-145.
        Vegetarianism as a sound basis for healthful and
    ethical living.

77 Beard, Sidney Hartnoll.   A comprehensive guide-book to
    natural, hygienic and humane diet. New York, Thomas
    Y. Crowell and Co., 1900.
        Noting increased interest in and influence of vege-
    tarian diets, author provides information on planning
    nutritious meals based on fruits, nuts, and grains;
    appeals to the reader to join in the Crusade against
    Carnivorism.

78 Bell, Ernest.   "Vegetarianism: an essential step."
    Vegetarian Messenger and Health Review 47 (Jan.

1950): 12-13.
   Abolition of exploitation of animals for food is seen
as essential step toward accomplishment of social re-
forms.

79 Bell, Robert. "The dietetics of cancer." Dietetic and
    Hygienic Gazette 22, 12 (Dec. 1906): 705-711.
       Advances arguments for diet consisting in large
    measure of uncooked fruits and vegetables as means
    of preventing cancer.

80 Bertholet, Edouard. Végétarisme et occultisme; vertus
    curatives des légumes et des fruits. Neuchâtel, Edi-
    tions Rosicrociennes, 1950.
       Physiological, economic, religious, and historical
    perspective; therapeutic properties of fruits and vege-
    tables. (In French.)

81 Besant, Annie. "Vegetarianism in the light of Theos-
    ophy." In: National Vegetarian Convention, 1st,
    Bombay, 1964. Souvenir..., p. 29-39.
       Man's relation to physical and spiritual order of
    the universe; with few exceptions, man is viewed as
    the disorderly element in nature. (Originally pub-
    lished in 1932.)

82 Beveridge, J. M. R.; Connell, W. F.; and Mayer, G.
    A. "Dietary factors affecting the level of plasma
    cholesterol in humans: the role of fat." Canadian
    Journal of Biochemistry and Physiology 34 (1956):
    441-455.
       Dietary experiments revealed that diets containing
    significant amounts of beef drippings, chicken fat,
    lard and butter elevate plasma cholesterol, whereas
    similar diets high in corn oil cause a drop in choles-
    terol levels.

83 Bidwell, Randolph G. "An early vegetarian society."
    Vegetarian Messenger and Health Review 43 (July
    1946): 136-138.
       Author's research uncovers little-known vegetarian
    religious community in England in the 15th century.

84 Billig, Herbert. "Die deutsche Volksernährung; leben
    wir heute vegetarisch?" Natur und Nahrung 3, 11-12
    (June 1949): 17-18. (In German.)

85 Bircher, Max Edwin. "The influence of vegetarian diet,
    predominantly raw, on the viscosity of the blood, the
    hemoglobin content and the blood pressure." Part I
    Schweizerische Medizinische Wochenschrift 58, 40
    (1928): 987-993.

86 Bircher, Max Edwin. "The influence of vegetarian diet,
    predominantly raw, on the viscosity of the blood, the
    hemoglobin content and the blood pressure." Part II
    Schweizerische Medizinische Wochenschrift 58, 41
    (1928): 1010-1014.
       Vegetarian diet appeared to normalize viscosities
    of the blood, hemoglobin and blood pressure.

87 Blomerus, Yvonne. "Vegetarianism." Woman and Her
    Home 4 (Nov. 1952): 257-258.
       Precautions and disadvantages to be considered in
    relation to vegetarian diet.

88 Bolt, J. H. "The aim of vegetarianism." Vegetarian
    Messenger and Health Review 43 (Oct. 1946): 197-
    199.
       Beginning on the individual level, vegetarianism
    endeavors to extend feelings of responsibility beyond
    one's own self and species to animals, plants, and
    the cosmos.

89 Bolt, J. H. "The Netherland and the Dutch Vegetarian
    Society." Vegetarian Messenger and Health Review
    47 (Feb. 1950): 58-62.
       Historical and cultural development and status of
    vegetarianism in the Netherlands.

90 Branson, J. R. B. Eating for victory; suggestions for
    war-time economy in food-stuffs. Bordon, Branson's
    Publications, 1940.
       Author relates experiences using fresh grass-mow-
    ings to augment his vegetarian diet and to make the
    best of food rationing during World War II; includes
    recipes.

91 Branson, J. R. B. Vegetarianism for health, energy,
    and economy, with patriotism, humanitarianism and
    long life thrown in. London, Branson's, 1943.

92 Braune, R. Über den Einfluss fleischloser Kost auf die
    Geistestätigkeit des Menschen. Berlin, R. Schotz,
    1935. (In German.)

93 Brockhaus, Wilhelm. Von der Ehrfurcht vor dem Leben
    und dem Recht der Tiere. Liedenscheid, Verlag
    Rudolf Beucker, 1953. (In German.)

94 Broun, Heywood. "The passing of Shaw's mentor."
    New Republic 98 (May 3, 1939): 375-376.
       Biographic tribute to Henry S. Salt, the father of
    modern vegetarianism, who influenced both Mohandas
    Gandhi and George Bernard Shaw.

95 Bush, Maxine Conwell. Diet for health. Mehoopany,
    PA, n. p. , 1951.

96 Buttner, Jacques Louis. A fleshless diet; vegetarian-
    ism as a rational dietary. New York, Frederick A.
    Stokes Co. , 1910.
       Anatomical, hygienic, health, and practical con-
    siderations.

97 Carbonell, J. Fernando. El vegetarianismo teórico y
    práctico, tratado razonado sobre la ciencia y el arte
    de la alimentación vegetariana. Montevideo, Biblio-
    teca de la revista Natura, 19--.

98 Carqué, Otto. The folly of meat-eating; how to con-
    serve our food supply; a plea for saner living. St.
    Catherines, Ont. , Provoker Press, 1970.
       Booklet originally written in the 1910's presents
    economic, ecological, and nutritional arguments for
    vegetarianism. Bound with Food preservation and
    fruitarianism; the social and economic aspects of the
    meatless diet, by Henry E. Lahn.

99 Carqué, Otto. The key to rational dietetics; funda-
    mental facts about the prevention of disease, the
    preservation of health, the prolongation of life. Los
    Angeles, The author, 1930.
       Therapeutic, health-enhancing benefits from vege-
    tarian foods, exercise, rest, fresh air, sunlight and
    pure water.

100 Carqué, Otto. Vital facts about foods; a guide to
    health and longevity with 200 wholesome recipes and
    menus and 250 complete analyses of foods. Los
    Angeles, The author, 1933.
       Manual of food reform covers importance of sim-
    ple vegetarian diet, fresh air, pure water, exercise,

rest; also acid and alkaline foods, treatment of disease, and food preparation.

101 Carrington, Hereward. The natural food of man, being an attempt to prove from comparative anatomy, physiology, chemistry and hygiene, that the original, best and natural diet of man is fruit and nuts. London, C. W. Daniel, 1912.

102 Carrington, Hereward. "Proper food for perfect health." Cosmopolitan 49 (Aug. 1910): 326-330.
    Personal account of a weak, sickly childhood, experiments with diet of raw nuts and fruits, and restoration of endurance, energy and health. Notes prominent vegetarian athletes of the day.

103 Carson, Gerald. Cornflake crusade. New York, Rinehart and Co., 1957.
    History of the 19th-century vegetarian food reform movement which led to the development of breakfast cereals and other foods by Sylvester Graham, J. H. Kellogg, C. W. Post and others.

104 Caspari, W. "Physiological studies with vegetarians." Archiv für die Gesamte Physiologie des Menschen und der Thiere 109 (1905): 473-595. (In German.)

105 Castro, José. Mis reformas e innovaciones al naturismo. Rosario, Argentina, Editorial Naturists "Devinir," 1950.

106 Chase, Alice. "The debate on vegetarianism." American Mercury 70 (June 1950): 763, 766.
    Letter disputes viewpoint presenting the case against vegetarianism.

107 Chase, Alice. Nutrition for health. New York, Parker Publishing Co., 1954.
    Advocates vegetarian diet as means of improving health and prolonging life; stresses use of fresh raw fruits and vegetables, dairy products and eggs. Contains chapter entitled, "The case against animal meats," p. 186-189.

108 Chattopadhyaya, Basanta Kumar. "The saving of modern civilization." Indian Philosophy and Culture 2 (S 1957): 133-135.
    Explanation of the doctrine of ahimsa (non-violence)

with reference to abstinence from the killing or eating of animals.

109 Chesterton, Gilbert Keith. "The meaning of mock turkey." In: Chesterton, G. K. Fancies versus fads. 2nd ed. London, Methuen, 1925, p. 35-45. Essay critiques philosophical viewpoints expressed in a vegetarian pamphlet.

110 Chhuttani, P. N. "Vegetarians and malnutrition." Indian Medical Gazette 89, 5 (1954): 289-292. Meat-eating soldiers had lower incidence of anemia than vegetarians, and the addition of weekly meat rations improved their overall state of nourishment.

111 Chittenden, Russell Henry. Physiological economy in nutrition with special reference to the minimal proteid requirement of the healthy man; an experimental study. New York, Frederick A. Stokes Co., 1904. Pioneering series of studies demonstrating that optimal protein and calorie requirements are much lower than had previously been believed; outlines injurious effects of diets high in protein.

112 Christian, Eugene. Why die. New York, E. Christian, 1928.

113 Christian, Eugene, and Christian, Mollie Griswold. Uncooked foods and how to use them; a treatise on on how to get the highest form of animal energy from food, with recipes for preparation, healthful combinations and menus. 7th ed. New York, The Health-Culture Co., 1904. Authors report complete restoration of health after adopting dietary plan based on raw fruits, vegetables, grains, and nuts.

114 Clark, David Lee. "The date and source of Shelley's, 'A vindication of natural diet.'" Studies in Philology 36 (Jan. 1939): 70-76. Essay asserts that "A vindication of natural diet" was Shelley's earliest work on vegetarianism, and that he had been influenced by Ritson's "An essay on abstinence from animal food" far more than had been previously recognized.

115 Clubb, Henry Stephen. Thirty-nine reasons why I am

a vegetarian. Philadelphia, The Vegetarian Society of America, 1903.
Spiritual and moral aspects of the vegetarian life.

116   Colborn, William H. Why let them die? Los Angeles, DeVorss and Co., 1950.
Lack of sodium and chlorine, and an excess of uric acid and carbonic acid are seen as the causes of disease, which may be corrected by a vegetarian diet.

117   Colvin, Bernard. "National Service for a vegetarian." Vegetarian News 36, 295 (Mar. -May 1957): 4-9.
Recommendations for improving the vegetarian's lot in the armed forces.

118   Comstock, Belle Jessie Wood. Three times a day. Takoma Park, Washington, DC, Review and Herald Publishing Co., 1937.

119   Coville, Marion E. An appeal against slaughter; are you able to hear? 2nd ed. Syracuse, C. W. Bardeen, 1914.
Ethical and religious arguments against the "injustice, cruelty, and degradation" of animal slaughter for food, fashion and sport.

120   Crichton-Browne, James. Parcimony in nutrition. London, Funk and Wagnalls Co., 1909.
Critical analysis refutes Chittenden's research on minimal protein requirement; advocates high protein and meat intakes for optimal health.

121   Cummings, Richard Osborn. "Prejudices and reformers (1830-1840)." In: Cummings, Richard Osborn. The American and his food: a history of food habits in the United States. Rev. ed. Chicago, University of Chicago Press, 1941, p. 43-52.
History of the early 19th-century vegetarian food reform movement.

122   Cutter, Ephraim, and Cutter, John Ashburton. "Food: its relation to health and disease." Dietetic and Hygienic Gazette (Mar. 1906): 151-156.
Recounts virtues of beef consumption, from the prevention of leprosy to maintenance of physical and mental manhood.

123 Dalemont, Julien. Enquêtes sur le végétarisme; quelques principes d'hygiène alimentaire et leurs conséquences sociales pour le bonheur des peuples. Paris, Les Editions du Cèdre, 1955.
     Vegetarian nutrition and foods; review of studies of vegetarian monasteries; menus. (In French.)

124 Damrau, Frederic. "Eat all the meat you want." Independent 121 (Sept. 29, 1928): 303-304, 312.
     Convictions of vegetarians and others that meat is harmful to the health are grounded in tradition and mere superstition.

125 Damrau, Frederic. "The folly of vegetarianism." Hygeia 5 (Sept. 1927): 439-442.
     Vegetarianism is based on myth, superstition, fancy, the unchecked imagination, and is nothing more than a "burlesque on dietetics."

126 Davies, John. "Vegetarianism and secularism." Vegetarian Messenger and Health Review 48 (Feb. 1951): 34-36.
     Based on ethical considerations, vegetarianism from a secular motivation is more realistic, basic, and universal than the dogmas or doctrines of organized religion.

127 Davis, Max. The case for the vegetarian conscientious objector. Brooklyn, Tolstoy Peace Group, 1944.
     Writing in 1944, a 22-year-old imprisoned vegetarian appeals for conscientious objector status on the basis of his vegetarian pacifist philosophy. Foreword by Scott Nearing.

128 de Coti-Marsh, Charles. Prescription for energy. London, Thorsons, 1959.

129 deFleury, M. "The regime and diet of a man engaged in intellectual work." Societé Scientifique d'hygiene Alimentaire et l'Alimentation Rationelle de l'Homme. Revue 3 (1906): 855-878.
     Overeating, lack of exercise, abuse of meat, fatty foods, alcohol, tea, coffee, tobacco and other stimulants are blamed for cases of nervous exhaustion among sedentary workers. (In French.)

130 de Raadt, O. L. E. "Where is urea formed in the body?" Nederlands Tijdschrift voor Geneeskunde 74,

2 (1930): 4323-4329.
Most of the urea is formed in the liver with a vegetarian diet, and in the tissues with a meat diet. (In Dutch.)

131 de Wijn, J. F.; Donath, W. F.; and van der Meulen-van Eyspergen, H. C. "A study of the effects of completely vegetarian diets on human subjects." Nutrition Society. Proceedings 13 (1954): xiv-xv.
Dietary study of vegans revealed low intakes of calories, protein, calcium, riboflavin; amino acid composition and vitamin B12 levels were normal. (Meeting abstract.)

132 Dessau, Kaj. "The future of the international vegetarian movement." Vegetarian Messenger and Health Review 47 (Sept. 1950): 261-265.
Outlines weaknesses and shortcomings of the vegetarian movement.

133 Dhopeshwarkar, G. A.; Trivedi, J. C.; Kulkarni, B. S.; Satoskar, R. S.; and Lewis, R. A. "The effect of vegetarianism and antibiotics upon proteins and vitamin B12 in the blood." British Journal of Nutrition 10, 2 (1956): 105-110.
Plasma protein and vitamin B12 levels in blood were determined for five vegetarians and five non-vegetarians.

134 Dickinson, Roy. "Common-sense vegetarianism." Vegetarian News 32 (Spring 1953): 19-21.
Practice and principles of balanced vegetarian diet.

135 Dickinson, Roy. "Vegetarianism and graceful old age." Vegetarian News 33 (Summer 1954): 43-44.
Practical assistance and reassurance regarding diets for elderly vegetarians.

136 Donath, W. F.; Fischer, I. A.; van der Meulen-van Eysbergen, H. C.; and de Wijn, J. F. "Health, nutrition and veganism." Voeding 14, 3 (Mar. 15, 1953): 153-178.
Dietary study of 60 vegans found lower intakes of calories, total protein, calcium, vitamin B12, vitamin D; and lower levels of cholesterol, basal metabolism, and body weight. Medical control urged for

vegan diets, since macrocytosis, carotenaemia and
relatively high alkaline serum phosphatase were observed. (In Dutch.)

137 Drake, Muriel E. "Forward--or backward?" Vegetarian News 32 (Summer 1953): 48-50.
      Role of veganism in the vegetarian movement.

138 Drake, Muriel E. "Veganism in 1952--from a vegan's
point of view." Vegetarian News 31 (Summer 1952):
49-52, 60.
      Physical, mental and spiritual changes resulting
from vegan diet.

139 Drew, Mary. "Why need we be poisoned?" Contemporary Review 109 (Apr. 1916): 452-461.
      The author, an arthritic, undertakes a fruitarian
diet.

140 Drew, Mary. "Why need we be poisoned? II." Contemporary Review 111 (Jan. 1917): 76-86.
      Author describes cases of health restoration, her
own and that of others, following adoption of the
fruitarian diet.

141 Drews, George Julius. Unfired food and tropho-therapy
(food cure). 9th ed., rev. Chicago, The Apyrotroph-
er Publishing House, 1924.
      Physical and spiritual health through the use of
raw foods.

142 Dunkel, Joan. "The effect of vitamin B12 in a certain
vegetarian diet." Walla Walla College Publications
of the Department of Biological Sciences and the Biological Station 1, 4 (Dec. 10, 1952): 59-64.
      Describes vegetarian diet developed for rats which,
even with vitamin B12 supplementation, was unable
to sustain animals beyond the seventh generation.

143 Dunlap, Knight. "A possible dietary predisposition to
stammering." Science 80, 2070 (Aug. 31, 1934):
206.
      Author posits that a vegetarian diet predisposes
children to stammering and stuttering, and that a
meat diet alleviates these conditions.

144 Easterbrook, L. F. "Alcohol and meat." Nineteenth
Century and After 95 (Feb. 1924): 306-314.

Slaughterhouse cruelties lead the author to conclude that the prohibition of meat is more justifiable
than the prohibition of alcohol.

145 Eckhardt, H. "Studies of children on a vegetarian
diet." Zentralblatt für die gesamte Physiologie und
Pathologie des Stoffwechsels 1 (1907): 617-622.
Dietary study of three healthy vegetarian children
in an orphanage. (In German.)

146 Edmunds, Albert J. "Pigs in a vegetarian Sunday
School." Open Court 22 (Aug. 1908): 477-479.
Account of slaughterhouse operating in building
formerly occupied by the vegetarian Bible Christian
Church of Philadelphia, 1823-1891.

147 Efron, Edith. "Heydays for the vegetarians." New
York Times Magazine (Apr. 8, 1945): 17, 32.
Briefly describes various vegetarian philosophical
positions.

148 Egerod, Oluf. "Vegetarianism in Denmark." Vegetarian Messenger and Health Review 43 (Sept. 1946):
187-188.
History, organization and activities of the Danish
Vegetarian Society.

149 Ehret, Arnold. A scientific method of eating your way
to health; Prof. Arnold Ehret's mucusless diet healing
system. 8th ed. Los Angeles, Ehret Literature
Publishing Co., 1924.
Therapeutic system based on fasting and diet designed to prevent mucus formation.

150 Evans, Newton, and Risley, E. H. "High protein ra-
tion as a cause of nephritis." California and Western
Medicine 23, 4 (Apr. 1925): 437-442.
Rats fed series of high-protein diets invariably
showed kidney damage; authors urge limited use of
meat and increased use of fruits and vegetables in
the prevention and treatment of nephritis.

151 Faulkner, James. The unfired food diet simplified; a
simple practical guide for those who are interested
in unfired foods. Pasadena, CA, The author, 1923.

152 Fauvel, P. "The vegetarian diet." Société Scientifique
d'Hygiene Alimentaire et de l'Alimentation Rationelle

de l'Homme. Revue 3 (1906): 972-978.
Report of beneficial mental and physical effects of
a vegetarian diet of five years duration to a 40-year-
old man. (In French.)

153 Fellows, Alfred. "Vegetarian guest." Living Age 250
(Aug. 11, 1906): 346-353.
Trials and tribulations of inviting a vegetarian to
dinner.

154 Fisher, Irving. "Diet and endurance at Brussels."
Science 26, 669 (Oct. 25, 1907): 561-563.
Studies of strength and endurance in vegetarians
and meat-eaters found little difference as far as
strength was concerned, but remarkable differences
in the area of endurance, the vegetarians surpassing
the meat-eaters by 50 to 200 percent. Vegetarians
were able to work on the ergograph two to three
times longer before exhaustion, and were able to
recover from fatigue far more quickly than the meat-
eaters.

155 Fisher, Irving. The effects of diet on endurance.
New Haven, Yale University Press, 1918. First
published in Connecticut Academy of Arts and Sciences. Transactions 13 (May 1907): 1-46.

156 Fisher, Irving. "The influence of flesh eating on endurance." Yale Medical Journal 13, 5 (Mar. 1907):
205-221.
Vegetarian athletes and non-athletes easily sur-
passed meat-eating athletes in series of endurance
tests.

157 Fletcher, Horace. The A. B. -Z. of our own nutrition.
New York, Frederick A. Stokes, 1903.
Food reformer advocates not only vegetarian diet,
but also prolonged and excessive chewing of food.

158 Forward, Charles Walter. Food of the future; a summary of arguments in favor of a non-flesh diet. London, George Bell and Sons, 1904.
Ethical, economic, physiological, nutritional advantages of vegetarian diet; historical and literary
writings favoring vegetarianism.

159 Freeman, Peter. "Vegetarianism or world famine."
Vegetarian 3 (July-Aug. 1955): 92-94.

Vegetarianism viewed as economic and political factor in the prevention of war and famine.

160 Friedmann, R. , and Raab, W. "Behavior of the circulatory organs in vegetarians and in alcoholics."
Zeitschrift für Klinische Medizin 130 (1936): 505-534.
Diet excluding meat, but not eggs and milk, did not prevent arteriosclerosis, but did tend to normalize blood pressure; alcoholism did not promote arteriosclerosis or high blood pressure. (In German.)

161 Gandhi, Mohandas Karamchand. An autobiography; the story of my experiments with truth. London, Phoenix Press, 1949.
Includes author's motivations and experiments with vegetarian diet.

162 Gandhi, Mohandas Karamchand. Diet and diet reform.
Ahmedabad, India, Navajivan Publishing House, 1949.
Collection of essays and correspondence on diet, including "The moral basis of vegetarianism," p. 8-12.

163 Gandhi, Mohandas Karamchand. The moral basis of vegetarianism. Ahmedabad, India, Navajivan Publishing House, 1959.

164 Gill, Dorothy. "Christianity and vegetarianism."
Vegetarian News 32 (Summer 1953): 45-47.
Christian ethic of pity, mercy, peace and love supports vegetarianism.

165 Gordon, Wilmer Ingalls. How to live 100 years; or, the new science of living. Cleveland, Suggestive New Thought Publishing Co. , 1903.

166 Gould, Symon. "The debate on vegetarianism." American Mercury 70 (June 1950): 761-763.
Letter asserts that the strength of vegetarianism lies in its ethical position.

167 Grabo, Carl H. Shelley's eccentricities. Albuquerque, University of New Mexico Press, 1950. (University of New Mexico Publications in Language and Literature, no. 5.)
Biographical analysis of Shelley's personal life and habits, including his vegetarian diet.

168 Graefe, Gerd. "Vernünftige rohkost." Reich der
    Landfrau 17 (Apr. 29, 1954): 135-136. (In German.)

169 Graefe, Gerd. "Vernünftige rohkost." Reich der
    Landfrau 18 (May 6, 1954): 142. (In German.)

170 Grosse-Brockhoff, F., and Haase, H. J. "Nitrogen
    balance and blood proteins during vegetarian or
    lactovegetarian diet." Deutsches Archiv für Klinische
    Medizin 197 (1950): 378-392.
        Account of a 397-day personal experiment on vege-
    tarian diet. (In German.)

171 Gulick, Luther H. "Mistake of eating meat." Ladies'
    Home Journal 26 (Mar. 1909): 36.
        Cites letter from reader whose headaches and
    heart trouble were cured by a diet devoid of "purins"
    (meats, peas, beans, coffee, tea and chocolate).

172 Hall, A. D. "Some aspects of vegetarianism."
    Harper's Monthly Magazine 123 (July 1911): 208-213.
        Examination of major arguments and motives of
    vegetarians.

173 Hall, Charlotte. Nature's pyramid to health. Denver,
    n.p., 1938.
        Author's personal system of vegetarian diet, hy-
    giene, and grooming; also natural treatment of array
    of chronic diseases.

174 Hardinge, Mervyn G. A nutritional study of vegetari-
    ans and non-vegetarians. Ph.D., Harvard Univer-
    sity, 1952.
        Landmark study of dietary habits and nutritional
    status of lacto-ovo-vegetarians, pure vegetarians,
    and non-vegetarians in three groups: older adults,
    adolescents, and pregnant women.

175 Hardinge, Mervyn G., and Stare, Frederick J. "Nu-
    tritional studies of vegetarians. I. Nutritional,
    physical, and laboratory studies." Journal of Clini-
    cal Nutrition 2, 2 (Mar.-Apr. 1954): 73-82.
        Comparative study of vegetarian and non-vegetari-
    an adults, adolescents, and pregnant women found no
    statistical differences in height, weight, blood pres-
    sure, childbirth and hematological data. Pure vege-
    tarians weighed an average of 20 pounds less than

lacto-ovo-vegetarians and non-vegetarians, despite similar caloric intakes and physical activity. Dietary intakes of all groups, except the adolescent pure vegetarian, approximated or exceeded amounts recommended by the National Research Council.

176 Hardinge, Mervyn G., and Stare, Frederick J. "Nutritional studies of vegetarians. II. Dietary and serum levels of cholesterol." Journal of Clinical Nutrition 2, 2 (Mar.-Apr. 1954): 83-88.
Dietary cholesterol intakes and serum cholesterol levels were highest in non-vegetarians and lowest in pure vegetarians.

177 Hardinge, Mervyn G.; Stare, Frederick J.; Chambers, Alma C.; and Crooks, Hulda. "Nutritional studies of vegetarians. III. Dietary levels of fiber." American Journal of Clinical Nutrition 6, 5 (Sept.-Oct. 1958): 523-525.
Lacto-ovo-vegetarians consumed nearly twice as much fiber as non-vegetarians, and a little less than half that of the strict vegetarians.

178 Harris, G. Kingsland. "Natural diet." Vegetarian News 25 (Summer 1946): 124-125.
Advocates vegetarian diet based on fresh foods.

179 Harrison, William. The Bible against flesh eating; Jesus a non-flesh eater. Manchester, England, n.p., 1907.
Over 500 biblical references in support of the author's contention that the vegetarian diet is divinely appointed.

180 Hartmann, Arthur. Rohkost und fleischlose Ernaehrung. München, J. F. Lehmann, 1928.
Discusses health merits of vegetarian regimen, presents sample diets and menus. (In German.)

181 Hashimoto, Hirotoshi. "Carotinoid pigmentation of the skin from a vegetarian diet." American Medical Association. Journal 78, 15 (Apr. 15, 1922): 1111-1112.
Brief description of yellowish discoloration of the skin in some Japanese consuming diets high in yellow vegetables.

182 Hauser, Bengamin Gayelord. Food science and health, including the famous Hauser elimination feeding sys-

tem. New York, Tempo Books, Inc. , 1930.
 Cleansing and detoxifying the body of wastes through
raw fruit and vegetable diet.

183 Hauser, Bengamin Gayelord. Here's how to be healthy.
New York, Tempo Books, Inc. , 1934.
 Therapeutic uses of fruit and vegetable juices;
recipes.

184 Haussleiter, J. Der Vegetarismus in der Antike.
Berlin, A. Popelmann, 1935.

185 Hegsted, D. M. ; Trulson, Martha F. ; White, Hilda S. ;
White, Philip L. ; Vinas, Eduardo; Alvistur, Enrique;
Diaz, Cesar; Vasquez, Juan; Loo, Angelica; Roca,
Amalia; Collazos Ch. , Carlos; and Ruiz, Alejandro.
"Lysine and methionine supplementation of all-vege-
table diets for human adults. " Journal of Nutrition
56 (1955): 555-576.
 Study of amino acids and nitrogen intake and ex-
cretion in young adult vegetarians with and without
supplementation with lysine and methionine.

186 Hegsted, D. M. ; Tsongas, A. G. ; Abbott, D. B. ; and
Stare, F. J. "Protein requirements of adults. "
Journal of Laboratory and Clinical Medicine 31 (1946):
261-284.
 Comprehensive study of nitrogen balance, digest-
ibility and biologic value of low-protein diets, one of
which was devoid of animal protein, the other replac-
ing one third of the protein by meat; concludes that
protein deficiency is most unlikely in healthy adults
consuming diets containing no animal products; finds
that the RDA of 70 grams of protein daily could be
safely lowered to 30-50 grams for a man weighing 70
kilograms.

187 Heinrich, H. "Obstbau und vegetarische Bewegung. "
Obstbau 71 (Feb. 1, 1952): 23.

188 Henderson, F. K. "Substitutes for dairy produce. "
Vegetarian News 24 (Spr. 1946): 96-97.

189 Henry, Moira. "Via vegetarianism. " Vegetarian Messenger and Health Review 42 (Nov. 1945): 211-212.
 Account of author's conversion to vegetarianism.

190 Hill, Leonard. "A strict vegetarian diet." British Medical Journal (Aug. 20, 1938): 417.
      Case of 9-year-old strict vegetarian boy with remarkable endurance, stamina, and physical and mental health.

191 Hindhede, M. "The effect of food restriction during war on mortality in Copenhagen." American Medical Association. Journal 74, 6 (Feb. 7, 1920): 381-382.
      Severe food restrictions during World War I necessitated that the population of Denmark live on a low-protein, nearly vegetarian diet consisting of bran bread, barley, potatoes, greens and milk. During this period, the death rate from disease fell 34 percent to the lowest levels in decades.

192 Hodson, Geoffrey. "Radiant health on a meat-free dietary." Vegetarian 10, 2 (July-Aug. 1954): 118-122.
      Summarizes six major arguments for vegetarianism.

193 Holbrook, Stewart H. "The vegetarians of Octagon City." Woman's Day 13, 3 (Dec. 1949): 58-59, 116-117, 119.
      Account of ill-fated vegetarian settlement in Kansas.

194 Hough, James. "The foundation and growth of the vegetarian movement in Britain." Vegetarian News 34 (June-Aug. 1955): 59-67.
      History of the vegetarian movement in Great Britain from its founding in 1809.

195 Hough, James. "Vegetarianism and the healthy life." Vegetarian Messenger and Health Review 49 (Nov.-Dec. 1952): 188-190.
      Physical, mental and moral fitness are enhanced by the vegetarian diet.

196 Hyatt, Harold. "Vegetarian heritage." Vegetarian 6, 3 (May-June 1958): 67-70.
      Christian and Hebrew writings on the treatment of animals.

197 Ioteyko, I., and Kipiari, V. "A physiological study of vegetarians." Société Scientifique d'Hygiene Aliment-

aire et de l'Alimentation Rationelle de l'Homme.
Revue 3 (1906): 114-207.
 Forty-three vegetarians in Brussels had greater
endurance than comparable group of meat-eaters.
Lung capacity, body size, psychological measurements, kinds and amounts of foods eaten were studied;
authors conclude that meat should be considered a
drug and its use regulated. (In French.)

198 Jaffa, M. E. "Further investigations among fruitarians
at California Agricultural Experiment Station, 1901-
1902." U.S. Department of Agriculture. Office of
Experiment Stations. Bulletin (1902): 1-81.

199 Jaffa, M. E. "Nutritional investigations among fruitarians and Chinese at the California Agricultural Experiment Station, 1899-1901." U.S. Department of
Agriculture. Office of Experiment Stations. Bulletin
(1901): 1-43.
 Dietary study of six healthy fruitarians, 6-30 years
of age, living almost exclusively on raw fruits and
nuts.

200 James, W. S. "A vegetarian in central Africa."
Vegetarian News 35 (Mar.-May 1956): 5-9.
 Impressions from author's tour of Africa.

201 Jast, L. Stanley. "Why I am not a vegetarian." In:
Jast, L. Stanley. Libraries and living: essays and
addresses of a public librarian. Freeport, NY, Books
for Libraries Press, 1969, p. 236-247.
 Address before a vegetarian organization in 1927
identifies vegetarianism with a Mephistophelean negative view of life; characterizes vegetarians as uncon-
vivial, anti-social, overly-concerned with the wicked-
ness of meat-eating, with no palate for food or drink,
and riddled with inconsistencies.

202 Jolliffe, Norman, and Archer, Morton. "Statistical
associations between international coronary heart disease death rates and certain environmental factors."
Journal of Chronic Diseases 9, 6 (June 1959): 636-
652.
 International food and mortality statistics support
hypothesis that coronary heart disease mortality is
positively associated with intake of saturated fats, and
to a lesser extent, with intake of animal protein.

203 Jones, H. H. "Food and fads." Vegetarian Messenger and Health Review 49 (Jan. -Feb. 1952): 31-34.
Critique of recent speech by Dr. Charles Hill on vegetarian and vegan diets.

204 Jones, Herbert Hilton. Food and famine; a survey of the world food problem. Manchester, England, The Vegetarian Society (U. K.), 1953.
Economic examination of world food supplies and production with regard to world population; recommends less land devoted to livestock production; international control of staple foodstuffs; soil conservation; and elimination of speculation in food.

205 Jones, Joseph. "Transcendental grocery bills: Thoreau's Walden and some aspects of American vegetarianism." Texas Studies in English 36 (1957): 141-154.
Comparison of the vegetarian dietary principles of William Alcott and Henry David Thoreau.

206 Kantha, Joseph; Kurien, P. P.; Swaminathan, M.; and Subrahmanyan, V. "The metabolism of nitrogen, calcium and phosphorus in children on a poor vegetarian diet based on ragi (Eleusine coracana). Annals of Biochemistry and Experimental Medicine 18, 6 (1958): 195-200.
All subjects maintained positive balance for nitrogen, calcium, and phosphorus.

207 Kantha, Joseph; Rao, M. Narayana; Ganapathy, Sita; Swaminathan, M.; and Subrahmanyan, V. "Studies on the nutritive value of rice and rice diets. II. Metabolism of nitrogen, calcium and phosphorus in children on poor vegetarian diets containing husked, undermilled and milled raw rice." Annals of Biochemistry and Experimental Medicine 18, 2 (1958): 51-58.
Study of metabolism of three nutrients in seven girls consuming rice diets found all subjects in positive balance.

208 Kaunitz, Hans. "Mineral excretion after loading with various salts and its relation to 'serous inflammation' by vegetarian diet." Biochemische Zeitschrift 293, 1-2 (Sept. 24, 1937): 142-156.
Raw vegetable diet mitigated effects of serous inflammation of the parenchyma. (In German.)

209   Keith, M. Helen. "Is vegetarianism based on sound
       science? Theories and results briefly reviewed."
       Scientific American Suppl. 82, 2135 (Dec. 2, 1916):
       358-359.
            Reviewing animal studies, author judges vegetarian
       diet to be inferior and more dangerous than the mixed
       diet.

210   Keleny, Eugene. "Vegetarianism in Hungary." Vege-
       tarian News 37 (Sept.-Nov. 1958): 101-105.
            Origins and leadership of Hungarian Vegetarian
       Society which was abolished in 1951 by the Minister
       of the Interior.

211   Kellogg, John Harvey. The Battle Creek Sanitarium
       diet list. Battle Creek, MI, Modern Medicine Pub-
       lishing Co., 1909.

212   Kellogg, John Harvey. The miracle of life. Battle
       Creek, MI, Good Health Publishing Co., 1904.
            Work by breakfast cereal magnate and vegetarian
       food reformer contains information on health, nutri-
       tion, physiology, first aid; includes chapter entitled,
       "Shall we slay to eat?", p. 161-196.

213   Kellogg, John Harvey. The natural diet of man. Bat-
       tle Creek, MI, Modern Medicine Publishing Co.,
       1923.
            Health, ethical, historical and scientific objections
       to meat consumption; addresses popular myths sur-
       rounding flesh foods.

214   Kellogg, John Harvey. The new dietetics; a guide to
       scientific feeding in health and disease. Rev. ed.
       Battle Creek, MI, Modern Medicine Publishing Co.,
       1923.
            Principles of physiology, metabolism, dietetics and
       vegetarian nutrition in health and disease as practiced
       at the Battle Creek Sanitarium.

215   Kent, Margaret. "Diet in a vegetarian school." Vege-
       tarian News 27 (Spr. 1948): 13-14.
            Successes and difficulties experienced by dietician
       in vegetarian boarding school.

216   Kent, Margaret R. "Vegetarian food reform." Vege-
       tarian News 30 (Summer 1951): 56-59.

Essence of food reform is the consumption of
raw, whole, alkaline-forming foods.

217 Keys, Ancel. "Diet and the epidemiology of coronary
heart disease." American Medical Association.
Journal 164, 17 (Aug. 24, 1957): 1912-1919.
Evaluation of medical evidence to date supports
hypothesis that dietary fat is associated with coronary
heart disease.

218 Kingsford, Anna Bonus. Addresses and essays on vegetarianism. London, J. M. Watkins, 1912.
Letters, speeches and essays address full range of
vegetarian issues, from historical, physiological,
hygienic, ethical and philanthropic perspectives.

219 Klewitz, F., and Habs, H. "Die Rohkost." Gesell-
schaft zur Befoerderung der Gesamten Naturwissen-
schaften. Sitzungsberichte 66 (1931): 13-35.
Nutritional significance and composition of raw
vegetable diet of six vegetarians. (In German.)

220 Konemann, E. "Ernährungs-merkblatt." Bionomica 5
(June 1954): 84. (In German.)

221 Kuppuswamy, S. "Supplementary value of Indian multi-
purpose food to poor vegetarian diets based on different cereals and millets." Food Science 6, 4 (Apr.
1957): 84-86.

222 Lane, Dorothy Engelhard. "The nutrition of twins on a
vegetable diet during pregnancy, the nursing period
and infancy." American Journal of Diseases of Children 42 (1931): 1384-1400.
Vegan diet proved satisfactory in all respects for
the nutrition of the mother during pregnancy and for
twins.

223 Lankester, Edwin Ray. "Vegetarians and their teeth."
In: Lankester, Edwin Ray. Science from an easy
chair. 2nd series. New York, Methuen, 1911-
1913, p. 159-169.
Examination of the debate over man's teeth and
his proper diet.

224 Lattie, Athelstan. "Ninety-four years a vegetarian."
Vegetarian Messenger and Health Review 42 (Nov.

1945): 216-218.
Reflections of bishop who served as missionary in the East Indies and the Orient.

225 Law of God. An appeal. By a vegetarian. London, Richard J. James, 1915.

226 Lawrance, Hannah E. "Feeding the school child." Vegetarian News 25 (Summer 1946): 121-123.
Problems of food service in schools during wartime austerity.

227 Leadsworth, J. R. Diet and endurance. n. p. , 19--? (Life and Health Series, no. 3.)

228 Lederman, E. K. "Food in relation to character, taste and health." Vegetarian Messenger and Health Review 44 (Apr. 1947): 76-80.
Ethical, sensual, and scientific aspects of diet.

229 Levinson, Samuel A. "The effect of a relief vegetable protein diet on 'normal' human subjects." American Dietetic Association. Journal 22 (Nov. 1946): 987-994.
Study describes vegetable protein diet designed for starving people in post-World War II Europe; following extensive clinical investigation, diet was found to be adequate in all respects.

230 Liebstein, A. M. , and Ehmke, Neil L. "The case for vegetarianism." American Mercury 70 (Apr. 1950): 398-407.
Health, ethical and economic arguments for vegetarianism.

231 Lightowler, Ronald. "The vegetarian testimony." Vegetarian News 30 (Autumn 1951): 75-77.
The diet which is ethically right cannot be scientifically wrong.

232 Lightowler, Ronald. "Vital aspects of vegetarianism." Vegetarian News 34 (Autumn 1955): 98-100, 106.
Vegetarian food reform for physiological, psychological, economic and ecological well-being.

233 Lin, Kuo-Hao. "Nutritive value of vegetable diets from an economic standpoint." National Medical Journal of

China 17 (1931): 200-209.
Feeding experiments show that cost of milk-wheat-vegetable diet in China is four times that of a legume-cereal-vegetable diet.

234 Lin Yutang. "Confessions of a vegetarian." In: Lin Yutang. With love and irony. New York, The John Day Co., 1940, p. 99-103.
Rationalizations of a "vegetarian" who eats meat on occasion.

235 Loma Linda University. School of Dietetics. Lesson outlines in nutrition and cookery. 2nd ed. Mountain View, CA, Pacific Press Publishing Association, 1949.
Guidelines in outline format for teaching principles of healthful vegetarian nutrition and cookery.

236 Lyman, Benjamin Smith. Vegetarian diet and dishes. Philadelphia, Ferris and Leach, 1917.
Physiological, economical, and ethical advantages of vegetarianism; vegetarian food and recipes, and principles of preparation.

237 Mendel, Lafayette B. "Some historical aspects of vegetarianism." Popular Science 64 (Mar. 1904): 457-465.
Ethical and philosophical arguments for vegetarianism as expressed in literary works.

238 Miles, Eustace Hamilton. Failures of vegetarianism. New York, E. P. Dutton, 1902.
Vegetarian author inveighs against the extravagant claims, excesses, dogmatism and faddishness of the vegetarian movement; portrays vegetarians as frequently pugnacious, petulant, peevish and anemic.

239 Moore, Robert. "The Meat Trust defends womanhood." New Masses (Dec. 21, 1937): 15-16.
Arguments of the Meat Trust for resisting compulsory meat grading.

240 Moore-Patalieka, B. "What not to eat; the bad aspects of English diet." Vegetarian News 24 (Spr. 1946): 110-111.

241 Morgan, Agnes Fay. "Shall we eat meat?" Woman's
    Home Companion 62 (Mar. 1935): 65, 70.
        Advantages of meat in the diet.

242 Morgan, Sampson. "Fruits for health, strength, and
    longevity." Fortnightly Review 106 (July 1916): 145-
    156.
        Nutritive advantages of fruits and nuts over meats.

243 Nicolici, Dumitru. The original diet. 4th impression.
    Summer Hill, Australia, Religious Liberty Publish-
    ing Association, 1951.
        Quoting extensively from biblical scriptures and
    the writings of Ellen G. White, this work presents
    principles of vegetarian dietetics; and details adverse
    effects on health and character from consumption of
    meats, dairy products, eggs, alcohol, spicy condi-
    ments, and stimulants of all kinds; contains recipes
    for fruit, nut, grain and vegetable dishes.

244 Nolfi, K. Y. Levende føde; rakostens betydning for
    sundheden. 7th ed. Kobenhavn, n. p., 1951.

245 Oldfield, Josiah. "Dangers of meat eating." West-
    minster Review 166, 2 (Aug. 1906): 195-200.
        Essay notes difficulties of avoiding consumption of
    diseased meat; advocates fruitarian dietary.

246 Ortmann, B. Vegetarisme in de oudheid. Soest, Neth-
    erlands, J. H. Littooij, 1956.

247 Our holy commandments. By a vegetarian. London,
    Morton, Burt and Sons, 1926.

248 Paget, J. B. "The health of the nation." English Re-
    view 38 (Mar. 1924): 377-385.
        British military officer traces the deterioration of
    physique and stamina of his countrymen to overcon-
    sumption of meat, refined foods and tea.

249 Pink, C. V. "The position of veganism in 1952."
    Vegetarian News 31 (Spr. 1952): 4-8.
        Examination of successes and possible causes of
    failure of veganism in some individuals.

250 Pink, C. V. "Vegetarianism in infancy." Vegetarian
    News 25 (Summer 1946): 136-137.

Having observed nearly 3,000 vegetarian babies and children, writer concludes that they tend to be healthier, freer from childhood ailments, satisfactory in growth, and more physically and mentally alert than omnivorous children.

251 Poucel, J. "Le naturisme et la vie; la joie d'etre sains." Journal des Debats 40, 2 (July 14, 1933): 65-68.

252 Powell, Milton. "Veganism." Vegetarian Messenger and Health Review 44 (Apr. 1947): 80-82.
Reply to criticism by Watson (q.v.) of author's views on veganism.

253 Powell, Milton. "Veganism critically examined." Vegetarian Messenger and Health Review 44 (Feb. 1947): 33-37.
Attacks claims that milk is deleterious to the health, and that veganism is the most effective means of ending animal exploitation.

254 Powell, Milton. "Vegetarianism and psychology." Vegetarian Messenger and Health Review 42 (June 1945): 107-110.
Advancing the cause of vegetarianism by understanding and purging the unconscious mind of its aggressive, war-making, meat-eating impulses.

255 Pritchard, Florence, and Pritchard, Edgar W. Scientific meatless diet; being the principles and practice of lacto-vegetarianism based on the latest scientific discoveries with original recipes. 4th ed. Marryatville, Australia, The authors, 1953.
Advantages of lacto-vegetarian diet; recipes.

256 Reddy, S. K.; Doralswamy, T. R.; Sankaran, A. N.; Swaminathan, M.; and Subrahmanyan, V. "Effects on the general health and nutritional states of children of partial replacement of rice in a poor vegetarian diet by tapioca flour." British Journal of Nutrition 8, 1 (1954): 17-21.

257 Register, U. D. "Are non-flesh proteins adequate?" Review and Herald (Aug. 7, 1958): 16-19.
Review of research indicating the nutritional adequacy of vegetable proteins.

258 Reid, Marion. "Psychology and vegetarianism." Vegetarian Messenger and Health Review 44 (Apr. 1947): 82-84.
     Psychological effects on animal-loving children of learning the origins of the meat they eat.

259 Retlaw, George S. "The vegetarian miracle." Vegetarian Messenger and Health Review 45 (June 1948): 121-122.
     Account of worker's life being saved through vegetarian diet.

260 Robertson, T. Brailsford; Hicks, C. Stanton; and Marston, Hedley R. "A comparison of the utilization of nucleic acids of animal and vegetable origin." Australian Journal of Experimental Biology and Medical Science 4, 3 (1927): 125-150.
     Absorption study of nucleic acids of plant and animal origin on human subjects concludes that a meat diet is preferable to a vegetable diet if reduced uric-acid production is desired.

261 Roper, Dora Cathrine Christine Liebel. Vegetarian supplement to scientific feeding. Oakland, CA, Buckner Printing Co., 1915.
     Hygienic food preparation and combinations, stressing exercise and raw foods; menus, recipes.

262 Rotondi, Pietro. Your vegetarian baby; its care and development. Hollywood, CA, The author, 1953.
     Introduction to prenatal and child care emphasizes hygiene, emotional control, animal-free foods, and consistent training of the child.

263 Rumpf, T. "The therapeutic use of a vegetarian diet." Zeitschrift für Diätetische und Physikalische Therapie 4 (1901): 25-37.
     Case of an apparently healthy man consuming a strict vegetarian diet; also discusses therapeutic uses of vegetarian diet. (In German.)

264 Russell, Hon. R. Strength and diet; a practical treatise with special regard to the life of nations. London, Green and Co., 1905.

265 Sale, George. "Eat or be eaten." English Review 42 (June 1926): 830-835.

Author dreams world becomes vegetarian by the
year 1950, and that by 2000, total chaos reigns, with
extremism, fanatacism and veganism rampant.

266 Salt, Henry Stephens. The logic of vegetarianism; essays and dialogues. 2nd ed., rev. London, G. Bell
and Sons, 1906.
Puts forth the logical case for vegetarianism on
the grounds of historical, physiological, religious,
asthetic, economic, and humanitarian concerns; answers commonly raised objections to vegetarianism.

267 Schouteden, H. "Ergographie de la main droite et de
la main gauche." Société Royale des Sciences Medi-
cales et Naturelles de Bruxelles. Annales 1, 5
(1904): 1-28.
Vegetarians averaged almost twice as many right-
hand contractions on an ergograph before exhaustion
compared to meat-eaters, and recovered from exhaustion more rapidly. (In French.)

268 Semple, Dugald. "The food crisis." Vegetarian Messenger and Health Review 43 (Aug. 1946): 158-159.
Calls for reductions in food waste, both individual-
ly and nationally in view of food shortages, rationing,
and other privations.

269 Semple, Dugald. "Why be vegetarian?" Vegetarian
Messenger and Health Review 48 (June 1951): 141-
143.
Vegetarianism and a renewed interest in the cultivation of the soil seen as alleviating world food
shortages.

270 Semple, Dugald. "Why food reform?" Vegetarian
News 24 (Winter 1945-1946): 84-85.
Changes in diet and food consumption patterns
brought about by war-time food shortages and rationing.

271 Shaw, George Bernard. "The vegetarian diet according
to Shaw." Vegetarian Times (Mar.-Apr. 1979): 50-
51.
Reprint from the Daily Chronicle, March 1, 1918,
presents Shaw's thoughts on diet.

272 Sheldon, Charles M. "The confessions of a vegetarian."
Independent 60 (June 21, 1906): 1457-1458.

Author describes his conversion to vegetarianism and his convictions that Americans eat too much and spend too much time and energy in the preparation of meals.

273 Shupper, Frances. Why grow old? Rockaway Beach, NY, Juvend Publishing Co. , 1928.

274 Simons, Madeleine A. "Rousseau's natural diet." Romantic Review 45, 1 (Feb. 1954): 18-28.
Although never a vegetarian, Rousseau espoused principles of a simply-prepared meatless diet of seasonal fruits and vegetables.

275 Simoons, Frederick J. "The distribution and origin of widely held prejudices against certain animal foods in the Old World." Association of American Geographers. Annals 48, 3 (Sept. 1958): 289.
Abstract of paper dealing with prohibitions against the eating of beef, pork and dog flesh, and evaluation of explanations for their being held over widespread areas of the world.

276 Sinclair, Upton. "Fasting experiments and experiences." Physical Culture 29 (Mar. 1913): 227-232.
Article on fasting by the 20th-century vegetarian writer and social activist.

277 Sinclair, Upton. The jungle. New York, Vanguard Press, 1926.
Injustices and deplorable conditions of American meat packing industry in the early 20th century.

278 Sinclair, Upton Beall. The fasting cure. New York, Mitchell Kennerly, 1911.
Fasting guidelines and benefits, based on author's personal experiences; also, opinions on the use of meat in the diet.

279 Staehelin, Rudolf. "Investigations on vegetarian diet, with special regard to the nervous system, circulation of the blood and diuresis." Zeitschrift für Biologie 49 (1907): 199-282.
Experiments performed on the author and other patients determined that meat had a decided diuretic effect, that blood viscosity was sometimes lower on a vegetarian diet, and that the pulse was frequently

higher after a large vegetarian meal than after a meat meal. (In German.)

280 Stevens, Henry Bailey. The recovery of culture. New York, Harper and Brothers, 1949.
Cultural and social history explains how man became a meat-eating and war-waging species.

281 Stoddard, Alan. "A vegetarian in the merchant navy." Vegetarian Messenger and Health Review 43 (Sept. 1946): 176-178.
Adventures of vegetarian ship's surgeon during World War II.

282 Stolzenberg, Günther. "Das vegetarische Lindenblatt." Neue Lebensordnung 7, 9 (Sept. 1956): 14-17. (In German.)

283 Strøm, Axel, and Jensen, R. Adelsten. "Mortality from circulatory diseases in Norway 1940-1945." Lancet 260 (Jan. 20, 1951): 126-129.
During the war years, in spite of increased nervous strain and anxiety, Norway experienced a well-defined decline in deaths from heart disease, which correlated with a decline in the consumption of meats, dairy products, eggs, and fats; a decline in protein consumption, and total calories consumed.

284 Subrahmanyan, V.; Bhagawan, R. K.; Doralswamy, T. R.; Joseph, K.; Bains, G. S.; Bhatia, M.; Sankaran, A. N.; and Swaminathan, M. "Effect of replacement of rice in a poor vegetarian diet by tapioca macaroni on the general health and nutritional status of children." Food Science 7, 4 (Apr. 1958): 87-89.

285 Tallarico, Giuseppe. "The vegetarian regimen is suitable for mid-life." Agricoltura 1, 10 (Oct. 1952): 45-50.
Guidelines for vegetarian diet after age forty. (In Italian.)

286 Taylor, Alonzo Englebert. "Is vegetarianism capable of world-wide application?" Popular Science 79 (Dec. 1911): 587-593.
Philosophical and practical arguments for and against vegetarianism.

287 Taylor, S., and Farrington, W. M. "Annual report
of the Vegetarian Society for the year ended 31st
August, 1946." Vegetarian Messenger and Health
Review 43 (Dec. 1946): 238-245.
　　Lectures presented, literature published, affiliated
societies, financial statements, etc. of the Vegetarian
Society.

288 Thomas, K. "Protein requirement and a vegetarian
diet." Umschau 14 (1910): 67-70.
　　Author asserts that a vegetarian diet would suffice
for agricultural regions, but animal foods are prefer-
able for urban populations; questions the rationality of
the vegetarian diet.

289 Tissier, H. "A vegetable diet utilizing animal fat followed during two years." Société de Biologie.
Comptes Rendus des Seances 68 (1910): 12-14.
　　Two adults lived two years on a vegetarian diet of
42-50 grams protein, 103-143 grams fat, and 225-249
grams carbohydrate daily, which proved ample for
both sedentary and physically demanding lifestyles.
(In French.)

290 Trueman, Kenneth. "Vegetarianism--England, 1888."
Vegetarian News 29 (Winter 1950): 103-108.
　　The social, political, and economic climate for
vegetarianism in 1888.

291 United States. Library of Congress. Division of Bibliography. List of references on vegetarianism.
Washington, DC, 1922. (Selected list of references,
no. 629.)
　　Selected bibliography covering general references,
cookbooks, and periodicals.

292 Valle, Adrian. "Influencia moral de la alimentación
vegetariana." Pro-Vida 25, 280 (Dec. 1944): 3-4.

293 Van Voast, Ellen. Eating for life, health and happiness. Washington, DC, Wednesday Club, 1916.

294 Velasco, Jose. "El vegetarismo de la post-guerra."
Pro-Vida 25, 273 (May 1944): 7.

295 Venkat Rao, S.; Pantulu, A. J.; Swaminathan, M.; and
Subrahmanyan, V. "Supplementary value of low-fat

groundnut flour to poor vegetarian diets based on jowar (Sorghum vulgare) and ragi (Eleusine cora- cana)." Annals of Biochemical and Experimental Medicine 18, 1 (1958): 33-38.

The addition of 10-20 percent groundnut flour to poor vegetarian diets produced a marked improvement in the growth-promoting value of the diets.

296 Wakeham, Glen, and Hansen, Louis. "The basal meta- bolic rates of vegetarians." Journal of Biological Chemistry 97, 1 (1932): 155-162.

Average basal metabolic rates dropped after six to eight years in subjects consuming vegetarian diets.

297 Wakeham, Glen, and Hansen, Louis. "The basal- metabolic rates of vegetarians." Science 74, 1909 (July 17, 1931): 70-71.

Basal metabolic rates of young women who had been vegetarians for at least five years were signifi- cantly lower than in non-vegetarians.

298 Walker, Norman Wardhaugh. Become younger. St. George, UT, Norwalk Press, 1949.

Evangelistic style urges vegetarianism and naturo- pathic healing; the phrase "Become Younger" appears in bold type at least twice on each page.

299 Wan, Shing. "Chemical composition of bones of vege- tarian and omnivorous rats." Chinese Journal of Physiology 7, 1 (1932): 23-24.

Omnivorous rats were larger than vegetarian rats, but there was little difference in the chemical com- position of the bones.

300 Wassersug, Joseph D. "The case against vegetarian- ism." American Mercury 70 (Apr. 1950): 407-413.

Arguments against reputed health benefits of vege- tarian diet.

301 Watson, Donald. "Veganism." Vegetarian Messenger and Health Review 44 (May 1947): 103-104.

Further reply to Milton Powell (q. v.).

302 Watson, Donald. "Veganism--a reply to Milton Pow- ell." Vegetarian Messenger and Health Review 44 (Mar. 1947): 55-60.

Challenges views expressed by Powell (q. v.) on veganism.

303 Weinmann, Ingeborg, and Schuphan, Werner. "Ernäh-
rungsversuche mit pflanzlicher Mischkost zur Ermitt-
lung der Aufwertbarkeit von pflanzlichen Eiweisstof-
fen." Qualitas Plantarum et Materiae Vegetebiles 5,
1-2 (Dec. 18, 1958): 85-94.
   Nitrogen balance studies in men and rats demonstrated the satisfactory protein quality in vegetarian
diets. (In German.)

304 Wells, Dorothy. "Vegetarianism of the Hindus."
Vegetarian News 34 (Dec. 1955-Feb. 1956): 162-165.
   State of vegetarianism among high-caste Hindus.

305 Wheldon, Rupert H. No animal food; and nutrition and
diet with vegetable recipes. New York, Health Culture Co., 1910.
   Appeal for vegetarianism based on ethics, aesthetics, economics, and physiology; advocates exclu-
sion of all foods of animal origin; also, section on
nutrition, dietetics, food values, recipes.

306 White, Alma Bridwell. Why I do not eat meat. Zare-
phath, NJ, The Pentecostal Union, 1915.
   Biblical interpretation and personal testimony in
support of vegetarian diet.

307 White, Ellen Gould Harmon. Counsels on diet and
foods; a compilation from the writings of Ellen G.
White. Takoma Park, MD, Review and Herald Publishing Association, 1938.
   Subject arrangement of quotations on matters of
diet and food reform by the founder of the Seventh-
day Adventist faith.

308 White, Julius Gilbert. Abundant health: expounding
the learn-how-to-be-well system of daily living. 3rd
ed. Madison College, TN, Julius Gilbert White Publications, 1942.
   Maintenance of physical and mental health through
the vegetarian diet and wholesome living.

309 Whiting, Harry. "How to reform your dietary."
Vegetarian Messenger and Health Review (Apr. 1951):
89-91.
   Steps include elimination of white flour, white
sugar, tea, coffee, meats, and then adopting diet
based on an abundance of salads, fruits, and con-
servatively cooked vegetables.

310 Wilkerson, Clennell. "The vegetarian dilemma." Outlook 58 (Nov. 6, 1926): 429.
Vegetarians find themselves in a predicament because, in spite of their protestations to the contrary, they probably still crave meat, and furthermore must deal with the guilt of killing plants for food.

311 Williams, H. S. "Vegetable versus meat diet." Hearst's Magazine 22 (Sept. 1912): 106.
Brief review of studies of vegetable and meat diets in rats.

312 Williams, Howard. The ethics of diet; a biographical history of the literature of humane dietetics from the earliest period to the present day. Abridged edition. Manchester, England, Albert Broadbent, 1907.
Classic of vegetarian literature traces writings in support of vegetarianism from ancient Greece to the nineteenth century.

313 Wishart, G. M. "Efficiency and performance of a vegetarian racing cyclist under different dietary conditions." Journal of Physiology 82 (1934): 189-199.
Ergometer experiments found the best performance on a high-protein vegetarian diet.

314 Wokes, F. "The direct use of plant materials by man." British Journal of Nutrition 6 (1952): 118-124.
Review of land requirements for various diets; protein and other nutrients in vegetarian diets; aspects of vegetable substitutes for animal products.

315 Wood, Francis. Reply to Dean Inge's defence of flesh-eating. London, C. W. Daniel Co., 1934.

316 Wright, Celeste Turner. "Much taboo about nothing." Hygeia 18 (Dec. 1940): 1088-1090.
Personal account of vegetarian for 20 years who went back to eating meat.

317 Wynne-Tyson, Esmé. "Approaches to vegetarianism." Vegetarian Messenger and Health Review 49 (May-June 1952): 79-81.
Discussion of shortcomings of adopting vegetarianism from intellectual, self-perfecting motivations alone.

318 Wynne-Tyson, Esmé. "The significance of vegetarian-
     ism." Vegetarian 1 (May-June 1953): 90-92.
         By renouncing violence toward his fellow man and
     fellow creatures, the humane vegetarian becomes the
     outward expression of conscience and applied com-
     passion.

319 Yukawa, G. "The absolute vegetarian diet of Japanese
     Bonzes." Archiv für Verdauungs-Krankheiten 15
     (1910): 471-524.
         Dietary study of 12 strict vegetarian Buddhist
     monks in Japan. (In German.)

320 Zeuger, Hans. "A cooperative community for vege-
     tarians." Cooperative Living 2 (Fall 1950): 13-15.
         Guidelines for organizing vegetarian farming set-
     tlements.

PART II:

RECENT WORKS: 1960-1980

GENERAL INTEREST

321 Airola, Paavo. How to get well; Dr. Airola's hand-
     book of natural healing. Phoenix, Health Plus Pub-
     lishers, 1974.
     Outlines vegetarian foods, supplements, fasting as
     therapy for common ailments.

322 Alexander, Alice. "The Farm." Atlanta Journal and
     Constitution Magazine (Apr. 8, 1979): 12-13, 33-34.
     Description of highly successful vegan community
     in Summertown, Tennessee.

323 Altman, Nathaniel. "Can a non-meat diet enhance your
     love life?" Vegetarian Times (May-June 1977): 10-
     12.
     Another plus for the healthful and humane diet.

324 Altman, Nathaniel. Eating for life; a book about vege-
     tarianism. Wheaton, IL, Theosophical Publishing
     House, 1973.
     Comprehensive coverage of all aspects of vege-
     tarianism.

325 Altman, Nathaniel. "The Meat Board has been feeding
     you a lot of baloney about nutrition." Vegetarian
     Times (Jan. -Feb. 1978): 10-13.
     Rebuttal to pamphlet issued by The National Live
     Stock and Meat Board extolling the virtues of meat-
     eating and warning of potential health hazards of
     vegetarianism.

326 Altman, Nathaniel. "Statement of Nathaniel Altman,
     American Vegetarians, Inc." In: Diet related to killer
     diseases, III. Hearings before the Select Committee
     on Nutrition and Human Needs of the United States
     Senate, 95th Congress, 1st session; response to diet-

49

ary goals of the United States: Re meat, Mar. 24, 1977, p. 321-322.
    Letter addresses health hazards posed by DDT, pesticides, and chemical additives found in meat.

327   Anon.   "Bringing vegetarianism into the gourmet lime-light." Vegetarian Times (Jan. -Feb. 1980): 28-32, 34-35.
    Feature article on vegan world class chef, Brother Ron Pikarski.

328   Anon.   "Diet theory: basic arguments in favor of vegetarianism." Vegetarian Times (May-June 1979): 32, 34-35.
    Nutritional and health arguments for eliminating meat from the diet.

329   Anon.   "Dieticians to testify on diet of children of vegetarian parents." Detroit News (Mar. 7, 1980): sec. B, p. 3.

330   Anon.   "Find out the facts on vegetarians." Current Health 4 (Mar. 1978): 30-31.
    Mother and son dialogue on vegetarianism.

331   Anon.   "For vegetarians." Chemistry 45, 7 (July 1972): 2.
    Brief summary of medical and environmental arguments for vegetarianism.

332   Anon.   "The future of vegetarianism." Vegetarian Times (Jan. -Feb. 1980): 37-42.
    Readers present their wide-ranging thoughts on the future of vegetarianism.

333   Anon.   "Helen and Scott Nearing: living the good life at 95." Vegetarian Times (Jan. -Feb. 1978): 38-39.
    Philosophy and lifestyle of vegetarian homesteaders and lifelong political activists.

334   Anon.   "The kosher of the counterculture." Time 96 (Nov. 16, 1970): 59-60, 63.
    Examination of the flourishing vegetarian, macro-biotic and natural foods movements.

335   Anon.   "Marcia Pearson." Vegetarian Times (Dec. -Jan. 1977): 44.
    Sketch of vegetarian activist and model.

336 Anon. "Michigan assumes custody of children whose
     parents are vegetarians." Detroit News (Mar. 3,
     1980): sec. B, p. 1.

337 Anon. "Michigan vegetarians receive permanent custody
     of their children." Detroit News (May 8, 1980):
     sec. C, p. 12.

338 Anon. "Michigan vegetarians restored custody of chil-
     dren with court warning." Detroit News (Mar. 14,
     1980): sec. B, p. 1.

339 Anon. "Nutrition and vegetarianism." Dairy Council
     Digest 50, 1 (Jan. -Feb. 1979): 1-6.
          Describes types and motivations of present-day
     vegetarians, as well as potential health hazards of
     very restrictive diets. Reprinted in Canadian Home
     Economics Journal 30 (Winter 1980): 10-14.

340 Anon. "Nutrition as therapy." Consumer Reports
     (Jan. 1980): 21-24.
          Urges caution in attributing therapeutic or pre-
     ventive qualities to megavitamins, vegetarianism,
     food fads and the like.

341 Anon. "One man's experience: fighting for the Green
     Revolution on the path to the Green Berets." Vege-
     tarian Times (Mar. -Apr. 1979): 52-53.
          Maintaining a vegetarian diet in the Army's Ranger
     School.

342 Anon. "PKU: PKU is shorthand for phenylketonuria,
     a rare disorder that robs kids of their intelligence."
     Chicago Tribune (July 8, 1979): sec. 12, p. 1.
          Report on rare, inherited infant disease which can
     be arrested by vegetarian diet and synthetic protein
     supplements.

343 Anon. "Sentence in death of boy, 4, upheld." New
     York Times (May 8, 1980): sec. 2, p. 4.
          Brief article on child's death after being fed re-
     stricted diet of only ground vegetables for several
     months.

344 Anon. "Study of vegetarianism fleecing the public?"
     Christian Science Monitor 71 (Oct. 30, 1979): 2.
          Briefly notes Senator William Proxmire's "Golden

Fleece" award to the U. S. Dept. of Agriculture for
study of behavioral determinants of vegetarianism.

345   Anon.   "A talk with Dick Gregory." Essence 10 (Aug.
      1979): 114.
        Brief interview with vegetarian social activist
      Dick Gregory.

346   Anon.   Vegan mothers and children.   Surrey, England,
      Vegan Society, 1973.
        Articles by ten vegan mothers describing their
      diets, pregnancies and children's development.

347   Anon.   "Vegetarian diets gain popularity." Futurist
      10 (Aug. 1976): 219.
        Increasing number of Americans from all walks of
      life are turning to vegetarianism as a result of eco-
      nomic, ecological, ethical and health concerns.

348   Anon.   "Vegetarian wins Nobel Prize for literature."
      Vegetarian Times (Jan. -Feb. 1979): 6.
        Profile of ethical vegetarian Isaac Bashevis Singer.

349   Anon.   "Vegetarians." New Yorker 55 (Sept. 17,
      1979): 36-37.
        Views following a visit to the 1979 National Vege-
      tarian Conference held at the Vegetarian Hotel in the
      Catskills.

350   Anon.   "Vegetarians: out of the closet." CNI Weekly
      Report 6, 14 (Apr. 1, 1976): 4-6.
        Examines evidence from several studies indicating
      vegetarians are well-nourished and perhaps in better
      health than omnivores.

351   Bacialli, S.   "When a vegetarian diet can be danger-
      ous." Good Housekeeping 182, 5 (May 1976): 211.
        Summarizes nutritional adequacy of three cate-
      gories of vegetarian diets.

352   Baer, Wilma F.   Secretos de la buena mesa.   Mexico,
      Ediciones Interamericanas, 1965.

353   Baker, Jay.   "What's your beef?   Going vegetarian
      without hasseling your family." Seventeen 39 (Aug.
      1980): 70.
        Six tips for teenage vegetarians.

354 Baldwin, Bernell E. , and Baldwin, Marjorie V. "Can eating meat cause disease?" Ministry (Nov. 1976): 32-36.
Report of a tour of a federally inspected slaughterhouse finding cattle carcasses condemned in whole or part due to various cancers, parasites, and infectious diseases; reviews meat inspection methods and relationship between meat-eating and chronic diseases.

355 Bargen, Richard. The vegetarian's self-defense manual. Wheaton, IL, Theosophical Publishing House, 1979.
Witty, irreverent bibliographic essay evaluates and interprets medical literature on vegetarianism; extensive bibliography.

356 Barkas, Janet. "It's super vegetable!" Family Health 7, 1 (Jan. 1975): 44-48.
Historical, nutritional and economical aspects of vegetarian diet.

357 Barkas, Janet. "The new vegetarians." McCalls 102 (Sept. 1975): 38.
Brief survey of upsurge in popularity of vegetarianism and tips for vegetarian meal preparation.

358 Bender, A. E. "Health foods." Nutrition Society. Proceedings 38, 1 (May 1, 1979): 163-171.
Critical discussion of claims and pricing of products (vegetarian, whole foods, additive-free, etc.) in health food stores.

359 Benjamin, Harry. Commonsense vegetarianism. 2nd ed. Wellingborough, England, Thorsons, 1974.

360 Bergan, James G. , and Brown, Phyllis T. A review of vegetarianism and the "new" vegetarians. (Second recording.) Chicago, American Dietetic Association, 1976. (Cassette-a-month-6, 1976.)
Review of medical studies notes health hazards and benefits of vegetarian diet; emphasis on studies of macrobiotics practicing Eastern religions in a communal setting; history of vegetarianism also presented.

361 Berry, Rynn, Jr. "Cloris!" Vegetarian Times (May-June 1979): 14-16, 18-20.
Interview with vegetarian actress Cloris Leachman.

362   Berry, Rynn, Jr.   The vegetarians.   Brookline, MA,
      Autumn Press, 1979.
        Insightful interviews with fourteen prominent vege-
      tarians in the fields of entertainment, literature, re-
      ligion, medicine, and social activism.

363   Bircher-Benner, Max Oskar.   The prevention of incur-
      able disease.   New Canaan, CT, Keats Publishing,
      1978.
        Chronic diseases may be prevented or cured by
      diet rich in raw fruits, vegetables, and nuts, with
      limited quantities of animal foods, and the elimination
      of alcohol, coffee, salt, and sugar.

364   Blair, Betty.   "Fruitarians squeeze diet to the limits."
      Detroit News (Jan. 2, 1979): sec. D, p. 1.
        Philosophy and nutritional value of fruitarian diet.

365   Blair, Betty J.   "New vegetarianism takes on flavor of
      respectability."   Detroit News (Apr. 9, 1978): sec.
      C, p. 1.
        Article on upsurge of popularity of vegetarianism
      notes health benefits, vegetarian researchers, and
      vegetarian organizations.

366   Blau, Eleanor.   "Schooling the new vegetarians."   Nu-
      trition Today 9, 1 (Jan.-Feb. 1974): 26.
        Description of Hare Krishna boarding school in
      Dallas, Texas.

367   Bohan, Paul.   "Nuts."   Manchester Medical Gazette
      54, 1 (Autumn 1974): 10.
        Humorous portrayal of the behavior of vegetarians
      at parties and social events.

368   Bower, Joanne.   "Poisoned meat."   New Ecologist 5
      (Sept.-Oct. 1978): 155-156.
        Hazards of hormone implants for growth promotion
      in livestock and poultry.

369   Braunstein, Mark.   "On being radically vegetarian."
      Vegetarian Times (Mar. 1980): 72-73.
        Essay presents the moral necessity of carrying the
      vegetarian diet to its logical conclusions.

370   Braunstein, Mark.   "Vegetarianism in art."   Vegetarian
      Times (Sept. 1980): 20, 22-24.
        Vegetarian sensibilities portrayed in works of art.

371 Brown, Harold R. "Vegetarianism and food reform. "
     Soil Sense 9, 10 (Dec. 1972): 19-20.
     Discussion of types of vegetarian diets, health
     benefits and hazards; warns against extremism in
     diet.

372 Calkins, Alice. "Observations on vegetarian dietary
     practice and social factors: the need for further re-
     search. " American Dietetic Association. Journal
     74, 3 (Mar. 1979): 353-355.
     Review of the literature related to social char-
     acteristics and motivations of vegetarians.

373 Callizo, G. R. La salud a través de la filosofía y la
     dieta vegetarianas. Barcelona, De Vecchi, 1975.

374 Candeias, Olegário Ribeiro. Sojo, vegetarianismo e
     saúde (diálogo com o povo). São Paulo, Composto e
     impresso pela Duplicadora Gráfica Batico, 1970.

375 Carter, Angela. "The new vegetarians. " New Society
     35, 700 (Mar. 4, 1976): 501-502.
     Pokes fun at the moral superiority, rituals and
     philosophical outlook of macrobiotics and vegetarians.

376 Castro, José. 60 secretos para prolongar la juventud.
     Torrente, Spain, Ediciones Castro, 1975.

377 Chen, Philip Stanley. The joy of being a vegetarian.
     Mountain View, CA, Pacific Press Publishing Associ-
     ation, 1977.
     Comprehensive presentation of major physiological,
     medical and ecological benefits of vegetarian diet;
     three sections of vegetarian recipes.

378 Cherry, Laurence. "Food for thought: is vegetarian-
     ism the better way?" Glamour 75 (Oct. 1977): 164,
     166, 169-170.
     Motivations and advantages of vegetarian diet.

379 Cherry, Laurence. "Make mine a broccoli steak. "
     Ms 6 (Feb. 1978): 68-72.
     Summary of health, economic, and ethical argu-
     ments for vegetarianism.

380 Clinkard, C. E. The uses of juices extracted from
     raw fruits and vegetables. Auckland, N. Z. , Whit-
     combe and Tombs, 1973.

381 Cox, Jeff. "The raw food, feel-good diet." Organic
     Gardening and Farming 25 (July 1978): 48-54.
          Health advantages of raw food vegetarian diet;
     recipes.

382 Cox, Michael, and Crockett, Desda. The subversive
     vegetarian; tactics, information and recipes for the
     conversion of meat eaters. Wellingborough, England,
     Thorsons, 1979.

383 Day, Harvey. About yoga diet. London, Thorsons,
     1969.
          Yoga philosophy as related to vegetarianism; dis-
     cusses history, protein; recipes.

384 Dextreit, Raymond. Initiation à l'alimentation végé-
     tarienne moderne. Les raisons, des conseils pra-
     tiques. 75 menus, 70 recettes. Paris, Editions de
     la revue "Vivre en harmonie," 1967.

385 Dorfman, Peter. "Vegetarians: who are they and
     what do they want from you?" Health Foods Busi-
     ness (Aug. 1980): 49-56.
          Analysis of the increasing significance of vegetar-
     ianism as a force in the health food market.

386 Dosti, Rose. "Vegetarian diet: idea with flaws."
     Los Angeles Times (Jan. 8, 1976): sec. 6, p. 1.
          Interview with biochemist and nutritionist J. W.
     Meduski stresses hazards of improperly planned vege-
     tarian diet, and need for nutritional knowledge and
     education.

387 Douglas, Gary D. "Too much at steak: the virtues
     of man the carnivore." Analog 98 (Mar. 1978):
     101-104.

388 Ealey, David. "Neglected vegetarian: I enjoy a good
     meal too." Sunday Times (London) (Feb. 10, 1980):
     19.
          Letter decries lack of tolerance, and limited
     restaurant menus for vegetarian diners.

389 Elrick, Harold; Crakes, James; and Clarke, Sam.
     Living longer and better: guide to optimal health.
     Mountain View, CA, World Publications, 1978.
          Preventive medicine through changes in lifestyle

and dietary habits; contains chapter on vegetarian diet with sample menus.

390 Faale, Ingrid. Råkostboken. Oslo, Forfatteren (Bok-centralen), 1969.

391 Ferrándiz, V. L. Armonías alimenticias: la buena combinación de los alimentos. 5th ed. Viladrau, Spain, Cedel, 1972.

392 Findhorn Garden, by the Findhorn Community. New York, Harper and Row, 1975.
   Account of vegetarian spiritual community in northern Scotland.

393 Fiske, Edward B. "Marijuana part of religion at commune in Tennessee." New York Times (Feb. 17, 1973): 33.
   Features controversial agricultural and religious vegan community in Tennessee.

394 Fleshman, Ruth P. "Eating rituals and realities." Nursing Clinics of North America 8, 1 (Mar. 1973): 91-104.
   Explores differing ways in which food is viewed; relates experiences of working at California free clinic; discusses diets with symbolic or spiritual meanings, which tend to be variations of the vegetarian theme.

395 Focus on health maintenance and prevention of illness. Wakefield, MA, Contemporary Publishing, 1975.
   Contains 18 essays on preventive medicine, including one discussing vegetarianism from historical, biological, and contemporary viewpoints.

396 Fulton, Alvenia M. Vegetarianism--fact or myth? Eating to live. Chicago, B.C.A. Publishing Corp., 1978.
   Introduction to vegetarianism, therapeutic dietary principles; recipes.

397 Fussell, B. H. "A tiny hamlet is vegetarians' hub." New York Times (June 11, 1978): sec. 11, p. 16-17.
   Profile of Jay and Freya Dinshah, founders of the North American Vegetarian Society and the American Vegan Society.

398 Fussell, B. H. "Vegetarians find their faith bearing
     fruit." New York Times (Aug. 2, 1978): sec. 3,
     p. 7.
          Report on the 4th annual congress of the North
     American Vegetarian Society.

399 García Bellsolá, Domingo. Los 50 lumbreras de la
     humanidad fueron vegetarianos: (los avaladores del
     naturismo). 2nd ed. Barcelona, Instituto Naturista
     Bellsolá, 1974.

400 Garfield, Eugene. "The vegetarian alternative." Cur-
     rent Contents (Mar. 14, 1977): 5-13.
          Editorial presents review of vegetarian philosophy
     and dietary principles.

401 Garten, Max Otto. "Civilized" diseases and their cir-
     cumvention. San Jose, CA, Maxmillion World Pub-
     lishers, 1978.
          Links diseases of Western civilization with faulty
     nutrition; raw foods, vegetarian diet, fasting suggested
     as therapeutic agents; extensive treatment of hazards
     of amalgam dental fillings.

402 Gerber, Charles. Alimentazione e salute. Sedici il-
     lustrazioni a colori e in nero fuori testo. Otto tab-
     elle nel testo. Firenze, Italy, A. D. V. , 1971.

403 Giehl, Dudley. Vegetarianism, a way of life. New
     York, Harper and Row, 1979.
          Thoroughly researched work covering environmen-
     tal, economic, ethical, health and religious issues,
     in addition to chapter tracing the theme of vegetarian-
     ism through the world's literature; biographical infor-
     mation on famous vegetarians.

404 Girard, Penny. "Vegetarian diet called ideal for space
     colonies." Los Angeles Times (Oct. 2, 1978): sec.
     1, p. 16.
          Brief account of second World Vegetarian Day con-
     ference held in Washington, DC.

405 Glick, Ruth. "Do you need all that red meat?" Es-
     sence 10 (June 1979): 58, 60.
          Health advantages of cutting back on meat con-
     sumption.

406 Goldberg, Jeanne. "Vegetarianism." Family Health
    10, 4 (Apr. 1978): 30-31.
        Brief review of history of vegetarianism, motiva-
    tions for becoming a vegetarian and nutritional ade-
    quacy of different types of vegetarian diets.

407 Golikere, R. K. Vegetarian vs. nonvegetarian. Bom-
    bay, India, Popular Book Depot, 1960.
        Discussion of various types of animals eaten by
    man; hazards of animal foods; maintaining balanced
    vegetarian diet; and state of vegetarianism in India.

408 Grosvenor, Verta Mae. "The vegetarians are coming!
    The vegetarians are coming!" Essence 8 (Oct. 1977):
    112-114, 116, 118.
        Advice on making the best of the coming vegetarian
    revolution.

409 Grotta-Kurska, Daniel. "Before you say 'Baloney'...
    Here's what you should know about vegetarianism."
    Today's Health 52, 10 (Oct. 1974): 18-21, 73-74.
        Notes reasons for vegetarianism, especially health
    and economic advantages.

410 Gsundi Choscht. Wegweiser zu naturnaher Ernährung.
    Winterthur, Switzerland, Verband schweizerischer
    Kneippvereine, 1968.

411 Hershaft, Alex. "The government should promote
    vegetarianism for health." Vegetarian Times (June
    1980): 37-38.
        Testimony regarding health aspects of vegetarian
    diet presented before Senate Subcommittee on Health
    and Scientific Research.

412 Hershaft, Alex. "How many vegetarians?" Washing-
    ton, DC, Vegetarian Information Service, n. d.
        Results of 1978 Roper poll indicated that U. S.
    vegetarians number seven to nine million, with 78
    percent of Americans surveyed acknowledging the
    merits of vegetarianism.

413 Hershaft, Alex. "Public information on meatless nu-
    trition." In: Nutrition Education. Hearings before
    the Subcommittee on Domestic Marketing, Consumer
    Relations, and Nutrition of the Committee on Agricul-
    ture, House of Representatives, 95th Congress, 1st

Session, Sept. 28, 1977, part 1, p. 441-445.
Statement recommends implementation of two-phase program of nutritional education and unbiased nutritional research; presents evidence for nutritional and environmental superiority of meatless diet.

414 Hershaft, Alex. "Statement of Alex Hershaft, President, Vegetarian Information Service, Inc." In: Nutrition Education: National Consumer Nutrition Information Act of 1978. Hearings before the Subcommittee on Domestic Marketing, Consumer Relations, and Nutrition of the Committee on Agriculture, House of Representatives, 95th Congress, 2nd Session, on H.R. 11761 and H.R. 12428, Jan. 31, 1978, part 2, p. 346-348.
Presents problems in conducting nutrition policy and nutrition education; objections and recommendations with regard to H.R. 12428.

415 Hershaft, Alex. "Statement of Alex Hershaft, President, Vegetarian Information Service, Inc." In: Nutrition Labeling and Information Amendments of 1979 to the Federal Food, Drug, and Cosmetic Act. Hearings before the Subcommittee on Health and Scientific Research of the Committee on Labor and Human Resources, United States Senate, 96th Congress, 2nd Session, on S.1652, Feb. 20, 1980, p. 65-67, 124-132.
Testimony on the role of meat and animal fat in the incidence of killer diseases; traces influence of meat industry in the U.S.; recommends five-point plan for nutrition education, food labeling and meatless alternatives in public feeding programs.

416 Hershaft, Alex. "Statement of Alex Hershaft, Vegetarian Information Service." In: Diet related to killer diseases, III. Hearings before the Select Committee on Nutrition and Human Needs of the United States Senate, 95th Congress, 1st Session, Response to Dietary Goals of the United States: Re Meat, Mar. 24, 1977, p. 322-334.
Documents evidence linking meat consumption and incidence of heart disease, cancer and other chronic diseases; presents advantages of vegetarian diet.

417 Hershaft, Alex. "When government tries to tell us what to eat." New York Times (Feb. 18, 1980):

sec. A, p. 16.
Letter on dietary guidelines promulgated by U. S.
Department of Agriculture.

418 Hewitt, Jean. "Teen-agers choose the meatless diet."
New York Times (June 5, 1972): 39.
Comments by high-school vegetarians.

419 Hillenius, D. Tegen het vegetarisme. Amsterdam,
G. A. van Oorschot, 1968.

420 Holzer, Hans W. The vegetarian way of life: how the
proper foods determine your outlook, health and ful-
fillment. New York, Pyramid Books, 1973.
Basic introduction to vegetarian principles and
philosophy.

421 Hube, Isolde. Moderne Reform- und Heildiät bei Gicht und
Rheuma. Wiesbaden, Germany, Falken Verlag, 1966.

422 Hur, Robin. Food reform: our desperate need. Aus-
tin, TX, Heidelberg Publishers, 1975.
Evidence linking chronic, degenerative diseases to
a high protein, fat and meat diet; advocates vegan
diet based on sprouts, greens, and small amounts of
algae.

423 Johnson, Marilyn. "Groatsed out." Esquire 94 (Oct.
1980): 126.
Reminiscences of a college Granolahead.

424 Johnson, Paul, and Johnson, Judeth. "An inexpensive,
modern, vegetarian horticultural project." North
American Pomona 10, 1 (Winter 1977): 34-37.
Description of authors' hand-built home, cultivation
of variety of wild and domestic plants, and vegan lifestyle in the mountains of West Virginia.

425 Johnston, Charley M. "Nutrition and life style. III.
Nutrition and contemporary communal living." American Dietetic Association. Journal 63, 3 (Sept. 1973):
275-276.
Brief observations on nutritional attitudes and
practices in ten vegetarian and macrobiotic communes
in the Pacific Northwest and British Columbia.

426 Kandel, Randy Frances. Rice, ice cream and the guru:
decision-making and innovation in a macrobiotic com-

munity. Ph. D. , City University of New York, 1976. Dissertation conducts sociological study of change, adaptation, innovation and decision-making in a vegetarian community in a large American city.

427 Karström, Henning. Vägen till hälsa. Stockholm, Svenska Vegetariska Föreningen, 1966.

428 Klemesrud, Judy. "Vegetarian: growing way of life, especially among the young." New York Times (Mar. 21, 1975): 43.
Health and ethical reasons for rising popularity of vegetarianism; lists a number of prominent vegetarians; comments by noted researchers and nutritionists.

429 Klemesrud, Judy. "World vegetarians meet to talk-- and eat." New York Times (Aug. 22, 1975): 37.
Article on the 1975 World Vegetarian Congress held in Maine and attended by over 1500 people from 30 countries.

430 Kulvinskas, Viktoras P. Nutritional evaluation of sprouts and grasses. Wethersfield, CT, OMango D'Press, 1978.

431 Lavarde, Thora. Din mad-din medicin. Vejledning om råkost og vegetarkost. Allerød, Forlaget Ny Tid og Vi (D. B. K.), 1966.

432 Lawson, Donna. The vegetarian diet. New York, Bantam, 1978.

433 Lehnert, Dick. "Those gentle vegetarians are scary folks." Michigan Farmer 273, 6 (Mar. 15, 1980): 70.
Editorial considers trend toward decreased consumption of animal products in the American diet.

434 Leo, John. "How to beat the beef against meat." Time 114, 19 (Nov. 5, 1979): 112.
Advice to concerned parents for combatting vegetarian tendencies in their teenage children.

435 Living the good life with Helen and Scott Nearing. (Motion picture). Bullfrog Films, n. d. (30 mins. 16mm. sound, color)
Visit with vegetarian pacifists Helen and Scott

Nearing, who, 45 years ago, left city life for self-sufficiency and homesteading.

436   Loercher, Diana. "Vegeterians gain on meat-eaters."
      Houston Post (Oct. 18, 1978): sec. D, p. 3.
      Remarks on the increasing popularity of vegetarian
      diets.

437   Logsdon, Gene. "From lawn to miracle garden."
      Organic Gardening and Farming 26, 1 (Jan. 1979):
      54, 56, 58, 60, 62, 64.
      Vegetarian gardener Michael McConkey maintains
      over 300 varieties of fruits, nuts and vegetables.

438   Lund, Gunnar. Folk og føde. Om fullverdig kompost-
      jordbruk og vegetarkost, giftfaren, folketilveksten og
      jordas ressurser. Oslo, Bryde, Forfatteren, 1965.

439   McCarthy, Colman. "If the Senator had sworn off
      beef...." Washington Post (Aug. 10, 1977): sec.
      B, p. 1.
      Relates media gaffe portraying Senator John
      Melcher as a vegetarian, instead of a veterinarian.

440   McCarthy, Colman. "Meatless meals: a change in
      America's menu." Washington Post (Jan. 13, 1976):
      19.
      Notes various reasons for increasing numbers of
      vegetarians in the U.S.: health, ethics, economics,
      and ecology.

441   McCarthy, Colman. "The vegetarian state of mind."
      San Francisco Chronicle (Jan. 23, 1976): sec. 4,
      p. 21.
      Cites rising popularity of vegetarianism, and dis-
      cusses philosophical motivations for becoming a
      vegetarian.

442   McCarthy, Colman. "Vic Sussman: the complications
      of simplicity." Washington Post Magazine (Nov. 5,
      1978): 32-33.
      Profile of Vic Sussman, author of The Vegetarian
      Alternative.

443   McClure, Jon A. Meat eaters are threatened. New
      York, Pyramid Books, 1973.
      Exposé of mishandling, contamination, adulteration,

lack of sanitation and bribery in the meat depart-
ments of 60 retail supermarkets in which the author
worked over a ten-year period.

444 Majumder, Sanat K. "Vegetarianism: fad, faith, or
fact?" American Scientist 60, 2 (Mar. -Apr. 1972):
175-179.
Historical, ecological, economic, nutritional aspects of vegetarianism.

445 Mascheville, Maria L. C. Coma bem e viva com
saúde; orientaçao prática sôbre alimentos sadios,
vegetarianos e iogues, receitas para cozinhar, in-
dicações para crianças, doentes e sôbre jejum e
desintoxicações. São Paulo, Sociedade Beneficente
S. Camilo, Departamento Gráfico, 1966.

446 Maurin-Rouyre, Hélène. Le secret de la santé selon
les lois divines; les légumes, les fruits, les plantes
et leurs propriétés, suivi du langage des fleurs et
des proverbes en dialecte cévenol. Anduze, France,
Languedoc éditions, 1969.

447 Mayer, Jean. "Are 'faddists' weird or wise?" Los
Angeles Times (Jan. 16, 1975): sec. 6, p. 21.
Columnist feels the term "food faddist" is over-
used and inappropriate for vegetarians.

448 Mayer, Jean, and Dwyer, Johanna. "Practicing vegetarianism." Washington Post (Dec. 16, 1976): sec.
E, p. 6.
Brief column discusses reasons for adopting vegetarian diet, and evaluates nutritional aspects of vegetarianism.

449 Maynard, Joyce. "Abstinence without tears." New
York Times (Nov. 10, 1976): sec. 3, p. 3.
Article on the author's change to vegetarianism.

450 Meat and the vegetarian concept; the case for meat in
the human diet: a review of the evidence. 2nd ed.
Chicago, National Live Stock and Meat Board, 1977.
Pamphlet examines motivations for vegetarian
diets, notes potential shortcomings of vegetarianism
and advantages of meat-centered diet.

451 Mellor, Constance. How to be healthy, wealthy and
wise. London, C. W. Daniel, 1976.

452 Meritt, Bill. "Why I don't eat meat." Vegetarian
Times (July-Aug. 1979): 20-21.
Three accounts of changing to a meatless diet.

453 Meyerowitz, Steve. "Steve Meyerowitz: sprout man,
raw foodist." Vegetarian Times (Aug. 1979): 24,
26-27.

454 Meyers, Nechema. "Tel Aviv talks of health food; the
vegetarian 'religion'." San Francisco Chronicle (May
24, 1978): 53.
Israeli Vegetarians' Association criticizes government for subsidy of eggs and meat which are thought
to contribute to Israel's high heart attack rate.

455 Mossé, Arlette. "Que faut-il penser des régimes
végétariens et végétaliens?" Revue du Practicien 25,
55 (Dec. 1, 1975): 4449-4458.
Reviews health advantages and disadvantages of
various types of vegetarian diets. (In French.)

456 Muggeridge, Malcolm. "The butchers' gala banquet,
and how the vegetarians swallowed it whole." Times
(London) (Dec. 22, 1977): 10.
Disputes, dialogues and joint banquets of the Wor-
shipful Company of Butchers and local vegetarian
group.

457 Nader, Ralph. "Tainted meat." New Republic 167
(Dec. 2, 1972): 9-10.
Brief account of abuses in the meat and poultry
industries, including filth, disease, and pesticide and
hormone residues.

458 National Vegetarian Convention, 1st, Bombay, 1964.
Souvenir of the First National Vegetarian Convention,
1964. Bombay, Indian Vegetarian Congress, 1964.
Collection of brief essays on nutritional and ethical
aspects of vegetarian diet.

459 Nearing, Helen, and Nearing, Scott. Continuing the
good life; half a century of homesteading. New York,
Schocken Books, 1979.
Homesteading philosophy and practical experiences
of vegetarians Helen and Scott Nearing.

460 Nearing, Helen, and Nearing, Scott. Living the good
life; how to live sanely and simply in a troubled

world. New York, Schocken Books, 1970.
From their departure from New York City in 1932
for farms in Vermont and Maine, the authors have
pursued a lifestyle embracing self-sufficiency, sim-
plicity, pacifism and vegetarianism.

461 Newman, Leslea. "Natural wonder." Vegetarian
Times (Mar.-Apr. 1979): 80.
Sketch of 10-year-old vegetarian Demitri Diatchen-
ko.

462 Noorbergen, Rene. Programmed to life: a scientific
confirmation of health reform. Mountain View, CA,
Pacific Press Publishing Association, 1975.
Quoting extensively from medical research and the
writings of Ellen G. White, this book states the case
against meat, alcohol, tobacco, caffeine and sugar.

463 North American Vegetarian Society. Facts of vegetarianism. Malaga, NJ, n.p. 1977.
Brief articles discuss world food crisis, health
and ethical aspects of vegetarianism. Recipes, vegetarian organizations, and sources of information are
listed.

464 Null, Gary. The new vegetarian: building your health
through natural eating. New York, Morrow, 1978.
Containing tips on buying and preparing meats,
fish, poultry, hot dogs, and ice cream, only in
broadest terms could this book be considered a book
on vegetarianism; provides information on abuses of
the food industries, in addition to information on
combining complementary proteins.

465 Obis, Paul. "An interview with McDonald's Ray Kroc."
Vegetarian Times (July-Aug. 1977): 16-18.
Vegetarian Times discusses food and business with
the president and founder of McDonald's.

466 Oudinot, Pierre. La conquête de la santé, précis de
diététique naturiste. 4th ed. Paris, Dangles, 1970.

467 Parham, Barbara. What's wrong with eating meat?
Denver, Ananda Marga Publications, 1979.
Summarizes health, ecological, economic, politi-
cal, and ethical reasons for vegetarian diet.

468 Perl, Lila. Eating the vegetarian way: good food
     from the earth. New York, Morrow, 1980.
       Reasons for and types of vegetarianism; discusses
     modern meat-producing techniques as influence of
     change in American diet. Also includes protein-rich,
     meatless recipes.

469 Peters, Jane S. "Vegetarianism in England." Vege-
     tarian Times (Mar. 1980): 32-34.
       Current status and activities of vegetarians in the
     United Kingdom.

470 Phillips, David A. From soil to psyche. Santa Bar-
     bara, CA, Woodbridge Press, 1977.

471 Pines, Maya. "Meatless, guiltless." New York Times
     Magazine (Nov. 24, 1974): 48, 50, 52, 54, 58, 60,
     62.
       Discusses reasons why she and her family are ex-
     perimenting with vegetarian diet.

472 Pioneers of the new age; accounts by twelve vegans of
     longstanding of how they have fared through the years.
     Surrey, England, Vegan Society, 1974.
       Personal testimonies of vegans of 10-30 years re-
     garding motivations, experiences, present food habits,
     and state of health.

473 Proctor, Stoy E., Jr., and Proctor, Leilani. Unmeat;
     the case for vegetarianism. Nashville, Southern Pub-
     lishing Association, 1973.
       Booklet presents seven reasons for the vegetarian
     diet.

474 Register, U. D., and Zolber, Kathleen. Vegetarian-
     ism. (Audiotape). Chicago, American Dietetic As-
     sociation, 1972.
       Cassette covers history, motivations, and nutri-
     tional guidelines; also reviews published research
     dealing with such vegetarian issues as protein, vita-
     min B12, and the world food shortage.

475 Reynolds, Sid. "Is eating bad for your health? Live-
     stock producers vs. vegetarians." Michigan Farmer
     273, 6 (Mar. 15, 1980): 6-8, 12-13, 39-40.
       Vegetarians spar with the livestock industry through
     research, the media, and consumer groups.

476 Rigby, Andrew, and Turner, Bryan S. "Communes, hippies and secularized religion." Social Compass 20, 1 (1973): 578.
   Sociological and religious examination of two British vegetarian communes. (In French.)

477 Rinehart, Lynn. "What's wrong with meat?" Fitness for Living (May-June 1972): 62-70.
   Presentation of potential health hazards from growth-promoting DES and antibiotic residues in meat.

478 Rodale, Robert. "Good words for meat." Prevention 32, 12 (Dec. 1980): 20-25.
   Editorial asserts that increased meat consumption could dramatically improve the health of Americans.

479 Rodale, Robert. "Ideas for vegetarian gardeners." Organic Gardening and Farming 22, 7 (July 1975): 28-32.
   Editorial describes vegetarianism as the wave of the future for Americans, then discusses possibility of zinc deficiency in vegetarians.

480 Rudd, Geoffrey L. Why kill for food? Madras, Indian Vegetarian Congress, 1973.
   Compendium of arguments for vegetarianism on health, economic, aesthetic, and religious grounds; history of vegetarianism from ancient times.

481 Scharffenberg, John A. The meat debate. (Sound recording). n.p., 1979. (Health Leadership Seminar, 7-28-79.)
   Account of debate on the pros and cons of meat consumption held at the annual meeting of the American Association for the Advancement of Science; cites numerous medical studies demonstrating the relationship between meat consumption and chronic diseases.

482 Scharffenberg, John A. Problems with meat. Santa Barbara, CA, Woodbridge Press, 1979.
   Addresses potential health hazards and nutritional problems of meat consumption; nutritional status of vegetarians and the economics of meat and vegetarian diets.

483 Schwantje, Magnus. Gesammelte Werke. München, Hirthammer, 1976.

484 Seiler, Michael. "A trial by fire for Louie and Boney."
Los Angeles Times (Nov. 9, 1973): sec. 4, p. 1.
Interview with Louis Marvin III, wealthy vegetarian
who saved his numerous animals from forest fire.

485 Short, J. Gordon. Can vegetarianism be justified?
(Sound recording) Waco, TX, Spenco Medical Corp.,
1976.
Discussion of practical and health advantages of
vegetarianism.

486 Shriver, Nellie. "Statement of Ms. Nellie Shriver,
American Vegetarians." In: Nutrition Education.
Hearings before the Subcommittee on Domestic Marketing, Consumer Relations, and Nutrition of the
Committee on Agriculture, House of Representatives,
95th Congress, 1st session, Sept. 28, 1977, part 1,
p. 446-447.
Exhorts federal government to educate the public
on the health hazards and inefficiency of meat consumption; advocates fruitarian diet.

487 Shulman, Martha. "A very French, French bean."
Texas Monthly 5, 11 (Nov. 1977): 178, 180, 182,
185.
Vegetarian dining, or nearly so, in France's haute
cuisine restaurants.

488 Simoons, Frederick J. Eat not this flesh; food avoidances in the Old World. Madison, University of Wis-
consin Press, 1961.
Research into the cultural preferences for and abstinence from various flesh foods: pork, beef,
poultry, horse, camel and dog flesh.

489 Simoons, Frederick J. "Fish as forbidden food: the
case of India." Ecology of Food and Nutrition 3, 3
(1974): 185-201.
Study of cultural and historical attitudes in India and Asia against fish-eating identifies vegetarianism as one of three factors influencing fish
avoidance.

490 Simross, Lynn. "Dick Gregory: thought for food."
Los Angeles Times (Jan. 14, 1975): sec. 4, p. 1.
Interview with vegetarian social activist Dick
Gregory.

491 Sims, Laura S. "Food-related value-orientations, atti-
       tudes, and beliefs of vegetarians and non-vegetarians."
       Ecology of Food and Nutrition 7, 1 (June 1978): 23-
       35.
            Study of factors influencing food consumption be-
       havior found that although vegetarians and non-vege-
       tarians differed very little on some variables, vege-
       tarians had higher food-related value-orientations of
       ethics, religion and health than non-vegetarians.

492 Smith, Althea. "A farewell to chitterlings; vegetarian-
       ism is on the rise among diet conscious blacks."
       Ebony 29, 11 (Sept. 1974): 104-112.
            Vegetarianism among black celebrities.

493 Smith, John Clark. "Vegetarianism as art." Vege-
       tarian Times (Sept. -Oct. 1979): 20-21.

494 Smith, Scott. "For Susan Richardson, plant foods are
       enough." Vegetarian Times (June 1980): 18-20.
            Interview with ethical vegetarian actress and star
       of "Eight is Enough."

495 Smith, Scott S. "Statement of Scott S. Smith, As-
       sistant Editor, Vegetarian World Nutrition Research-
       er." In: Diet Related to Killer Diseases, III.
       Hearings before the Select Committee on Nutrition
       and Human Needs of the United States Senate, 95th
       Congress, 1st session. Response to Dietary Goals
       of the United States: Re Meat, Mar. 24, 1977, p.
       335-336.
            Argues that reduced meat consumption would re-
       sult in better health for Americans and a decrease
       in the incidence of such diet-related conditions as
       obesity, lack of energy, premature aging, cancer and
       arthritis.

496 Smith, Torney. "Susan Smith Jones; more than just a
       pretty face." Vegetarian Times (Dec. 1979): 20-24.
            Plan for achieving optimal health through combina-
       tion of exercise, vegetarian diet, and positive mental
       attitude.

497 Snellman, Teo. Suomalainen ihanneravinto; laktovege-
       taarinen keittokirja, ravinto-ohjeita terveille ja sair-
       aille. Hämeenlinna, Finland, Karisto, 1970.

498 Snyder, Jean. "What you'd better know about the meat
     you eat." Today's Health 49 (Dec. 1971): 38-39,
     67-69.
         Controversial issues in the meat industry include
     lack of sanitation, questionable wholesomeness of
     ground meat, short-weighting in supermarkets, and
     hormonal fattening agents added to the feed of beef
     cattle.

499 Sokolov, Raymond A. "Meat-eating, 230-pound doctor
     is now 175-pound vegetarian." New York Times
     (Aug. 12, 1971): 38.
         Sketch of vegetarian M. D., Andrew T. Weil, au-
     thority on hallucinogenic drugs and meditation.

500 Sonken, Lori. "Carol Tucker Foreman: the USDA's
     highest ranking woman is a friend of vegetarians and
     consumers, but the bane of the meat industry."
     Vegetarian Times (Mar. 1980): 28, 30.
         Interview with long-time foe of meat industry
     abuses and supporter of consumer causes.

501 Sonken, Lori. "Fred Richmond: a progressive con-
     gressman with vegetarian concerns." Vegetarian
     Times (July 1980): 36-37.
         Profile of congressional advocate of improved nutri-
     tion education and protection of laboratory animals.

502 Sonken, Lori. "Vegetarianism comes to Western Jr.
     High." Vegetarian Times no. 40, (n. d.): 26-28.
         Reactions from seventh-graders following a week-
     long meatless diet.

503 Steinway, Frederick. "The day I became a vegetarian."
     In: Feroe, Paul, ed. Silent voices; recent American
     poems on nature. St. Paul, MN, Ally Press, 1978,
     p. 69.

504 Stephens, William. "The vegetarian's passion--more
     than losing weight." Los Angeles Times (Apr. 8,
     1973): sec. 6, p. 4.
         Motivating factors, history, shortcomings of vege-
     tarian regimen.

505 Stevens, Henry Bailey. Para-Desa. Los Angeles,
     Vegetarian World Publishers, 1975.

506 Stoia, Rose Greer. If you don't eat meat, what do
     you eat? Loma Linda, CA, Seventh-day Adventist
     Dietetic Association, 1973.
         Brochure summarizes ecological, economic, and
     health reasons for vegetarian diet.

507 Stroud, D. H. "Meat is a contribution to health, not
     a hazard." Supermarketing 32 (May 1977): 28-29.

508 Sussman, Vic. "Health and your diet." Vegetarian
     Times (July-Aug. 1978): 24-27, 29-37.
         Reprint of chapter from The Vegetarian Alternative
     covers scientific and medical evidence for the sound-
     ness of the vegetarian diet.

509 Sussman, Vic S. The vegetarian alternative: a guide
     to a healthful and humane diet. Emmaus, PA, Rodale
     Press, 1978.
         Comprehensive presentation of all aspects of vege-
     tarianism, especially moral and ethical issues.

510 Sutton, Suzanne. "Superstars." Vegetarian Times
     (Mar.-Apr. 1977): 36-37.
         Prominent vegetarian celebrities and athletes.

511 Suzineau, René. Le végétarisme. Paris, Seghers,
     1977.

512 Székely, Edmond Bordeaux. Treasury of raw foods.
     San Diego, CA, Academy Books, 1973.

513 Thomas, Adeline. "What meat buyers should know."
     Review and Herald (Mar. 14, 1968): 8-9.
         Grocery store employee reports first-hand on the
     recycling of spoiled meats and packaging ploys to
     maximize gross profits.

514 Thomsen, Nora. Sund mad. Odense, Denmark, Dansk
     Bogforlag, 1968.

515 Thrash, Agatha M. Nutrition for vegetarians. Seale,
     AL, Yuchi Pines Institute, 1978.
         Vegetarianism recommended for prevention and
     control of disease, for enhanced mental ability, sound
     moral actions, and realization of spiritual potential.

516 Tobe, John H. The miracle of live juices and raw

foods. St. Catherines, Ont. , Provoker Press, 1977.
Therapeutic uses of raw foods and fruit and vegetable juices.

517 Todhunter, E. Neige. "Food habits, food faddism and
nutrition. " World Review of Nutrition and Dietetics
16 (1973): 286-317.
Factors influencing food habits and types of food
fads; discusses vegetarianism as a cult diet. Reprinted in: Rechcigl, Miroslav, Jr. , ed. Nutrition
and the world food problem. Basel, S. Karger,
1979, p. 267-294.

518 Toorn Van-Dam, Martine van den. De waarheid over
het vegetarisme. Emmen, Netherlands, De Ark,
1970.

519 Trop, Jack Dunn. You don't have to be sick! Nature's
secrets for better health, longer life, and more joyful
living. New York, Julian Press, 1961.
Expounds principles of Natural Hygiene system of
exercise, rest, fasting, and vegetarian diet emphasizing raw foods.

520 Valnet, Jean. Organic garden medicine: the medical
uses of vegetables, fruits and grains. New Paltz,
NY, Erbonia Books, 1975.
Condensed translation of author's Traitement des
maladies par les légumes, les fruits, et les céréales
identifies health benefits, therapeutic uses and preparation notes of fruits and vegetables.

521 Valnet, Jean. Thérapeutic journalière par les légumes
et les fruits. Paris, Librairie Maloine, 1967.

522 Valnet, Jean. Traitement des maladies par les légumes, les fruits, et les céréales. 4th ed. Paris,
Librairie Maloine, 1973.

523 Vegetarian way. Madras, Indian Vegetarian Congress,
1967. (World Vegetarian Congress, 19th, Delhi,
1967.)
Special issue of the 19th World Vegetarian Congress consisting of hundreds of brief articles on
ethical vegetarianism, famous vegetarians, practical
aspects of vegetarianism, vegetarianism in various
countries, quotations from literature, etc.

524 Vegetarianism: Life and Health supplement. Washington, DC, Review and Herald Publishing Association, 1973.
Compilation of nine articles on various vegetarian dietary concepts, plus an interview with 84-year-old vegetarian international ski champion.

525 Vegetarianism in a nutshell. (Filmstrip with cassette.) Farmington, CT, Polished Apple, 1976.
Fourteen minute filmstrip with cassette discusses reasons for becoming a vegetarian, nutritional implications and proper planning of vegetarian diet. Concludes that both meat-centered and vegetarian diets can be nutritionally adequate.

526 Venditto, Gu. "Energy efficient rock 'n' roll." Vegetarian Times (Apr. 1980): 26-30.
Vegetarianism among members of rock group, The B-52's.

527 Waerland, Ebba Langenskiold. Rebuilding health; the Waerland method of natural therapy, with case histories. New York, Devin Adair Co., 1961.
Diet therapy system combines lacto-vegetarian diet with raw foods and exercise.

528 Walker, Fai. "Live food eating: ask your Grandma." Essence 10 (Nov. 1979): 58, 61-62.
Discusses merits of raw foods and vegetarian diet.

529 Walker, Norman Wardhaugh. Diet and salad suggestions: for use in connection with vegetable and fruit juices. Rev. ed. Phoenix, Norwalk Press, 1971.

530 Walker, Norman Wardhaugh. Raw vegetable juices: what's missing in your body? Rev. ed. Phoenix, Norwalk Press, 1970.
Therapeutic properties of raw fruit and vegetable juices, with combinations of ingredients for specific illnesses.

531 Weintraub, Michele, and Weintraub, Michael. "An interview with Dr. Paavo Airola." Vegetarian Times (Sept.-Oct. 1979): 45-51.
Renowned nutritionist presents views on wide range of topics of interest to vegetarians.

532 White, Philip Louis, and Selvey, Nancy. Let's talk about food; answers to your questions about foods and nutrition. Acton, MA, Publishing Sciences Group, 1974.
Question and answer format contains brief entry on vegetarianism, p. 39-40.

533 Wilson, Frank Avray. Food fit for humans. London, Daniel, 1975.

534 Winick, Myron. "The vegetarian diet." Nutrition and Health 2, 1 (1980): 1-6.
Surveys types of vegetarian diets, potential pitfalls, protein combining, and medical studies.

535 Winski, Joseph M. "Too fat? Thin? Tired? Fad diets are pushed as cures for our ills." Wall Street Journal (June 30, 1977): 1.
Describes a number of alternative diets.

536 Wolff, Robert J. "Who eats for health?" American Journal of Clinical Nutrition 26, 4 (Apr. 1973): 438-445.
Surveys cultural attitudes, opinions, and motivations of customers at health food stores.

537 Woolsey, Raymond H. Meat on the menu: who needs it? Washington, DC, Review and Herald Publishing Association, 1974.
Summary of major health arguments for vegetarianism.

538 Wynne-Tyson, Jon. Food for a future; the complete case for vegetarianism. New York, Universe Books, 1979.
Social, ecological, ethical and nutritional necessity of vegetarianism in relation to individual and societal values and commitment to humanitarian concerns; examines the logic of veganism and the environmental impact of eating habits.

539 Young, Jeff C. "Andrew Jacobs: the vegie on the hill." Vegetarian Times (Sept.-Oct. 1977): 38-39.
Interview with vegetarian member of Congress.

HISTORY OF VEGETARIANISM

(See also: 7, 8, 11, 13, 64, 83, 94, 103, 121,
146, 167, 193, 194, 237, 307, 403, 480.)

540 Alsdorf, Ludwig. Beiträge zur Geschichte von Vege-
tarismus und Rinderverehrung in Indien. Mainz,
Akademie der Wissenschaften und der Literatur; in
Kommission bei F. Steiner, Wiesbaden, 1962.

541 Axon, William Edward Armytage. Shelley's vegetarianism. New York, Haskell House Publishers, 1971.
The vegetarianism and lifestyle of Percy Bysshe
Shelley as revealed in his writings and those of his
family and contemporaries.

542 Barkas, Janet. "Frau Wagner." Opera News (July
1972): 20-21.
Vegetarian philosophy of composer Richard Wagner.

543 Barkas, Janet. The vegetable passion; a history of the
vegetarian state of mind. New York, Scribners,
1975.
Traces development of vegetarianism in various
cultures from its earliest manifestations to the present, with extensive coverage of vegetarian historical
figures.

544 Bolitho, Hector. "A note on Bernard Shaw and H. E.
Bates." Texas Quarterly 11 (Spr. 1968): 100-112.
Account and reprint of article by archvegetarian
George Bernard Shaw urging Royal Air Force air-
crews to eat more vegetables and avoid meat.

545 Calbet i Camarasa, Josep Maria. "Catalonian medicine and nutrition." In: Zangheri, Renato. Origens
del capitalisme. Esplugues de Llobregat, Editorial
Ariel, 1974, p. 249-261.
Essay traces Catalonian medical and political attitudes toward nutrition from the end of the 18th century to the present, including various groups cham-
pioning vegetarianism. (In Spanish.)

546 Carson, Gerald. "Vegetables for breakfast and lunch
and supper." Natural History 77 (Dec. 1968): 18-
20, 24, 78-81.

Historical perspective noting famous vegetarians and the philosophical basis of vegetarianism.

547 Foster, John W., Jr. "The members of the Vegetarian Society." Journal of the History of Medicine and Allied Sciences 29, 1 (Jan. 1974): 106-107.
Lithograph produced in 1853 portrays sick and feeble vegetarians being carried on stretchers into a restaurant for their annual banquet.

548 Gambone, Joseph G. "Octagon City." American History Illustrated 10 (Aug. 1975): 10-15.
Account of an ill-fated attempt to establish a vegetarian colony in Kansas in 1856.

549 Gandhi, Raj S. "The rise of Jainism and its adoption by the Vaishyas of India: a case study in Sanskritisation and status mobility." Social Compass 24, 2-3 (1977): 247-260.
Study of the historical influence of Jainism on vegetarianism as practiced today by the majority of Brahmins.

550 Garrett, James F. "George Bernard Shaw." Vegetarian Times (July-Aug. 1977): 38-39.
Brief survey of Shaw's vegetarian diet.

551 Hardinge, Mervyn G., and Crooks, Hulda. "Non-flesh dietaries. I. Historical background." American Dietetic Association. Journal 43 (Dec. 1963): 545-549.
Historical survey and background of vegetarian diet and philosophy.

552 Jones, Kenneth W. "Sources for Arya Samaj history: an exploratory essay." Indian Archives 18, 1 (1969): 20-36.
Information sources on the history, religious ideology, vegetarianism, and political activities of a 19th-century Indian religious and social movement.

553 Klaw, Spencer. "Pursuing health in the promised land; clues to why your grandfather probably was, and your daughter probably is, an ovo-lacto vegetarian." Horizon 18 (Spr. 1976): 24-29.
History of vegetarian and health food movements in the U. S.; interprets motivating factors of natural food enthusiasts.

554 Parluski, George. "The history of the vegetable pas-
    sion in the Orient." Vegetarian Times (Mar. -Apr.
    1977): 21-23.
         The meatless tradition in oriental religions and
    philosophies.

555 Prisco, Salvatore, III. "The Vegetarian Society and
    the Huashan-kut'ien Massacre of 1895." Asian Forum
    3, 1 (1971): 1-13.
         Historical description and interpretation of activ-
    ities and leadership of the Vegetarian Society, a
    secret political and terrorist group in 19th-century
    China.

556 Robertson, Constance Noyes. Oneida Community: an
    autobiography, 1851-1876. New York, Syracuse Uni-
    versity Press, 1970.
         Based on public and private writings of members,
    records early history of 19th-century vegetarian
    utopian community.

557 Robertson, Constance Noyes. Oneida Community: the
    breakup, 1876-1881. Syracuse, Syracuse University
    Press, 1972.
         Account of the dissolution of controversial 19th-
    century vegetarian community.

558 Salomon, Louis B. "The least-remembered Alcott."
    New England Quarterly 34 (Mar. 1961): 87-93.
         Biographical sketch of 19th-century vegetarian re-
    former William Andrus Alcott.

559 Sarkesian, Barbara. "Thoreau." Vegetarian Times
    (Dec. -Jan. 1977): 20.
         Vegetarian inclinations and sympathies of Henry
    David Thoreau.

560 Sheraton, Mimi. "History of American nutrition."
    New York Times (June 11, 1980): sec. 3, p. 14.
         Summary of history of nutrition in the U.S. in-
    cludes photo of vegetarian Bernarr McFadden.

561 Sutton, Suzanne. "Ellen White, Seventh-day Adventist
    and vegetarianism." Vegetarian Times (Nov. -Dec.
    1977): 39.
         Brief review of the vegetarian counsels of Ellen
    G. White, founder of the Seventh-day Adventist faith.

562 Todhunter, E. Neige. "Some aspects of the history of dietetics." World Review of Nutrition and Dietetics 18 (1973): 1-46.
Brief mention of vegetarianism. Surveys concepts of dietetics, diseases of dietary origin, diet therapy, emergence of dietetic profession.

563 Trager, James. "Nuts in the fruitcake." In: Trager, James. The enriched, fortified, concentrated, country-fresh, lip-smacking, finger-licking, international, unexpurgated foodbook. New York, Grossman Publishers, 1970, p. 455-485.
Chapter contains history of vegetarianism in the U.S.; states that there is "no convincing nutritional justification for vegetarianism."

564 Turner, Ernest Sackville. All heaven in a rage. New York, St. Martin's Press, 1964.
Inspired by a visit to a Chicago slaughterhouse, this work relates the history of British efforts against cruelty to animals.

565 Wesslowski, Daniel. "Henry Thoreau." Vegetarian Times (Nov.-Dec. 1977): 39.
Pro-vegetarian philosophy of Henry David Thoreau.

566 Whorton, James C. "'Tempest in a flesh-pot': the formulation of a physiological rationale for vegetarianism." Journal of the History of Medicine and Allied Sciences 32, 2 (Apr. 1977): 115-139.
Philosophy of the 19th-century vegetarian food reform movement, in which over-stimulation from any source was thought to be the origin of all physical and moral disease.

ATHLETICS, ENDURANCE

(See also: 17, 56, 102, 104, 154, 155, 156, 197, 227, 267, 313, 614.)

567 Anon. "Amby Burfoot: on the run." Vegetarian Times (Sept.-Oct. 1978): 39-43.
Interview with vegetarian winner of the 1968 Boston Marathon.

568   Astrand, Per-Olof. "Something old and something new
       ... very new." Nutrition Today 3, 2 (June 1968):
       9-11.
           High-carbohydrate, low-protein diets increase
       stamina of bicycling athletes by 300 percent.

569   Burfoot, Amby. "The joys of vegetarian carbohydrate-
       loading; for days before a marathon, vegetarians are
       suddenly emulated." Runner's World 14 (Jan. 1979):
       138.
           Guidelines based on author's experience with car-
       bohydrate-loading for maximum marathon performance.

570   Burfoot, Amby. "The meatless runner." Runner's
       World 13 (Feb. 1978): 48-55.
           Carefully maintained vegetarian diet is an asset
       to the runner.

571   Burfoot, Amby. "Vegetarian diets." In: The Com-
       plete diet guide for runners and other athletes.
       Mountain View, CA, World Publications, 1978, p.
       194-213.
           Practical discussion of the nutritional adequacy of
       a vegetarian diet, cultural aspects of diet, and athletic
       and fitness benefits of vegetarianism.

572   Creff, A. F. "Alimentation dans les sports de détente
       et les sports de fond." Medicina dello Sport 29, 6
       (June 1976): 219-220. (In French.)

573   Dickinson, Art. "Vegetarian diet." Nordic World 6,
       2 (Oct. 1977): 44.
           Suitability of vegetarian diet for cross-country
       skiers.

574   Ewald, Ellen Buchman. "How to go vegetarian."
       Backpacker 3, 4 (Winter 1975): 31-33.
           Suggestions and recipes for vegetarian hikers,
       campers and backpackers.

575   Goulart, Frances Sheridan. "Making it without meat."
       Bike World 6, 12 (Dec. 1977): 19.
           Shortcomings of meat in the diets of athletes and
       non-athletes.

576   Goulart, Frances Sheridan. "Making it without meat:
       enter the vege-athlete." Handball 28, 2 (Apr. 1978):

51-52.
Disadvantages of meat diets for athletes.

577 Goulart, Frances Sheridan. "Super foods for super
performance." Vegetarian Times (Mar.-Apr. 1979):
27-29.
Why meat is fading fast from the serious athlete's
diet.

578 Grasing, Robyn M. "John Marino: a world record
holder on nutrition and health." Vegetarian Times
(Jan.-Feb. 1979): 30-31.
Champion bicyclist discusses his philosophy of
diet and training.

579 Lamb, Julia. "The healthiest diet?" Sports Illustrated
46, 10 (Feb. 28, 1977): 68.
Brief mention of study determining that the healthiest individuals were vegetarian runners, followed by
vegetarian non-runners, non-vegetarian runners, and
then by non-vegetarian non-runners.

580 Lambert, P. "Nutrition: potions, notions and non-
sense." Volleyball Magazine 10 (Nov.-Dec. 1977):
47-48.

581 Lewanski, Bob. "Vegetarians who pump iron." Vegetarian Times (Mar.-Apr. 1979): 18-22.
Current and past champion vegetarian weight lift-
ers and body builders.

582 Murray, Jim. "Cauliflower mouths." Los Angeles
Times (Nov. 9, 1975): sec. 3, p. 1.
Sportswriter discusses vegetarianism among ath-
letes.

583 Newnham, Blaine. "Wow, like let's really try to win."
Sports Illustrated (Oct. 12, 1970): 50-54.
Article on Chip Oliver, vegetarian linebacker for
the Oakland Raiders.

584 Pessin, Donna Meryl. "Vegetarian backpacking: one
woman's experience." Vegetarian Times (Aug. 1979):
64-67.
Suggestions for foods and equipment, plus sample
menus.

585 Smith, Nathan. Food for sport. Palo Alto, CA, Bull
     Publishing Co. , 1976.
          Chapter Three deals with non-traditional diets and
     contains suggestions for the vegetarian athlete.

586 Sussman, Vic. "Outrunning the meat-eaters; why more
     and more athletes are becoming vegetarians." Run-
     ning Times 29 (June 1979): 24-25, 27, 29.
          Covers protein myths, endurance and health studies
     of vegetarians, and tips for changing to a meatless
     diet.

587 Weinstein, Lawrence. "Vegetable vs. meat ingestion:
     the effects on barpressing." Psychonomic Society.
     Bulletin 10, 1 (July 1977): 35-36.
          Rats fed a vegetarian diet performed at higher
     levels than those fed a meat diet.

588 Williams, Melvin H. "Vegetarian athletes." In: Wil-
     liams, Melvin H. Nutritional aspects of human physi-
     cal and athletic performance. Springfield, IL,
     Charles C. Thomas, 1976, p. 301-304.
          Brief review of vegetarianism in relation to ath-
     letics.

          PLANNING THE VEGETARIAN DIET: ADULTS

          (For vegetarian diets for the elderly, see
               135, 285, 613, 649.)

          (For medical studies of elderly vegetarians, see
               910, 911, 944, 950, 1096, 1100, 1101,
                    1106, 1108, 1338.)

589 Adams, Ruth. "Cooking to economize on proteins."
     Organic Gardening and Farming 22, 3 (Mar. 1975):
     98-100, 102-103.
          Food combining for complementary proteins.

590 Altman, Nathaniel. "Vitamins." Vegetarian Times
     (Mar. -Apr. 1977): 12-15.
          Summarizes functions, recommended allowances,
     and non-meat sources of vitamins.

591 Anon. "Everything's coming up vegetables." Family
     Health 10, 4 (Apr. 1978): 32-36.
     Tips and recipes for serving nutritious vegetarian
     meals.

592 Anon. "Going vegetarian? Be careful!" Changing
     Times 31, 11 (Nov. 1977): 31-33.
     Planning well-balanced vegetarian meals.

593 Anon. "Healthy up your diet with vegetarian meals."
     Glamour 77 (Jan. 1979): 146.
     Meal planning guidelines and descriptions of some
     staples of the vegetarian diet.

594 Anon. "How to be a healthy vegetarian." Mademoiselle
     85 (Aug. 1979): 92, 106.
     Lacto-ovo-vegetarian food group plans needing no
     special supplementation.

595 Anon. Meal plans for total vegetarians. Loma Linda,
     CA, Loma Linda University, Department of Nutrition,
     School of Health, n. d.
     Brochure of simple, inexpensive menus with cost
     and nutrient data; recipes and shopping suggestions.

596 Anon. Meals without meat. Loma Linda, CA, Seventh-
     day Adventist Dietetic Association, n. d.
     Brochure cites health advantages of vegetarian diet,
     discusses protein and meal planning.

597 Anon. "1-week test on lacto-ovo-vegetarian diet proves
     satisfying." Houston Post (Apr. 10, 1980): sec.
     AA, p. 20.

598 Anon. "Series on nutrition examines food groups for
     vegetarians." Detroit News (Mar. 26, 1980): sec.
     F, p. 1.

599 Anon. Vegetarianism. University Park, PA, Nutrition
     Information and Resource Center, Pennsylvania State
     University, 1979.
     Four-page booklet of guidelines for the vegetarian
     diet.

600 Anon. "Vegetarianism; can you get by without meat?"
     Consumer Reports (June 1980): 357-361.
     Review of the basics of vegetarianism, covering

types of vegetarian diets, the protein and vitamin
B12 issues.

601 Anon. "The wise vegetarian." Chemistry 50, 5 (June
1977): 21-22.
Combining complementary plant proteins to supply
essential amino acids in the vegetarian diet.

602 Baines, Maud. Vegetarianism for beginners. Cheshire,
England, Vegetarian Society (U. K.), 1963.

603 Bircher-Benner raw food and juices nutrition plan; a
comprehensive guide with suggestions for diet menus
and recipes. Translated by Timothy McManus. Los
Angeles, Nash Publishing, 1972.
Preparation, recipes and therapeutic uses of raw
foods and juices as practiced at the Bircher-Benner
Clinic in Zurich.

604 Brody, Jane. "Balanced vegetarian diets call for nutritional savvy." Chicago Tribune (Mar. 7, 1977):
sec. 2, p. 6.
Vegetarian diets require some degree of planning,
but may preserve health and prevent disease.

605 Brody, Jane E. "Living sensibly--or perilously--as a
vegetarian." New York Times (Mar. 2, 1977): sec.
3, p. 7.
Nutritional aspects of vegetarian diet.

606 Cobe, Patricia. "Eating the vegetarian way." Forecast for Home Economics 25 (Feb. 1980): 44-45, 64.
Protein combining; recipes.

607 Colorado. State University, Fort Collins. Student
Health Service. Vegetarian diet. Rev. ed. Fort
Collins, CO, The Service, 1976.
Guidelines and sample menus for obtaining adequate
nutrients from a lacto-ovo-vegetarian diet.

608 Dinshah, H. Jay. How to be a total vegetarian. Malaga, NJ, American Vegan Society, 1975. (Ahimsa
booklet, no. 1.)
Booklet describes health and ethical motivations
for vegetarian and vegan diets, has sample menus,
diet suggestions, and advice for changing to a vegan
lifestyle.

609 Doyle, Rodger P. The vegetarian handbook; a guide to
vegetarian nutrition. New York, Crown Publishers,
1979.
Nutritional guidelines for vegetarians of all ages;
discusses various types of vegetarian diets; recipes,
sources of vegetarian foods.

610 Eckstein, Eleanor F. "Vegetarians and fruitarians."
In: Eckstein, Eleanor F. Menu planning. 2nd ed.
Westport, CT, AVI Publishing Co., 1978, p. 312-
323.
Textbook on food service and menu planning with
section emphasizing culturally-based food preferences,
including vegetarianism.

611 Fortino, Denise. "Preventing cellulite: the diet solu-
tion." Harper's Bazaar (Mar. 1979): 126, 166.
Vegetarian diet for prevention and control of cellulite.

612 Gregory, Dick. Dick Gregory's natural diet for folks
who eat: cookin' with Mother Nature. New York,
Perennial Library, 1973.
Entertaining, informative guide to vegetarian and
fruitarian living.

613 Henderson, Fay K. Vegetarianism: the wellbeing of
the elderly. Cheshire, England, Vegetarian Society
(U.K.), 1974.
Pamphlet outlines guidelines for vegetarian diets
for the elderly.

614 Hodson, Geoffrey. Vegetarian foods, their nutrient
properties; plant foods and dairy products as sources
of full nutrition. Auckland, New Zealand Vegetarian
Society, 1960.
Brochure lists vegetarian sources of nutrients, and
contains practical information on food values, food
combinations, acid and alkaline foods; accounts of
famous vegetarian athletes.

615 Hunt, Janet. The raw food way to health: change
your eating habits and change your life. Wellingborough, England, Thorsons, 1978.

616 Jaffrey, Madhur. "How to be a good vegetarian."
Organic Gardening and Farming 25, 10 (Oct. 1978):

114, 116-118, 120, 122-125.
Helpful advice for switching to a vegetarian diet.

617 James, Nancy Ann. "The painless road to a healthy diet." Minneapolis-St. Paul 8 (May 1980): 122-123.
Reasons why vegetarians are becoming more assertive, and guidelines for making the transition from meat-based diet.

618 James, W. S. Outline of vegetarian nutrition. Cheshire, England, Vegetarian Society (U.K.), 1980.
Pamphlet summarizes nutrients, energy, fiber in the vegetarian diet.

619 Jannaway, Kathleen. First hand, first rate; five dozen hints, ideas and recipes for an economical diet. 4th ed. Leatherhead, England, Vegan Society, 1979.
Guidelines and recipes for healthful and economical vegan diet.

620 Jones, Susan Smith. The main ingredients: positive thinking, exercise and diet. Provo, UT, BiWorld Publishers, 1978.
Vegetarian nutritional information and recipes for physical and mental health.

621 Kunz-Bircher, Ruth; Bircher, Ralph; Kunz-Bircher, Alfred; and Liechti-von Brasch, Dagmar. Eating your way to health. Baltimore, MD, Penguin Books, 1972.
Vegetarian principles and recipes employed by the Bircher-Benner Clinic in Switzerland.

622 Latto, Barbara. Vegetarianism: slimplan. Cheshire, England, Vegetarian Society (U.K.), 1978.
Pamphlet outlines vegetarian reducing diet with menus and guidelines.

623 Lawrence, Lillian. The vegetarian diet. New York, Bantam Books, 1978.
Basic introduction to vegetarian diet, with recipes and meal planning guidelines.

624 Leneman, Leah. Slimming the vegetarian way. Wellingborough, England, Thorsons, 1980.

625 Levey, Gail A. "Fat facts for vegetarians." Vegetarian Times (Sept.-Oct. 1979): 22-24.

Vegetarians consuming dairy products must recognize importance of selecting foods low in fats and cholesterol.

626 Levey, Gail A. "Feast without fear; a common sense guide for effective weight control." Vegetarian Times (June 1980): 22-28.
Vegetarian weight control program concentrates on learning how to eat, not merely how to diet.

627 Levey, Gail A. "A vegetarian primer on dietary minerals." Vegetarian Times (Mar. 1980): 66-68.
Obtaining adequate minerals on a vegetarian diet.

628 Lewis, Clara M. Vegetarian diets, a self-instructional program. Chapel Hill, NC, Health Sciences Consortium, 1977.
Provides basic information, including such topics as types of vegetarian diets, health benefits and hazards, meal patterns and sample menus.

629 Lucas, Jack W. Vegetarian nutrition. Cheshire, England, Vegetarian Society (U.K.), 1979.
Comprehensive presentation of nutrients in the vegetarian diet.

630 Moore, Shirley T., and Byers, Mary P. A vegetarian diet; what it is; how to make it healthful and enjoyable. Santa Barbara, CA, Woodbridge Press Publishing Co., 1978.
Clarification of the vegetarian diet and practical suggestions for enhancing the vegetarian lifestyle.

631 Robertson, Laurel; Flinders, Carol; and Godfrey, Bronwen. Laurel's kitchen; a handbook for vegetarian cookery and nutrition. Berkeley, CA, Nilgiri Press, 1976.
Combination of cookbook and comprehensive handbook for vegetarian sources of nutrients; extensive tables, charts and information sources.

632 Seventh-day Adventist Dietetic Association. About nutrition. Nashville, TN, Southern Publishing Association, 1971.
Layman's guide to vegetarian nutritional principles, including food groups, menu planning, nutritional needs of different age groups.

633 Seventh-day Adventist Dietetic Association. Diet manual, utilizing a vegetarian diet plan. 5th ed. Loma Linda, CA, The Association, 1978.
Comprehensive looseleaf handbook for the planning, selection and coordination of vegetarian diets.

634 Shelton, Herbert McGolphin. Superior nutrition. 12th ed. San Antonio, TX, Dr. Shelton's Health School, 1978.
Natural Hygiene diet system based on raw foods, pure water, fasting.

635 Sherman, Carl. "Take a vacation from meat." Prevention 30, 6 (June 1978): 68-73.
Provides advice and encouragement to those contemplating giving up meat; points out health advantages of vegetarian diet.

636 Smith, Elizabeth B. "A guide to good eating the vegetarian way." Journal of Nutrition Education 7, 3 (July-Sept. 1975): 109-111.
Food planning and selection guide for lacto-ovo-vegetarian diet.

637 Sonnenberg, Lydia. Everyday nutrition for your family. Los Angeles, Seventh-day Adventist Dietetic Association, 1960.
Principles of vegetarian diet for all age groups.

638 Sonnenberg, Lydia, and Zolber, Kathleen. Food for us all; the vegetarian diet. Chicago, American Dietetic Association, 1973.
Home study course contains historical review of vegetarianism, collection of articles from scientific literature, principles and practice of balanced vegetarian diet.

639 Stern, Judith S. "How to stay well on a vegetarian diet and save money too!" Vogue 165 (Feb. 1975): 150-151.
Balancing protein in meatless meals.

640 Székely, Edmond Bordeaux. Scientific vegetarianism: guide to organic ecological nutrition. San Diego, CA, Academy Books, 1976.
Vegetarian dietary principles and guidelines as practiced at Rancho La Puerta health resort.

641 Taif, Betty. "Vegetarianism: the new view." Journal
     of Practical Nursing 26, 11 (Nov. 1976): 28-30.
     Suggestions for planning adequate vegetarian diets.

642 Trescher, Eloise R. "How to plan nutritionally sound
     vegetarian meals." House and Garden 147, 5 (May
     1975): 14, 16, 18.
     Guidelines and recipes for vegetarians.

643 Vollmer, Marion W. Food: health and efficiency; les-
     sons in nutrition and healthful food preparation. Rev.
     ed. Nashville, TN, Southern Publishing Association,
     1964.
     For use in vegetarian home economics classes,
     contains lessons and recipes for vegetarian meal
     planning, adequate protein, and healthful eating habits.

644 Williams, Eleanor R. "Making vegetarian diets nu-
     tritious." American Journal of Nursing 75, 12 (Dec.
     1975): 2168-2173.
     Health benefits of vegetarianism and guidelines for
     the planning of nutritionally adequate and palatable
     vegetarian meals.

PLANNING THE VEGETARIAN DIET:
PREGNANCY, INFANTS, CHILDREN

(See also: 250, 262, 346, 637.)

645 Anon. "Dietary advice for a pregnant, vegetarian pa-
     tient." British Medical Journal 3 (Sept. 29, 1973):
     689.
     Question and answer column replies that the preg-
     nant, lacto-vegetarian probably obtains an adequate
     supply of nutrients for herself and the fetus, but the
     vegan patient may become deficient in vitamin B12
     or other nutrients, unless supplements are taken.

646 Anon. "Parents." Vegetarian Times (Dec.-Jan. 1977):
     52-54.
     Responses by vegetarian parents outline guidelines
     for breast feeding, introducing foods, and dealing with
     unsympathetic family members and friends.

647 Anon. "Pregnancy and diet." Vegetarian Times (Sept. - Oct. 1978): 30-33.
Practical guidelines for meeting special dietary needs of pregnancy, with food guide chart for pregnant vegetarians.

648 Anon. Vegetarianism: infant feeding. Cheshire, England, Vegetarian Society (U. K.), 1979.
Pamphlet provides general advice and menu suggestions for infants up to one year of age.

649 Anon. Vegetarianism throughout the life cycle. University Park, PA, Nutrition Information and Resource Center, Pennsylvania State University, 1979.
Information sheet on vegetarian diets for infants, during pregnancy, and for the elderly.

650 Beer, Sherry. "What?! No meat?!" Pediatric Nursing 3, 3 (May-June 1977): 16-19.
Planning and preparing balanced vegetarian diets for infants and children.

651 Dinshah, Freya. Feeding vegan babies. 2nd ed. Malaga, NJ, American Vegan Society, 1975. (Ahimsa Booklet, no. 9.)
Vegan diets for nursing mothers and children; breastfeeding and introduction of solid foods; sources of additional information.

652 Gaskin, Ina May. "Spiritual midwifery on The Farm in Summertown, Tennessee." Birth and the Family Journal 5, 2 (Summer 1978): 102-104.
Prenatal care and home birthing in Tennessee vegan community.

653 Howard, Frances, and Howard, Friedenstern. Parents' handbook of breastfeeding and plant foods. 2nd ed. Hertfordshire, England, The Authors, 1975.
Guidelines for breastfeeding and vegan feeding of babies and children; methods of feeding, sources of information and plant-based infant foods.

654 Kenyon, Judy. Diet for a healthy baby; vegetarian food alternatives for your baby and young child. Van Nuys, CA, The Author, 1979.

655 Kitzinger, Shelia. The experience of childbirth. 4th ed. Middlesex, England, Pelican Books, 1978.

Vegetarian childbirth educator and mother of twins presents complete guide to pregnancy, labor, and childbirth.

656 Obis, Clare Barrett. "Vegetarian nutrition for pregnant and breastfeeding women." Vegetarian Times (Dec. 1979): 42, 44-46.
Meeting the special nutritional needs of pregnancy with a well-balanced vegetarian diet; covers vegetarian and vegan sources of nutrients.

657 Pipes, Peggy L. Nutrition in infancy and childhood. St. Louis, MO, C. V. Mosby Co., 1977.
Brief consideration of complementary proteins and food combining in vegetarian diets for children, pages 27-28.

658 Potterton, D. "Growing up a vegetarian." Nursing Times 74, 13, Suppl. (Mar. 30, 1978): viii-x, xi.

659 Skuratowicz, Paula, and Baginski, Yvonne. "Helping children improve their nutritional awareness." Vegetarian Times (Mar. 1980): 38-39.
Advice and suggestions for instilling sound nutritional habits in children.

660 Stoia, Rose Greer. Feeding the vegetarian infant. Loma Linda, CA, Seventh-day Adventist Dietetic Association, 1978.
Brochure provides practical information on feeding vegetarian babies, with emphasis on protein and iron-rich foods.

661 Vyhmeister, Irma B.; Register, U. D.; and Sonnenberg, Lydia M. "Safe vegetarian diets for children." Pediatric Clinics of North America 24, 1 (Feb. 1977): 203-210.
Guide for management of vegetarian diets for infants and children; charts of food groups with sources, sample menus for different age groups of children.

662 Yntema, Sharon. Vegetarian baby: a sensible guide for parents. Ithaca, NY, McBooks Press, 1980.
Practical nutritional information and advice for parents raising their children on meatless diets.

663 Zurbel, Runa, and Zurbel, Victor. The vegetarian family; with recipes for a healthier life. Englewood

Cliffs, NJ, Prentice-Hall, 1978.
Guidebook with recipes for preparing healthful
vegetarian meals using natural foods. Suggestions
for raising children on vegetarian diet.

PLANNING THE VEGETARIAN DIET: PETS

664 Berman, Kathy, and Forman, Dorothy. "Vegetarian-
     ism for the healthy cat and dog." Vegetarian Times
     (Jan. -Feb. 1979): 18-20, 22-23.
        Meeting nutritional requirements of cats and dogs
     with vegetarian diets.

665 Diamond, Stuart. "Vegetarian pets." Omni 2 (May
     1980): 36.
        Brief review of feeding vegetable diets to cats and
     dogs.

666 Goulart, Frances Sheridan. Bone appétit: natural
     foods for pets. Seattle, WA, Pacific Search Books,
     1976.
        Vegetarian and natural foods recipes for dogs and
     cats.

667 Goulart, Frances Sheridan. "Pet foods, the pure and
     the doggerel." Vegetarian Times (Dec. -Jan. 1977):
     8, 10-11.
        Problems with commercial pet foods; vegetarian
     recipes for pets.

668 Lloyd-Jones, Buster. "Cats, dogs, and vegetarian-
     ism." Vegetarian Times (Dec. -Jan. 1977): 9, 12.
        Reasons pets should not be changed to a vegetarian
     diet.

669 Pitcairn, Richard H. "Can your pet be a vegetarian?"
     Prevention 31, 10 (Oct. 1979): 132, 134, 136, 138,
     140-141.
        Guidelines and vegetarian protein combinations for
     cats and dogs.

FOOD TECHNOLOGY

670   Anon. "Food of the future." Hospitals 46, 1 (Jan. 1, 1972): 69.
      Brief article on vegetable protein imitation meats as a means of reducing incidence of heart disease.

671   Anon. "Vegetarian 'meats'." Consumer Reports (June 1980): 362-365.
      Samples of convenience food meat analogs showed variable quality of nutritional labeling, the addition of some food additives in some products, low levels of contamination by filth and extraneous matter, and little taste correlation with meat.

672   Bulkeley, William M. "Good old bean curd is suddenly popular, but you call it tofu; longtime food of the Orient now is providing protein to American vegetarians." Wall Street Journal (Apr. 12, 1979): 1, 31.
      Increasing popularity of tofu and soy products, with projected annual growth in sales of 25-30 percent.

673   Chen, Philip Stanley. Soybeans for health, longevity, and economy. 3rd ed. St. Catharines, Ont., Provoker Press, 1970.
      Nutritive value of soybeans, role of soybeans in the world food situation, preparation and uses of soy products, recipes.

674   de Cremiers, P. "New protein sources and their use in human nutrition." Paris. Ecole Française de Meunerie. Bulletin des Anciens Elèves 260 (1974): 82-87. (In French.)

675   Donovan, Sharon. "Hamburger fans use something other than meat between buns." Houston Chronicle (Nov. 22, 1979): sec. 4, p. 17.
      Some hamburger chain restaurants are testing vegetarian burgers and salad bars as additions to the menus.

676   Greenberg, Daniel S. "Slaughterhouse zero: how soybean sellers plan to take the animal out of meat."

Harper's 247 (Nov. 1973): 38-43.
Economics and marketing in the expanding soybean
simulated meats industry.

677 Hannigan, Kevin J. "Tempeh ... a super soy." Food
Engineering (Nov. 1979): 11.
High-protein soy food has endless possibilities as
an engineered food.

678 Hartman, Warren E. "Vegetarian protein foods."
Food Technology 20, 1 (Jan. 1966): 39-40.
Early developments in the textured soybean protein
industry.

679 Hellman, Hal. "The story behind those meatless
'meats'." Popular Science (Oct. 1972): 78-80, 164.
Description of the production of meat analogs
from soybeans, with account of economic and health
advantages.

680 Hutt, Peter Barton, and Sloan, A. Elizabeth. "FDA
regulation of vegetable protein products." Nutrition
Policy Issues (Jan. 1979): 1-2.
Background, history and major provisions of tenta-
tive FDA regulation of vegetable protein products.

681 Levey, Gail A. "An in-depth look at texturized vegetable protein." Vegetarian Times (Jan.-Feb. 1980):
56-59.
Processing and nutritional value of TVP.

682 Mayer, Jean. "TVP: can you tell the meat substitutes from the 'real' thing? (Only chickens, pigs
and cows know for sure.)" Family Health 8, 9
(Sept. 1976): 40-41, 69.
Description of soybean meat analogues: history,
how manufactured, and reasons for eating.

683 Shandler, Nina, and Shandler, Michael. How to make
all the "meat" you eat from wheat. New York, Rawson, Wade, 1980.

684 Shurtleff, William. "Soyfoods: protein source of the
future." Vegetarian Times (Jan.-Feb. 1980): 50,
52-53.
Soybean foods combine versatility, low cost, and
energy-efficiency with high nutritional value.

685 Shurtleff, William, and Aoyagi, Akiko. The book of
     miso. Brookline, MA, Autumn Press, 1976.

686 Shurtleff, William, and Aoyagi, Akiko. The book of
     tempeh. New York, Harper and Row, 1979.

687 Shurtleff, William, and Aoyagi, Akiko. The book of
     tofu. Brookline, MA, Autumn Press, 1976.

688 Shurtleff, William, and Aoyagi, Akiko. Miso produc-
     tion. Lafayette, CA, New-Age Foods, 1979.

689 Shurtleff, William, and Aoyagi, Akiko. Tempeh pro-
     duction. Lafayette, CA, New-Age Foods, 1980.

690 Shurtleff, William, and Aoyagi, Akiko. Tofu and soy-
     milk production. Lafayette, CA, New-Age Foods, 1979.

691 Singh, Kartar; Philip, Susan; Eapen, Sucy; and Philip,
     Thangam E. "Formulation of ready-made balanced
     meals." Indian Food Packer 30, 1 (1976): 40-43.
       Preparation, preservation and nutritional status
     of vegetarian and non-vegetarian ready-to-eat food
     items.

692 Wells, Patricia. "Zounds! The arrival of future
     foods!" New York Times (Jan. 10, 1979): sec. C,
     p. 1.
       Food trends of the future, including increased
     prominence of vegetarianism and aquaculture.

693 Zalcman, Mary. "New foods for special diets."
     Nutrition and Food Science 51 (Mar. 1978): 23-24.
       Describes new range of convenience foods for those
     suffering from food allergies; packages will be
     marked with symbols indicating vegetarian, gluten-
     free, cholesterol, refined sugar, albumen, milk,
     low-calorie, etc.

INSTITUTIONAL FOOD SERVICE

694 Anon. "Health foods enter student diets--naturally."
     College and University Business 52 (Mar. 1972): 51.

Food service professionals are responding to college students' increasing preference for natural foods and vegetarian menus.

695 Anon. "New meatless alternatives feature familiar ingredients and tempting flavor." Cooking for Profit (Aug. 1979): 40-41.
Guidelines, recipes, and marketing techniques for restaurants serving meatless dishes.

696 Anon. "Pick a pack of pickles and kraut." School Foodservice Journal 34, 6 (June-July 1980): 42, 44.
Lacto-ovo-vegetarian meals incorporating eggs, cheeses, peanut butter, nuts, seeds, grains as substitutes for the two-ounce meat requirement in school lunches.

697 Anon. "Soybean products: new vegetarian delights." School Foodservice Journal 34, 6 (June-July 1980): 48, 50.
Use of soy products including soy oil and tofu in the School Food Service Program in Santa Cruz, California.

698 Anon. "Special meals on campus." New York Times (Mar. 10, 1976): 47.
Brief description of vegetarian lunch program at Mt. Holyoke College.

699 Anon. "Vegetarian meals are a bit hit at MSU." Detroit News (Feb. 22, 1977): sec. B, p. D02.
Michigan State University serves over 90 meatless dishes in the school cafeteria.

700 Boss, Donna. "Vegetarianism on campus." Food Management 11, 4 (Apr. 1976): 44, 46, 64, 72, 81, 83, 85.
Vegetarian food service program at Princeton University.

701 Bush, Marlene Ellstrom. Adequacy of lacto-ovo-vegetarian diets in Seventh-day Adventist boarding academies. Master's thesis, University of Alabama, 1969.
Study of menus from 27 SDA boarding schools serving vegetarian diets concludes that well-planned vegetarian diets can be adequate in all nutrients.

702 Call, Susan L. "Healthy foods for healthy sales."
Cornell Hotel and Restaurant Administration Quarterly
20, 2 (Aug. 1979): 6-7.
Describes trend among restaurant diners toward
vegetarian, low-fat, low-calorie items, and away from
fatty meats and heavy dishes.

703 Cappadona, Marie V. "Student vegetarianism takes
root at UM." College and University Business 52
(Mar. 1972): 52-53.
Vegetarian food service plan at the University of
Massachusetts.

704 Carpenter, Carol. "UC signs nature into food contract." College and University Business 52 (Mar.
1972): 54-55.
Natural foods program at the University of California at Santa Cruz.

705 Chilson, Bennett D. , and Knickrehm, Marie E. "Nutrient intake of college students under two systems
of board charges--à la carte vs. contract." American Dietetic Association. Journal 63, 5 (Nov. 1973):
543-545.
Comparison of nutrient intakes of students from
two colleges operating lacto-ovo-vegetarian food
plans.

706 Darsch, G. A.; Young, R. G.; Shaw, C. P.; and
Tuomy, J. M. Entree production guides for modi-
fied diets at Walter Reed Army Medical Center.
Part IV. Meat substitute entrees. Final Report.
Army Natick Research and Development Command,
MA, 1979.
Hospital production guidelines for thirteen meatless
entrees. (NTIS AD-A079 958)

707 Fial, Anita. "Meatless menus: a marvelous alternative." School Foodservice Journal 34, 6 (June-July
1980): 79-80, 84.
Preparation and planning of vegetarian menus
should emphasize flavor, heartiness, and appearance.

708 Guley, Helen M. "A vegetarian program for students
on a college board plan." American Dietetic Association. Journal 71, 3 (Sept. 1977): 276-277.
Vegetarian meal program on the SUNY-Binghamton
campus.

709 Henning, Janet L. "Without meat, cost and cholesterol
     are low." Modern Hospital 120, 5 (May 1973): 107.
         Brief description of meatless meals served at
     Hinsdale (Ill.) Sanitarium and Hospital, which has
     had a vegetarian meal plan since 1904.

710 Johnson, Barbara. "At Hiram, the revolution is hap-
     pening in the kitchen." College Management 7, 6
     (June 1972): 33-34.
         Food service innovations at Hiram College, Hiram,
     Ohio, which was the first college in the U.S. to of-
     fer students a vegetarian meal program.

711 Kinsella, Susan. "A vegetarian option." In: Kinsella,
     Susan. Food on campus: a recipe for action; a
     step-by-step guide to improving your college food
     service. Emmaus, PA, Rodale Press, 1978, p. 33-
     48.
         Approaches and case histories of schools instituting
     vegetarian meal plans.

712 MacMillan, J. B. , and Smith, E. B. "Development
     of a lacto-ovo-vegetarian food guide." Canadian
     Dietetic Association. Journal 36, 2 (1975): 110-117.

713 Manning, Hilda H. , and Hammond, James. "Vege-
     tarian: variety and vitality." School Foodservice
     Journal 34, 6 (June-July 1980): 56, 58, 60.
         Use of ethnic foods as means of introducing stu-
     dents to vegetarian meals.

714 Robertson, Nan. "A campus natural: the 'Veggie
     Room'." New York Times (Mar. 2, 1977): sec. 3,
     p. 1.
         Notes increase in vegetarianism among students
     on American college and university campuses.

715 Robertson, Nan. "Veggies cultivate the campuses."
     Chicago Tribune (Mar. 7, 1977): sec. 2, p. 1.
         Discusses vegetarian meal plans for students on a
     number of colleges and universities across the U.S.

716 Shaw, Jane. "Yogurt keeps Yale students happy and
     healthy." College and University Business 52 (Mar.
     1972): 55-56.
         Vegetarian and health food meal service at Yale.

717 Werner, I. "Hospital food and possibilities of its im-
     provement." Bibliotheca Nutrio et Dieta. Aktuelle
     Probleme der Ernaehrung 19 (1973): 86-92.
     Recommendations for Swedish hospital diets for the
     average patient and those requiring special diets.

718 Zolber, Kathleen. "Producing meals without meat."
     Hospitals 49, 12 (June 16, 1975): 81-82, 84-86.
     Guide for health professionals for the planning of
     balanced vegetarian meals.

719 Zuhlke, Judy. "Students come first at St. Olaf."
     School Foodservice Journal 27, 5 (May 1973): 54-56.
     Since 1972, St. Olaf College in Northfield, Min-
     nesota has had successful vegetarian and natural
     foods menus for students.

CHILDREN'S MATERIALS

720 Blanchard, Marjorie P. The vegetarian menu cook-
     book. New York, Watts, 1979.
     Vegetarian dishes for variety of occasions, with
     calorie and nutritional information for each.

721 Brown rice. (Motion picture) Released by Time-Life
     Films, 1972.
     Teenagers' reactions to vegetarian meals, a flat
     tire, and school assignment to read The Art of Lov-
     ing.

722 Caruana, Claudia M. "A soda pop conspiracy." Vege-
     tarian Times (Sept. -Oct. 1979): 32-33.
     Story written for children tells of vegetarian
     youngster who is teased by his classmates.

723 Dinosaurs: plant eaters. (Motion picture) Walt Disney
     Productions, Santa Ana, CA, Doubleday Multimedia,
     1967.
     Portrayal of behavior of vegetarian dinosaurs (for
     primary and intermediate grades).

724 Freeman, Val. We're vegetarian too! Malaga, NJ,
     North American Vegetarian Society, 1975.

Children's coloring book of some North American
vegetarian wild animals.

725 Gay, Kathlyn; Gay, Martin; and Gay, Marla. Get
hooked on vegetables. New York, Julian Messner,
1978.
Written for grades 7 and up, discusses vegetarianism with sections devoted to starting the vegetarian
diet, kitchen tips, recipes, individual rights vs. junk
food advertising, and vegetarian organizations.

726 Hurwitz, Johanna. Much ado about Aldo. New York,
William Morrow and Co., 1978.
Story of an 8-year-old boy who decides to become
a vegetarian.

727 Montgomery, Charlotte Baker. My kindness coloring
book. Washington, DC, Humane Society of the United
States, 1971.
Coloring book of wild and domestic animals has
kindness message for each animal.

728 Perl, Lila. Eating the vegetarian way; good food from
the earth. New York, William Morrow and Co.,
1980.

729 Puffed-up dragon. (Motion picture) Sterling Educational
Films, 1966.
Story of friendly vegetarian dragon who eats wagon-
loads of food in a medieval kingdom, much to the
annoyance of the townspeople.

REFERENCE SOURCES

(See also: 39, 291, 355.)

730 Anon. Vegetarian food facts. Cheshire, England,
Vegetarian Society (U.K.), 1980.
Chart details nutritional composition of vegetarian
foods.

731 Anon. Vegetarian information sources. Washington,
DC, Vegetarian Information Service, 1980.

Leaflet lists sources of vegetarian information, foods, products and services.

732 Anon. The vegetarian unit. Ann Arbor, MI, National Health Systems, 1977.
Poster depicts vegetarian food sources and guidelines for balanced vegetarian nutrition.

733 Anon. A vegetarian's bookshelf. University Park, PA, Nutrition Information and Resource Center. Pennsylvania State University, 1979.
Four-page annotated list of books, cookbooks and pamphlets of interest to vegetarians.

734 Batt, Eva. Vegan shoppers guide. I. Surrey, England, Vegan Society, 1980.
Brand-name guide to vegan toiletries, footwear, household products.

735 Batt, Eva. Vegan shoppers guide. II. Surrey, England, Vegan Society, 1980.
Brand-name guide to food products acceptable to vegans.

736 Casale, Joan T. The diet food finder. New York, R. R. Bowker, 1975.
Sources of reliable information on therapeutic and special diets, nutrition education, recipes, food suppliers; section on vegetarianism contains annotated list of cookbooks and general works.

737 Cohlmeyer, David. A guide to vegetarian living in Toronto. Toronto, Ont., Pythagorean Press, 1979.
Restaurants, health food stores, gourmet shops and organizations in the Toronto area; listings of books, periodicals of interest to vegetarians.

738 Cronk, Loren Kennett. Annual directory of vegetarian restaurants, 1980. Angwin, CA, Daystar Publishing Co., 1980.
State-by-state directory of restaurants compiled from responses to questionnaires indicates types of vegetarian food served, whether preservatives, artificial color used, average prices.

739 Davis, Maxine W., and Tetrault, Gregory J. The organic traveler; a guide to organic, vegetarian, and

health food restaurants in the U. S. and Canada. Syracuse, NY, Grasshopper Press, 1975.
Based on personal experiences and responses to questionnaires, directory is arranged by state (or province) and city, with coded symbols to describe menu and atmosphere. Brief description of specialties, hours, prices, etc.

740 Housewright, Stephen. "A selective bibliography of books and other materials pertaining to vegetarianism." Unabashed Librarian 36, 3 (1980): 18-31.
Annotated bibliography of in-print books, cookbooks, and audiovisual materials related to vegetarianism, plus listings of vegetarian organizations and periodicals.

741 International vegetarian health food handbook, 1979-1980. Edited by Bronwen Humphries and Derek McEwen. Parkdale, England, Vegetarian Society (U. K.), 1979.
Biennial international directory of vegetarian restaurants, hotels, food stores, societies, publications, etc.

742 Kulvinskas, Viktoras. The new age directory: holistic health directory. 3rd ed. Survival Foundation, Wethersfield, CT, distributed by OMango D'Press, 1978.
Sources of vegetarian information, services, products, organizations, health resorts, publications, communes, and health and spiritual centers.

743 Magel, Charles R. A bibliography on animal rights and related matters. Washington, DC, University Press of America, 1980.
Over 3000 entries cover entire spectrum of issues related to ethics and the use of animals for food, sport, science, fashion, from the 10th century B. C. to the present. Included are books, journal articles, films, government documents, conferences, organizations, college courses on animal rights.

744 National Nutrition Education Clearing House. Vegetarians and vegetarian diets: resource list. Berkeley, CA, Society for Nutrition Education, 1974. (Nutrition education resource series, no. 8.)
Bibliography of selected educational materials and

professional resources on vegetarianism from books, journals, pamphlets, and audiovisual aids.

745 Nutrition Education Development Project. ESEA Title IVC Project. Pamphlet file. Washington, DC, U. S. Dept. of Health, Education, and Welfare, Office of Education, 1978.
      Subject listing of free or inexpensive educational materials in nutrition for elementary and secondary teachers contains seven entries for vegetarian materials. (ED 164 966)

746 Schwartz, Diane. Vegetable cookery; a selected annotated bibliography. New York, The Council on Botanical and Horticultural Libraries, Inc. , The New York Botanical Garden, July 1978. (Plant bibliography, no. 2.)
      Annotated bibliography of cookbooks containing vegetarian recipes using fruits, vegetables, nuts, grains, herbs, spices; notes relevance to vegetarians and indicates those also containing meat recipes.

747 Shorr, Ivy. The exciting world of natural food and vegetarian restaurants in southern California. Santa Monica, CA, Dennis Landman Publishers, 1974.
      Alphabetical listing of restaurants serving vegetarian and/or organic meals, with descriptions of specialties and atmosphere.

748 Simkowitz, Howie. Vegetarian and macrobiotic guide: Europe, 1973; or, The great European health food trip. Craftsbury, VT, Craftsbury Publishers, 1973.
      Directory of vegetarian and macrobiotic restaurants and food stores in the British Isles and Europe, with translation guide for vegetarian travelers.

749 Stoia, Rose M. Vegetarianism: cultural and nutritional aspects; a bibliography. Prepared for the Seventh-day Adventist Dietetic Association, Sept. 1979.
      Three-page bibliography of journal articles dealing with medical aspects of the vegetarian diet.

750 Vegetarian Society of Colorado. Bye bye burger. 2nd ed. Denver, CO, The Society, 1979.
      Brief articles on topics of interest to vegetarians: world food situation, animal welfare, ethics, travel,

protein, nutrition, etc., plus listings of publications, organizations, and Colorado vegetarian restaurants, health food stores.

751 Vegetarian Times guide to dining in the U.S.A. The editors of Vegetarian Times; compiled by Kathleen Moore. New York, Atheneum, 1980.
    Arranged by state, directory of over 500 restaurants serving vegetarian fare includes information on types of dishes served, prices, hours, methods of payment and reports from diners.

POSITION PAPERS ON THE VEGETARIAN DIET

752 American Academy of Pediatrics. Committee on Nutrition. "Nutritional aspects of vegetarianism, health foods, and fad diets." Pediatrics 59, 3 (Mar. 1977): 460-464.
    Vegetarian and vegan diets can be adequate if varied food selection is maintained; considers excellent health, rarity of obesity, and lower serum cholesterol levels of vegetarians; points out serious hazards of Zen macrobiotic diets and excess intakes of vitamins A, C, D and E, and protein.

753 American Dietetic Association. "Position paper on food and nutrition misinformation on selected topics." American Dietetic Association. Journal 66, 3 (Mar. 1975): 277-280.
    States that "the careful selection of foods for vegetarians can insure adequate nutrition for adults"; condemns Zen macrobiotic diets, high-protein diets for athletes, quick weight loss diets, and megavitamin therapy.

754 American Dietetic Association. "Position paper on the vegetarian approach to eating." American Dietetic Association. Journal 77, 1 (July 1980): 61-69.
    Reaffirms nutritional adequacy of well-planned vegetarian diets, and recognizes a positive relationship between vegetarian diets and the prevention of certain diseases, including coronary heart disease, obesity, osteoporosis, and gastrointestinal and reproductive cancers.

755 National Research Council. Committee on Nutritional
Misinformation. Food and Nutrition Board. "Vegetarian diets." American Dietetic Association. Journal 65, 2 (Aug. 1974): 121-122.
Examination of nutritional issues and nutritional
status of vegetarians concludes that a vegetarian can
be well-nourished if he eats a variety of plant foods
and gives attention to certain critical nutrients.

756 National Research Council. Committee on Nutritional
Misinformation. Food and Nutrition Board. Vege-
tarian diets: a statement of the Food and Nutrition
Board, Division of Biological Sciences, Assembly of
Life Sciences, National Research Council. National
Academy of Sciences, May, 1974.
Report covers types of vegetarian diets and the
health record of vegetarians.

PHILOSOPHICAL ASPECTS OF DIET:
ECONOMICS, ECOLOGY

(See also: 48, 159, 204, 268, 269, 270, 314, 538.)

757 Anon. "Dietary morality." Science 186 (Nov. 15,
1974): 614.
Brief review of book urging Americans to switch
to a semi-vegetarian diet in order to equalize world
food supplies.

758 Anon. "Labeling meat." Bureaucrat 6, 4 (Winter
1977): 61-64.
Harassment and intimidation of USDA meat inspector who exposed misgrading, certification of in-
ferior meat, bribery, and ineptitude in the meat
packing industry.

759 Anon. "President is scolded for vegetarian meal."
New York Times (Apr. 21, 1977): 18.
Meatless meal at the White House commemorating
Food Day is criticized by president of the American
National Cattlemen's Association.

760 Anon. "U.S. hiring of vegetarian angers the meat industry." San Francisco Chronicle (Apr. 13, 1978):

sec. 4, p. 18.
American Meat Institute strongly objects to hiring
of vegetarian Michael Jacobsen as USDA consultant.

761 Baldwin, R. L. Animals, feed, food and people; an
analysis of the role of animals in food production.
Boulder, CO, Westview Press, 1980. (AAAS selected symposia, no. 42.)
Papers examine efficiency and economics of animal
production, implications for international trade, resource allocation to livestock production, and a nutritionist's view of vegetable proteins, health concerns,
nutrition policy.

762 Bender, Arnold E. The role of plants in feeding man-
kind. Surrey, England, Vegan Society, 1980.
Pamphlet details economic and ecological advantages of plant-based diets.

763 Bodwell, C. E. "Evaluation of plant proteins to solve
nutritional problems of the Third World." Qualitas
Plantarum--Plant Foods for Human Nutrition 29, 1-2
(July 6, 1979): 135-162.
Recommendations for nutritional improvement of
plant sources of protein and calories in foods forming
the staple diets of the Third World; extensive bibliography.

764 Brown, Lester R., and Eckholm, Erik P. "Our dietary habits: should they be changed? For what reasons?" Vital Issues 24, 2 (Oct. 1974): 1-4.
Examines factors encouraging the shift from beef
and animal products to vegetable sources of protein:
economy, ecology, health, inefficiency and waste in
beef production. Chart of meat consumption by country, 1960 to 1972.

765 Burfoot, Ambrose J. "Vegetarian cause." New York
Times (July 5, 1976): 14.
Letter observes agribusiness influence on the
American diet, and ascribes increase in vegetarian-
ism to recognition of world protein shortage.

766 Chang, Hui-shyong. "Functional forms and the demand
for meat in the United States." Review of Economics
and Statistics 59, 3 (Aug. 1977): 355-359.
Statistical model for the estimation of meat demand
in the United States.

767 Collins, Jackie. "Statement of Jackie Collins, Vegetarian Activists of New York." In: National Nutrition Policy Study, 1974. Hearings before the Senate
Committee on Nutrition and Human Needs of the
United States Senate, 93rd Congress, 2nd session,
part 4A-Appendix to nutrition and food availability,
June 20, 1974, p. 1855-1857.
    Pleas for end to waste caused by meat consump-
tion and calls for immediate action to alleviate world
food crisis in poorer countries of the world.

768 Dickerson, J. W. T. Plant foods for human health,
with special reference to the diseases of affluence
and the needs of the developing world. Surrey, England, Vegan Society, 1979.
    Booklet summarizes health arguments for vegan
diet, also protein and energy needs of lesser developed countries.

769 Diet for a small planet. (Motion picture) Bullfrog
Films, 1973. (28 mins. 16mm, sound and color)
    Obtaining complete proteins by combining comple-
mentary non-meat foods; ecological and economic
factors in the world food problem. (See also no.
779.)

770 Eckholm, Erik P., and Record, Frank. The two faces
of malnutrition. Washington, DC, Worldwatch Institute, 1976. (Worldwatch paper, no. 9.)
    Adverse health risks of both undernutrition and
overnutrition.

771 Factory farming; a symposium, held 23 August 1968
in Dundee. Edited by V. R. Bellerby on behalf of
the British Association for the Advancement of Science. Oxford, England, Education Services, 1970.
    Papers cover legislation, antibiotics, economics
of intensive factory farming of food animals.

772 Fager, Charles E. "Vegetarianism: a force against
famine?" Christian Century 92, 35 (Oct. 29, 1975):
971-972.
    Critique of the 1975 World Vegetarian Congress.

773 Gay, Ruth. "The tainted fork." American Scholar 48
(Winter 1978): 83-88.
    Reviews literature related to various aspects of

diet: moral issues of world poverty, ecological issues of pollution and waste, and health hazards of modern diets.

774 Hamilton, W. J., III, and Busse, C. D. "Primate carnivory and its significance to human diets." BioScience 28, 12 (Dec. 1978): 761-766.
Ecological and behavioral hypotheses regarding the tendency of many primates, including humans, to increase the amount of animal products in the diet when economically feasible to do so.

775 Hershaft, Alex. "Solving the population/food crisis by 'eating for life'." Vegetarian Times (July-Aug. 1978): 64.
Vegetarian strategy for reducing world hunger and malnutrition through equalization of food supplies, reducing waste of natural resources involved in livestock production, and reducing incidence of chronic debilitating diseases.

776 Heupke, W. "The rapidly increasing spread of vegetarian nutrition in the world." Münchener Medizinische Wochenschrift 105 (Nov. 8, 1963): 2244-2248.
Predicts future importance and necessity of vegetarianism for economic reasons resulting from world food shortages. (In German.)

777 Hur, Robin. "Vegetarianism for a world of plenty." Moneysworth 9 (Mar. 1979): 18-19.
Environmental and economic issues involved in meat production.

778 Jackrell, Thomas. "Statement of Thomas Jackrell, Vegetarian Activist Collective of New York." In: National Nutrition Policy Study, 1974. Hearings before the Select Committee on Nutrition and Human Needs of the United States Senate, 93rd Congress, 2nd session, part 2A-Appendix to nutrition and the international situation, June 19, 1974, p. 468-470.
Addresses a number of topics related to economic aspects of diet.

779 Lappé, Frances Moore. Diet for a small planet. Rev. ed. New York, Ballantine Books, 1975.
Economic and ecological analysis of diet and protein requirements, with section of complementary protein recipes. (See also no. 769.)

780   Lappé, Frances Moore. "Protein from plants."
      Chemistry 46, 9 (Oct. 1973): 10-13.
      Clarifies misconceptions about the vegetarian diet;
      considers the inefficient, expensive meat diet of
      Americans the oddity, not the predominantly carbo-
      hydrate vegetable-centered diet of the majority of the
      world's population.

781   Loehr, Raymond C. Pollution implications of animal
      wastes; a forward oriented review. Washington, DC,
      U. S. Federal Pollution Control Administration, 1968.

782   Lucas, Jack. Vegetarianism: the world food problem.
      Cheshire, England, Vegetarian Society (U. K.), 1978.
      Booklet deals with world population growth, food
      shortages, and relative efficiency of plant-based pro-
      tein sources.

783   MacGillivray, John H. , and Bosley, James B. "Amino
      acid production per acre by plants and animals."
      Economic Botany 16, 1 (Jan. -Mar. 1962): 25-30.
      Comparative analysis of amino acid production by
      plant and animal foods finds that legumes have the
      highest percentage of amino acids and highest produc-
      tion of amino acids per acre, followed by animal
      foods and non-legume foods.

784   Rachels, James. "Vegetarianism and 'the other weight
      problem'. " In: World hunger and moral obligation.
      Edited by William Aiken and Hugh LaFollette. Engle-
      wood Cliffs, NJ, Prentice-Hall, 1977, p. 180-194.
      Author argues that in view of world food shortages,
      meat eating is immoral because of cruelty to animals
      and massive waste of resources in the production of
      meat; urges end of exploitation of animals which at
      the same time would increase the world's food supply.

785   Rensberger, Boyce. "Can eating less meat here re-
      lieve starvation in the world?" New York Times
      (Nov. 28, 1974): 44.
      Economic implications of reduced U. S. beef con-
      sumption.

786   Ross, Tamara. "Animal, vegetable, mineral. " Nurs-
      ing Mirror 151, 2 (July 10, 1980): 22-24.
      Summarizes ecological and ethical arguments for
      vegetarian and vegan diets.

787 Sabry, Z. I. "Coordinating food production with human needs." Chemistry in Canada 27, 2 (Feb. 1975):
16-19.
　　Factors such as the shortage of arable land, the
inefficiency of animal production, the direct competi-
tion between animals and humans for food, and the
size of the world population point to the inevitability
of vegetarianism as a global way of life.

788 Sanderson, Fred Hugo. Japan's food prospects and
policies. Washington, DC, Brookings Institution,
1978.
　　Economic impact of Japan's change in the past 20
years from a nearly vegetarian diet to one similar to
that of Western nations.

789 Schuck, Peter. "The curious case of the indicted meat
inspectors." Harper's Magazine (Sept. 1972): 81-88.
　　Miscarriage of justice in 40 Boston meat inspector
bribery cases.

790 Sinclair, H. M. "The human nutritional advantages of
plant foods over animal foods." Qualitas Plantarum--
Plant Foods for Human Nutrition 29, 1-2 (July 6,
1979): 7-18.
　　Outline of advantages and disadvantages of vegetable and animal foods, with attention to the world
food situation.

791 Stout, Perry R. "Fertilizers, food production and environmental compromise." In: Western Hemisphere
Nutrition Congress. III. Proceedings, Miami Beach,
FL, Sept. 2, 1971, p. 293-299.
　　Compares amount of land and other resources re-
quired to support vegetarian as opposed to meat-based
diet; discusses nitrogen pollution of water and various
sources of protein for human consumption.

792 Thompson, Susan, and Braun, Ernest. "Cropping for
plant-based agriculture." Food Policy 3, 2 (May
1978): 147-149.
　　Description of project evaluating the potential for
a transition from the current animal-based agricultural
system to a vegetarian food production scheme for
England and Wales.

793 Tudge, Colin. "An end to meat mythology." Food
Policy 2, 1 (Feb. 1977): 82-85.

Author attempts to debunk primary arguments supporting meat consumption, based on economics, biology, and politics.

794 Wedemeyer, Dee. "Food Day dinner at the White House offers the meat of controversy." New York Times (Apr. 22, 1977): sec. 2, p. 4.
Report of the vegetarian Food Day dinner buffet held at the White House.

795 Wellford, Harrison. Sowing the wind; a report from Ralph Nader's Center for Study of Responsive Law on food safety and the chemical harvest. New York, Grossman Publishers, 1972.
Influence of politics on meat packing industry, meat inspection, animal drugs, pesticides.

796 Wynne-Tyson, Jon; Allaby, Michael; Long, Alan; Blythe, Colin; Roberts, Peter; and Seymour, John. "Must an ecological society be a vegetarian one?" Ecologist 6, 10 (Dec. 1976): 356-375, 384.
Panel discussion and debate on the ecological aspects of vegetarianism.

797 Young, Vernon R.; Scrimshaw, Nevin S.; and Milner, Max. "Food from plants." Chemistry and Industry (July 17, 1976): 588-598.
Economic, ecological and nutritional considerations regarding plant sources of dietary protein and energy for the human population.

PHILOSOPHICAL ASPECTS OF DIET:
ETHICS, PHILOSOPHY, RELIGION,
ANIMAL RIGHTS

For works prior to 1900, see 3, 4, 5, 10, 15, 25, 28, 30, 31, 32, 33, 34, 35, 38, 41.

For works between 1900 and 1959, see 43, 45, 50, 54, 57, 63, 78, 81, 93, 108, 115, 119, 126, 127, 158, 163, 164, 166, 179, 196, 218, 237, 266, 278, 306, 312, 318.

For related contemporary works, see 403, 480, 509, 538, 743.

798 Agee, James. A mother's tale. (Motion picture) New
York, Learning Corporation of America, 1976.
Color 16 mm film based on short story of a bull
who escapes from the slaughterhouse and returns to
warn the others of what awaits them. (See also no.
45.)

799 Altman, Nathaniel. "Soul food." Vegetarian Times
(Nov.-Dec. 1977): 36-38.
Conveys the spiritual side of vegetarianism.

800 Animal rights and human obligations. Edited by Tom
Regan and Peter Singer. Englewood Cliffs, NJ,
Prentice-Hall, 1976.
Anthology of philosophical writings from ancient
times to the present arguing various sides of the
animal rights issue; also included are allegorical
works in which man is the consumed, not the consumer.

801 Animals, men and morals; an enquiry into the maltreatment of non-humans. Edited by Stanley Godlovitch, Roslind Godlovitch, and John Harris. New
York, Taplinger Publishing Co., 1972.
Collection of essays devoted to coverage of man's
interaction with the rest of the animal world, including the use of animals for food, sport, fashion, and
research; raises moral and philosophical issues involved and responds to arguments generated in support of meat eating.

802 Anon. "Is pain the price of farm efficiency? Areas
of disquiet." New Scientist (Oct. 18, 1973): 170-171.
Summary of commonly-used intensive farming
practices for different types of farm animals.

803 Anon. Jesus was a vegetarian; why aren't you? Im-
laystown, NJ, The Edenite Society, 1977.
Evidence and arguments from biblical scriptures,
Dead Sea scrolls, and Essene texts for a humane,
vegetarian Jesus.

804 Anon. "When keeping kosher isn't kosher enough."
New York Times (Sept. 14, 1977): sec. 3, p. 4.
Article on Jewish vegetarianism includes comments by members of North American Jewish Vegetarian Society and prominent vegetarians.

805 Auxter, Thomas. "The right not to be eaten." Inquiry
22, 1-2 (Summer 1979): 221-230.
    Employing the teleological-ethical theory that the
moral rightness or wrongness of an action is a function of the good produced, author argues that wild
animals have the right not to be eaten and that
domestication of animals for meat production should
cease.

806 Barriot, Claude Lucien. Tu ne tueras point ... tes
aliments: de l'interprétation du cinquième commande-
ment ... à la diététique. Prades, France, Collection
Serpolet, 1977.

807 Benson, John. "Duty and the beast." Philosophy 53
(Oct. 1978): 529-549.
    Comparison and assessment of the moral position
advanced by Peter Singer in Animal Liberation and
Stephen Clark in The Moral Status of Animals.

808 Berman, Louis A. "Why is Jewish vegetarianism different from all others?" Vegetarian Times (Apr.
1980): 42-47.
    Jewish dietary traditions and rituals against a
backdrop of compassion for animals and humans.

809 Bermont, G. "Comparative perspectives on the pigeon
to person problem." Philosophical Studies (Ireland)
23 (1975): 178-188.

810 Berry, J. W. "A psychocultural perspective." Philosophical Studies (Ireland) 23 (1975): 172-178.

811 Bon, B. H. "What Hinduism can offer to world fellowship." Indian Philosophy and Culture 11, 1 (Mar.
1966): 1-7.
    Abstention from animal foods and intoxicants is
viewed as necessary to proper worship and attainment
of spiritual freedom.

812 Bon, B. H. "What Hinduism can offer to world fellowship." Indian Philosophy and Culture 11, 2 (June
1966): 3-8.
    Notes vegetarianism as one element comprising
the superior spiritual position embraced by Hinduism.

813 Carpenter, Edward. Animals and ethics; a report of
the working party on animals and ethics. London,

Watkins, 1980.
    Outline of current uses of animals for food, research, pets, and recommendations for improvement of the lot of animals.

814 Clark, Stephen R. L. The moral status of animals. Oxford, England, Clarendon Press, 1977.
    Arguing for the principle of animal rights, author views vegetarianism as a necessary indicator of devotion to the moral life; regards meat-eating as a mere holdover from ancient ritual sacrifices.

815 Clooney, Francis X. "Vegetarianism and religion." America 140 (Feb. 24, 1979): 133-134.
    Religious significance of vegetarianism.

816 David, William H. "Man-eating aliens." Journal of Value Inquiry 10 (Fall 1976): 178-185.
    Allegorical situation is described in which vastly superior alien creatures arrive on earth and intend to use humans as their primary food source even though suitable alternatives are available. Presents human appeals on the grounds of prudence, sympathy and conscience as well as the aliens' viewpoint in response to these pleas.

817 Devine, Philip E. "The moral basis of vegetarianism." Philosophy 53 (Oct. 1978): 481-505.
    Examines the moral objections of the vegetarian to the rearing and slaughter of animals for food.

818 Diamond, Cora. "Eating meat and eating people." Philosophy 53 (Oct. 1978): 465-479.

819 Dickens, Eldon W., Jr. "Cruelty in vegetarianism." New York Times (June 26, 1976): 23.
    Argues against the moral basis of vegetarianism on the grounds that raising and killing plants for food is equally as cruel as raising and killing animals.

820 Dieges, Jon. No me, know me, no meat. n. p., 197?
    Poetic essays promoting heightened sensitivity to life discuss war, killing, eating animals, making love, drugs, silence.

821 Duncan, Ian. "Can the psychologist measure stress?" New Scientist (Oct. 18, 1973): 173-175.

Conditions of stress, frustration, and boredom in poultry produced by intensive farming methods.

822   Ewbank, Roger. "The trouble with being a farm animal." New Scientist (Oct. 18, 1973): 172-173.
Discussion of the difficulties involved in objectively measuring and dealing with signs of stress in livestock.

823   Ewer, Tom. "Farm animals in the law." New Scientist (Oct. 18, 1973): 178-179.
Review of legislation in the United Kingdom to protect the basic welfare of intensively-produced livestock.

824   Fox, Michael. "Animal liberation: a critique." Ethics 88 (Jan. 1978): 106-118.
Discusses philosophical issues and moral positions with regard to the treatment of animals in two publications, Animal Liberation, by Peter Singer and "The Moral Basis of Vegetarianism" by Tom Regan. Argues that the concept of moral rights cannot be extended to include animals.

825   Fox, Michael. "Animal suffering and rights: a reply to Singer and Regan." Ethics 88 (Jan. 1978): 134-138.
Further clarification of the author's view that animals do not have rights.

826   Fox, Michael. Suffering: the hidden cost of factory farming. Washington, DC, Humane Society of the United States, n. d.
Describes inhumane conditions of crowding, confinement, and disease in modern livestock production. (Reprinted from Humane Society News, Winter 1978.)

827   Francis, Leslie Pickering, and Norman, Richard. "Some animals are more equal than others." Philosophy 53 (Oct. 1978): 507-527.
Criticizes principle of equal consideration of the interests of animals as a moral basis for vegetarianism as put forward by Peter Singer in Animal Liberation.

828   Frey, R. G. "Rights, interests, desires and beliefs." American Philosophical Quarterly 16, 3 (July 1979): 233-239.

Argues against position that animals have desires, beliefs, and interests which entitle them to moral rights.

829 Gavin, E. A. "Human and nonhuman activity." Philosophical Studies (Ireland) 23 (1975): 198-209.

830 Green, Joe. Chalutzim of the Messiah. The text of a lecture delivered by Joe Green. The religious vegetarian concept as expounded by Rabbi Yitzchak Hacohen Kook.... Johannesburg, S. A., n. p., 1971.
Interpretation of Hebrew texts and laws expounding the ethical vegetarian position.

831 Green, Joe. The Jewish vegetarian tradition. 2nd ed. Johannesburg, S. A., Mimeographed printing, 1969.
Traces ethical, compassionate tradition from Biblical times to the modern Jewish vegetarian movement.

832 Harris, John. Vegetarianism: the ethics. Cheshire, England, Vegetarian Society (U. K.), 1978.
Booklet's question and answer format discusses ethical issues of diet.

833 Harrison, Ruth. Animal machines; the new factory farming industry. London, Vincent Stuart Ltd., 1964.
Classic of animal rights movement details conditions employed in the intensive factory farming methods of poultry, egg, veal, and beef production.

834 Harrison, Ruth. "Animal production and welfare: practical considerations." Animal Regulation Studies 2, 3 (Aug. 1980): 215-222.

835 Hartshorne, Charles. "The rights of the subhuman world." Environmental Ethics 1 (Spr. 1979): 49-60.
Philosophical argument that religion, philosophy and science support the rights of nonhuman life forms.

836 Head, Louis. "Vegetarianism and animal rights." Humanist 37, 5 (Sept. -Oct. 1977): 60.
Letter discussing possible solutions to the ethical dilemma of deciding between saving either a man or a wolf favors saving the wolf.

837   Herrick, Lynn.   "Vegetarianism and animal rights."
      Humanist 37, 5 (Sept. -Oct. 1977): 60.
      Letter considers vegetarian sensitivities somewhat
      misplaced in that plants have feelings also.

838   Hershaft, Alex.   "Vegetarianism and animal rights."
      Humanist 37, 5 (Sept. -Oct. 1977): 59.
      Letter disputes position of Michael Levin on ani-
      mal rights; discusses distinction between granted
      rights and seized rights.

839   Jackson, Jon A.   "The life and death of an American
      chicken."   Saturday Review (Sept. 2, 1972): 12-13.
      Assembly-line production of poultry.

840   Jussawalla, J. M.   Living the vegetarian way.   Bom-
      bay, Lalvani Publishing House, 1971.
      Spiritual and medical aspects of the vegetarian
      diet; excerpts from the writings of famous vegetari-
      ans.

841   Leadbeater, Charles Webster.   Vegetarianism and oc-
      cultism.   Adyar, Madras, Theosophical Publishing
      House, 1960.
      Evidence for the superiority of plant foods; em-
      phasizes moral considerations of slaughter and ad-
      herence to hidden laws of nature.

842   Leepson, Marc.   "Animal rights."   Editorial Research
      Reports (Aug. 8, 1980): 563-580.
      Treatment of animals in medical research and on
      factory farms; motivations for vegetarianism.

843   Lehman, H. S. , and Hurnik, J. F.   "On an alleged
      moral basis of vegetarianism."   Applied Animal
      Ethology 6, 3 (July 1980): 205-229.
      Editorial argues that if it is morally wrong to kill
      animals for food, it is equally wrong to kill plants
      for food.

844   Levin, Michael E.   "All in a stew about animals: a
      reply to Singer."   Humanist 37, 5 (Sept. -Oct. 1977):
      58.
      Further charges and counter-charges on the animal
      rights issue.

845   Levin, Michael E.   "Philosophical vegetarianism: con
      and pro; animal rights evaluated. "   Humanist 37, 4

(July-Aug. 1977): 12, 14-15.
Critique of <u>Animal Liberation</u> by Peter Singer states that "if we stopped eating animals and using them in research, the human race would be decimated." Asserts that since animals cannot reason or entertain goals, they have no natural rights.

846 Linzey, Andrew. <u>Animal rights; a Christian assessment of man's treatment of animals.</u> London, SCM Press, 1976.
Examination of moral issues involved in man's dealings with animals, especially those used for food and research; argues that animals have a moral right to live as animals on their own terms and in their own ways; vegetarianism thus becomes a moral necessity.

847 McLachlan, H. V. "Moral case of a carnivore." <u>Contemporary Review</u> 237 (July 1980): 19-24.

848 Magiawala, Kiran R. "Vegetarianism." <u>Humanist</u> 38, 3 (May-June 1978): 2, 39.
Letter comments on personal motives for becoming a vegetarian.

849 Martin, Michael. "A critique of moral vegetarianism." <u>Reason Papers</u> 3 (1976): 13-43.

850 Martin, Michael. "Vegetarianism, the right to life and fellow creaturehood." <u>Animal Regulation Studies</u> 2, 3 (Aug. 1980): 205-214.
Challenges moral arguments for vegetarianism which are based upon the right to life and the fellow creaturehood concepts.

851 Mason, James B. "Animals." <u>Vegetarian Times</u> (Mar. 1980): 52-53.
Highlights problems of confinement and disease resulting from the industrialization of livestock production.

852 Mason, James B. "Vegetarianism is a human rights struggle." <u>Vegetarian Times</u> (June 1980): 47-49.
Assessment of the magnitude of the struggle against oppression of human and non-human animals.

853 Mason, Jim, and Singer, Peter. <u>Animal factories.</u> New York, Crown Publishers, 1980.

Presentation of current factory farming methods
for the intensive production of livestock and poultry;
animals undergo stress, boredom, mutilation, over-
crowding, confinement, disease, and drugs in a system designed to maximize profits for agribusiness.

854 Monticone, George T. "Animals and morality." Dialogue 17, 4 (1978): 683-695.
Review of Animal Rights and Human Obligations
by Tom Regan and Peter Singer concludes that animals have the right to be spared torture and unnecessary pain since nearly all animals appear to be
capable of experiencing pain.

855 Morris, Jan. "Speciesism?" Encounter 53, 3 (Sept.
1979): 89-91.
Views on symposium on animal rights sponsored
by the RSPCA.

856 Morse, Mel. Ordeal of the animals. Englewood
Cliffs, NJ, Prentice-Hall, 1968.
Man's inhumane treatment of animals is examined
as it routinely occurs in the laboratory, rodeo, motion picture industry, cockfight, dogfight, and the
slaughterhouse.

857 Nevin, David. "Scientist helps stir new movement for
'animal rights'." Smithsonian 11, 1 (Apr. 1980):
50-59.
Efforts of Michael Fox for humane conditions on
factory farms and in research laboratories.

858 Nielsen, Kai. "Persons, morals and the animal kingdom." Man and World 11 (1978): 231-256.
Finds the argument that in relation to animals man
deserves preferential treatment or special consideration because of greater intrinsic worth or moral advancement to be humanocentric and without adequate
rational justification.

859 Obis, Paul. "Man vs. animals: the worse offense."
New York Times (Feb. 12, 1979): sec. 1, p. 16.
Letter considers present day animal husbandry
practices worse than hunting, although both are repre-
hensible.

860 Perry, Graham. "Can the physiologist measure
stress?" New Scientist (Oct. 18, 1973): 175-177.

Consideration of physiological and behavioral reactions to stress in farm animals.

861 Pybus, Elizabeth M., and Broadie, Alexander. "Kant and the maltreatment of animals." Philosophy 53 (Oct. 1978): 560-561.
Reply to Tom Regan's criticism of authors' interpretation of Kant's theory of the moral status of animals.

862 Pybus, Elizabeth M., and Broadie, Alexander. "Kant's treatment of animals." Philosophy 49 (Oct. 1974): 375-383.

863 Pyke, Magnus. Technological eating; or, where does the fish-finger point? London, John Murray, 1972.
Advances and changes in food production, processing and marketing over the last century; discusses ethical implications of factory farming, kosher foods and vegetarianism.

864 Rajnessh, Bhagwan Shree. "The spiritual side of vegetarianism." Vegetarian Times (Mar. 1980): 64.
Complexity, inter-relatedness, and interdependence of life forms forbid their destruction for food.

865 Regan, Tom. "Broadie and Pybus on Kant." Philosophy 51 (Oct. 1976): 471-472.
Disputes essay on Kant's views of animals by stating that Kant never maintained that it is wrong to use animals as a means, e.g. beast of burden, but rather that it is wrong to maltreat them because it predisposes people to mistreat other people in a similar way.

866 Regan, Tom. "Fox's critique of Animal Liberation." Ethics 88 (Jan. 1978): 126-133.
Noting misrepresentations and inconsistencies by Fox, author restates his position and arguments with regard to treatment of animals.

867 Regan, Tom. "McCloskey on why animals cannot have rights." Philosophical Quarterly 26 (July 1976): 251-257.
Rebuttal to arguments that animals do not possess either rights or interests.

868 Regan, Tom. "The moral basis of vegetarianism."
     Canadian Journal of Philosophy 5, 2 (Oct. 1975):
     181-214.
        Author attempts to establish a rational foundation
     for the vegetarian way of life by arguing that vege-
     tarianism is prima facie obligatory, that both ani-
     mals and humans can and do experience pain, and
     that both have an inherent right to live.

869 Regan, Tom. "Utilitarianism, vegetarianism and ani-
     mal rights." Philosophy and Public Affairs 9, 4
     (Summer 1980): 305-324.
        Argues that Singer's case for moral obligation for
     vegetarianism and the utilitarian concept of the treat-
     ment of animals require completely different sets of
     arguments.

870 Reiger, George. "The king and us." Field and
     Stream 82, 2 (June 1977): 20, 24.
        Citing hunting and trapping traditions from ancient
     times and the unchanging nature of man, author points
     out practical and moral inconsistencies of vegetarians
     and wildlife protectionists.

871 Report of the Technical Committee to Enquire into the
     Welfare of Animals Kept under Intensive Livestock
     Husbandry Systems. Command Paper 2836. London,
     Her Majesty's Stationery Office, 1965.
        Study of inhumane conditions on British factory
     farms; known as the Brambell Report.

872 Rudd, Geoffrey L. The Bible and vegetarianism and
     Holmes-Gore, V. A. Was the Master a vegetarian?
     Los Angeles, CA, Vegetarian Book Club, n. d.
        Religious and scriptural basis of vegetarianism.

873 Shriver, Nellie. "Going all the way." Vegetarian
     Times (Dec. -Jan. 1977): 24-25.
        Ethical and health superiority of the fruitarian diet.

874 Siderits, M. A. "Person vs. pigeon-monger; the vari-
     able of counteraction." Philosophical Studies (Ireland)
     23 (1975): 188-197.

875 Singer, Peter. Animal liberation; a new ethics for our
     treatment of animals. New York, Random House,
     1975.

Presents moral and philosophical arguments for
vegetarianism based on the suffering and exploitation
of animals used as laboratory experimental subjects
and as objects of intensive factory farming; advances
the utilitarian concept of actions based on the greatest
good and the least evil as the basis for the equal
consideration of the interests of animals.

876   Singer, Peter.   "Animals and human beings as equals."
      Animal Regulation Studies 2, 3 (Aug. 1980):   165-174.

877   Singer, Peter.   "The fable of the Fox and the unliber-
      ated animals."   Ethics 88 (Jan. 1978):   119-125.
         Rebuttal to Fox's critique cites misinterpretation
      of author's positions, and also contains counter-ar-
      guments to objections raised by Fox.

878   Singer, Peter.   "Philosophical vegetarianism: con and
      pro; a reply to Professor Levin."   Humanist 37, 4
      (July-Aug. 1977):   13, 16.
         Point-by-point rebuttal defends equal consideration
      of non-humans, discusses utilitarianism vs. absolut-
      ism in solving ethical dilemmas.

879   Singer, Peter.   "Utilitarianism and vegetarianism."
      Philosophy and Public Affairs 9, 4 (1980):   325-337.
         Defends and elaborates upon concept of utilitarian-
      ism as a basis for vegetarianism.

880   Society for Animal Rights.   A message to those con-
      cerned about animal suffering.   Clarks Summit, PA,
      The Society, n. d.
         Pamphlet expresses plea for vegetarianism on
      ethical, moral and humanitarian grounds.

881   Steel, C.   "Porphyrius' reactie tegen het amoralisme
      van de gnostici."   Tijdschrift voor Filosofie 37
      (July 1975):   211-225.   (In Dutch.)

882   Székely, Edmond Bordeaux.   The Gospel of peace of
      Jesus Christ by the disciple John; the Essene gospel
      of peace.   vol. 1.   San Diego, CA, Academy of
      Creative Living, 1971-1974.
         Prohibits the killing of man or beast, and admon-
      ishes man to eat only herbs, seeds, fruits, and
      milk, and to eat nothing which has been destroyed
      by fire, frost, or decay.

883   Tree of life; an anthology of articles appearing in the
      Jewish Vegetarian, 1966-1974. Edited by Philip L.
      Pick.   South Brunswick, NJ, A. S. Barnes, 1977.
      Anthology expresses vegetarian thought in the
      Jewish tradition.

884   Tudge, Colin.   "Farmers in loco parentis."   New Sci-
      entist (Oct. 18, 1973):   179-181.
      Anthropomorphism with regard to farm animals.

885   Tyler, Robert L.   "Plant liberation: the struggle
      against fauna chauvinism."   Humanist 38, 1 (Jan. -
      Feb. 1978):   30-32.
      Discusses moral issues of vegetarianism and puts
      forth the case for the liberation of plants from dis-
      crimination, suffering, and destruction.

886   Vidal-Naquet, Pierre.   "Plato's myth of the statesman;
      the ambiguities of the Golden Age and of history."
      Journal of Hellenistic Studies 98 (1978):   132-141.
      Analysis of widely varying interpretations of
      Plato's myth of the Golden Age includes historical
      and mythical accounts of vegetarian, non-vegetarian
      and cannibalistic diets, each portrayed as the pre-
      dominant diet during the Golden Age.

887   Vyas, Vaidya Vasudera Vitthal-prasad.   "Importance
      of vegetarianism in ayurveda."   Rural India 30, 2
      (Dec. 1967):   70-72.
      Discussion of the relationship of vegetarianism and
      ahimsa (non-violence) to ayurveda (science of life).

888   Watson, I. Bruce.   "Satyagraha: the Gandhian synthe-
      sis."   Journal of Indian History 55, 1-2 (1977):   325-
      335.
      Analysis of the humane philosophy of satyagraha,
      as practiced by Gandhi, incorporating the ideals of
      self-realization, non-violence, vegetarianism, and
      the avoidance of killing.

889   Wenz, Peter S.   "Act-utilitarianism and animal libera-
      tion."   Personalist 60 (Oct. 1979):   423-428.
      Argues that act-utilitarianism obstructs the vege-
      tarian cause, and that the moral arguments for vege-
      tarianism must rest on non-utilitarian ethical the-
      ories.

MEDICAL ASPECTS OF VEGETARIAN DIETS

General Interest
(See also: 1, 20, 21, 111, 174, 175,
191, 283, 297, 752-756.)

890 Anon. "Vegetarian diets." American Journal of Clinical Nutrition 27, 10 (Oct. 1974): 1095-1096.
Editorial asserts that vegetarians can be well
nourished if a variety of foods are eaten and if sufficient care is taken in planning the diet.

891 Anon. "Vegetarian diets." Medical Letter on Drugs
and Therapeutics 15, 7 (Mar. 30, 1973): 30-32.
Advises physicians of vegetarian patients to pre-
scribe vitamin B12 and to encourage milk and cheese
consumption.

892 Anon. "Vegetarian diets." Medical Letter on Drugs
and Therapeutics 21, 15 (July 27, 1979): 62-63.
Summary of nutritional aspects of vegetarian diet.

893 Anon. "Vegetarianism and nutrition." American Family Physician 20, 3 (Sept. 1979): 82, 85.
Editorial characterizes nutritional problems posed
by various vegetarian and cult diets as dependent
upon the restrictiveness of the diet.

894 Armstrong, Bruce K.; Davis, Richard E.; Nicol,
Darryl J.; van Merwyk, Anthony J.; and Larwood,
Carol J. "Hematological, vitamin B12, and folate
studies on Seventh-day Adventist vegetarians."
American Journal of Clinical Nutrition 27, 7 (July
1974): 712-718.
Vegetarians had higher folate levels and lower
vitamin B12 levels than non-vegetarians.

895 Barness, Lewis A. "Nutritional aspects of vegetarianism, health foods, and fad diets." Nutrition Reviews
35, 6 (June 1977): 153-157.
Reviews health considerations of various dietary
practices.

896 Bengtsson, Calle; Bruce, Ake; and Thunborg, Phebe.
"Nutritional intake and state of health in female vege-

tarians." Var Foeda 30, 3 (1978): 91-104.
Study of 22 vegetarian women found no significant
differences from controls, although vegetarians had
higher total iron binding capacity and lower serum
cholesterol levels. (In Swedish.)

897 Crosby, William H. "Can a vegetarian be well nourished?" American Medical Association. Journal 233,
8 (Aug. 25, 1975): 898.
Properly selected vegetarian diets can be nutritionally adequate.

898 Dickerson, J. W. T. , and Ellis, F. R. "Vegetarian-
ism--a clinician's view." Nutrition and Food Science
48 (July 1977): 6-8.
Review of medical literature indicates no harmful
effects from the consumption of balanced vegetarian
and vegan diets.

899 Dickerson, John W. T. , and Fehily, Ann M. "Bizarre
and unusual diets." Practitioner 222 (May 1979):
643-647.
Nutritional implications of vegetarian, vegan, fruitarian and Zen macrobiotic diets.

900 Duc, Ha Nguyet, and Tran, Phan The. "Nutrition of
Buddhist monks in Vietnam." Revue de L'institut
Pasteur de Lyon 8, 2 (1975): 173-182.
Analysis of Buddhist monks' vegetarian diets deter-
mined that all nutrients were adequate with the ex-
ception of calcium, iron, and vitamins A, B1, and
B2. (In French.)

901 Durnin, J. V. G. A. "Nutrition." Royal Society of
London. Philosophical Transactions. Biological Sci-
ences 274, 934 (July 1, 1976): 447-455.
Review of nutritional observations on various cul-
tures notes studies of vegetarians and vegans in the
U. K. finding no evidence of nutritional deficiency,
except for possible marginal deficiency of vitamin
B12.

902 Dwyer, Johanna. "Vegetarianism." Contemporary
Nutrition 4, 6 (June 1979): 1-2.
Overview of health aspects of vegetarianism. Re-
printed in New York State Journal of Medicine 80, 4
(Mar. 1980): 660-661; and Medical Society of New
Jersey. Journal 76, 10 (Sept. 1979): 687-689.

903 Gear, J. S.; Mann, J. I.; Thorogood, M.; Carter,
R.; and Jelfs, R. "Bio-chemical and haematological
variables in vegetarians." British Medical Journal
280, 6229 (June 14, 1980): 1415.
Measurement and comparison of 12 biochemical
and hematological factors in groups of vegetarians
and non-vegetarians.

904 Hardinge, Mervyn G., and Crooks, Hulda. "Non-flesh
dietaries. III. Adequate and inadequate." American
Dietetic Association. Journal 45 (Dec. 1964): 537-
542.
Summary of findings of a number of investigators
regarding adequate and inadequate vegetarian, vegan
and near-vegetarian diets.

905 Hardinge, Mervyn G., and Crooks, Hulda. "Non-flesh
dietaries. II. Scientific literature." American
Dietetic Association. Journal 43 (Dec. 1963): 550-
558.
Representative review of English language literature relating to experimental investigations, group
studies, health advantages and disadvantages of vegetarian diets.

906 Harland, B. F., and Peterson, M. "Nutritional status
of lacto-ovo-vegetarian Trappist monks." American
Dietetic Association. Journal 72, 3 (Mar. 1978):
259-264.
Analysis of four weeks' menus indicated sufficient
nutrients were provided.

907 Hitchcock, Nancy E., and English, Ruth M. "A comparison of food consumption in lacto-ovo-vegetarians
and non-vegetarians." Australian Institute of Anatomy. Food and Nutrition Notes and Reviews 20, 11-
12 (Nov.-Dec. 1963): 141-146.
Vegetarians had lower consumption of protein, fat,
total calories, vitamin A; higher consumption of calcium, thiamine, ascorbic acid, and fiber than non-
vegetarians.

908 Huijbregts, A. W. M.; van Schaik, A.; van Berge-
Henegouwen, G. P.; and van der Werf, S. D. J.
"Serum lipids, biliary lipid composition, and bile
acid metabolism in vegetarians as compared to normal controls." European Journal of Clinical Investi-

gation 10, 6 (Dec. 1980): 443-449.
Study of young healthy vegetarians found an association between vegetarian diet and bile acid conservation, but not between vegetarian diet and reduced
deoxychoate formation.

909 Jorge, Francisco Bastos; Cintra, Antonio Barros de
Ulhoa; and Soares, Ana Maria. "Studies of vegetable
diets. I. Nitrogen balance and some physiological
effects of vegetable diets on normal individuals."
Revista Paulista de Medicina 68, 3 (Mar. 1966):
140-147.
Subjects on a vegetarian diet experienced positive
nitrogen balance and reduced urea and cholestrol
concentrations in the blood. (In Portuguese.)

910 Kunkel, M. E.; Mason, R. L.; and Beauchene, R. E.
"Dietary intakes and physical and biochemical measurements in older, adult female vegetarians and non-
vegetarians." Federation Proceedings 38, 3 (1979):
711.
Comparison of nutrient intakes and physical and
biochemical parameters in vegetarian and nonvegetarian women aged 40 years and over. (Abstract
only.)

911 Kunkel, Mary Elizabeth. Relationships among age,
physical measurements and protein intake and metabolism in older adult female vegetarians and nonvegetarians. Ph. D., University of Tennessee, 1979.
Dissertation examines physical variables, protein
intake and the urinary excretion of protein-derived
metabolites in lacto-ovo-vegetarians, vegans, and
non-vegetarian women ranging in age from 40 to 92
years. Concludes that compared to non-vegetarian
diet, vegan diet may affect some physical measurements, protein intake and metabolism, although effect
of lacto-ovo-vegetarian diet is minimal.

912 Mason, Rossie L.; Kunkel, M. Elizabeth; Davis, Teresa
Ann; and Beauchene, Roy E. "Nutrient intakes of
vegetarian and nonvegetarian women." Tennessee
Farm and Home Science 105 (Jan. -Mar. 1978): 18-
20.
Study of dietary intakes of 78 vegetarian and non-
vegetarian women found that vegetarians consumed
significantly less total fat, saturated fat, cholesterol,

and niacin and significantly more calcium, fiber, and
thiamine than the nonvegetarians.

913 Raper, Nancy R. , and Hill, Mary M. "Vegetarian
diets. " Nutrition Program News (July-Aug. 1973):
1-4.
Nutritional adequacy of vegetarian diets. Reprinted
in Nutrition Reviews 32, Suppl. (July 1974): 29-33;
and condensed in Family Economic Review (Summer
1974): 14-16.

914 Register, U. D. , and Sonnenberg, L. "Vegetarian
diet. " American Dietetic Association. Journal 62,
3 (1973): 253-261.
Review of literature indicates vegetarian diet can
provide all essential nutrients. Reprinted in:
Sourcebook on food and nutrition. Scarpa, Ioannis
S. , and Kiefer, Helen Chilton, consulting editors.
Chicago, Marquis Academia Media, 1978, p. 220-
228.

915 Schultz, Terry D. , and Leklem, James E. "Vitamin
B6 status in Seventh-day Adventist vegetarians and
non-vegetarians. " Federation Proceedings 38, 3
(1979): 452.
Vitamin B6 status did not differ significantly in
vegetarians, non-vegetarians and controls. (Abstract
only.)

916 Sutnick, M. R. "Vegetarian diets. " Primary Care
2, 2 (June 1975): 309-315.
Vegetarian diets can supply the nutritional needs
of individuals of all ages, although strict vegetarians
avoiding all animal products should pay close attention to intakes of protein, calcium, riboflavin, and
vitamin B12.

917 Taber, Louise A. L. , and Cook, Richard A. "Dietary
and anthropometric assessment of adult omnivores,
fish-eaters, and lacto-ovo-vegetarians. " American
Dietetic Association. Journal 76, 1 (Jan. 1980):
21-29.
Comprehensive study of energy and nutrient intakes
and anthropometric measurements in three dietary
groups.

Cardiovascular System
(See also: 82, 85, 86, 160, 176, 202, 217, 1236, 1241,
1244, 1248, 1249, 1251, 1252, 1283, 1288, 1289, 1376.)

918   Anholm, Anne C.   The relationship of a vegetarian
      diet to blood pressure."   Preventive Medicine 7, 1
      (1978): 35.
      Vegetarian Seventh-day Adventists had significantly
      lower blood pressure levels for age and sex than non-
      vegetarian Mormons.

919   Anon.   "Altitude and hypertension."   Nutrition Reviews
      35, 8 (1977): 218-219.

920   Anon.   "Diet and stress in vascular disease."   Amer-
      ican Medical Association.   Journal 176, 9 (June 3,
      1961): 806-807.
      Citing studies indicating that a vegetarian diet
      could prevent 90 percent of thrombo-embolic disease
      and 97 percent of coronary occlusions, editorial con-
      cludes that stress has little or no effect on the de-
      velopment of heart disease provided the diet is low
      in animal fat.

921   Anon.   "Plant foods and atherosclerosis."   Nutrition
      Reviews 35 (1977): 148.

922   Anon.   "Plasma lipids and lipoproteins in vegetarians
      and controls."   Nutrition Reviews 33, 9 (Sept. 1975):
      285-286.
      Report of two studies suggesting that vegetarian
      diets may be of significant therapeutic value for per-
      sons with hyperlipoproteinemia and hypertension.

923   Armstrong, Bruce; Clarke, Helen; Martin, Craig;
      Ward, William; Norman, Nevoli; and Masarei, John.
      "Urinary sodium and blood pressure in vegetarians."
      American Journal of Clinical Nutrition 32, 12 (1979):
      2472-2476.
      Vegetarians had lower blood pressure readings
      than non-vegetarians, seemingly unrelated to dietary
      sodium intakes.

924   Armstrong, Bruce; van Merwyk, Anthony J.; and
      Coates, Harvey.   "Blood pressure in Seventh-day
      Adventist vegetarians."   American Journal of Epi-

demiology 105, 5 (May 1977): 444-449.
Seventh-day Adventist vegetarians had significantly
lower blood pressure readings than a comparable
group of non-vegetarians.

925 Barrow, J. Gordon; Quinlan, Carroll B.; Cooper,
Gerald R.; Whitner, Virginia S.; and Goodloe, Mary
H. R. "Studies in atherosclerosis. III. An epidemiologic study of atherosclerosis in Trappist and
Benedictine monks: a preliminary report." Annals
of Internal Medicine 52, 2 (Feb. 1960): 368-377.
Vegetarian Trappist monks derived 26 percent of
caloric intake from fats (43 percent from animal
sources and 57 percent from vegetable sources),
while omnivore Benedictine monks derived 45 percent
of caloric intake from fats (75 percent from animal
sources and 25 percent from vegetable sources);
vegetarian monks had lower serum cholesterol, free
cholesterol, esterified fatty acids, phospholipids and
total lipids.

926 Carroll, K. K.; Giovannetti, P. M.; Huff, M. W.;
Moase, O.; Roberts, D. C. K.; and Wolfe, B. M.
"Hypocholesterolemic effect of substituting soybean
protein for animal protein in the diet of healthy
young women." American Journal of Clinical Nutrition 31, 8 (Aug. 1978): 1312-1321.
Plasma cholesterol levels were found to be significantly lower on the plant protein diet as compared to
the animal protein diet.

927 Castro, José. La hipertensión arterial: su origen y
su homoterapia (nueva medicina biológica). Valencia,
Spain, Artes Gráf Unicrom, 1976.

928 Chen, Jui-san. "The effect of long-term vegetable
diet on serum lipid and lipo-protein levels in man."
Formosan Medical Association. Journal 65, 2 (Feb.
28, 1966): 65-77.
Chinese vegetarians had lower serum lipids, alpha-
beta lipo-protein ratios, and lower blood pressure
levels than Chinese non-vegetarians and those with
coronary heart disease. These levels tended to increase more slowly with age in vegetarians than in
non-vegetarians.

929 Connor, William E., and Connor, Sonja L. "The
alternative American diet." Advances in Experimental

Medicine and Biology 82 (1977): 843-849.
In an effort to prevent coronary heart disease and atherosclerosis, authors urge immediate steps be taken to phase out excessive consumption of meat and high-fat animal products in the American diet.

930 Crawford, M. A.; Crawford, S. M.; and Hansen, I. Berg. "Plasma structural lipids in groups at high and low risk to atherosclerosis." Biochemical Journal 122, 1 (Mar. 1971): 11P-12P.
Groups consuming animal fats but which are at low risk to atherosclerosis tend to eat fats rich in essential structural lipids, whereas high-risk groups tend to eat excessive amounts of adipose fat present in animals raised by modern intensive methods.

931 Crawford, Michael. "Dietary prevention of atherosclerosis." Lancet 2, 635 (Dec. 27, 1969): 1419-1420.
Letter states that carcasses of intensively raised food animals contain five times as much fat, less protein and less structural tissue than free-living counterparts.

932 Eastwood, Martin. "Dietary fibre and serum-lipids." Lancet 2, 632 (Dec. 6, 1969): 1222-1224.
Serum cholesterol levels decreased in groups of lacto-ovo-vegetarian monks receiving diets with various levels of cereal fiber.

933 Glueck, Charles J. "Dietary fat and atherosclerosis." American Journal of Clinical Nutrition 32, 12 (Dec. 1979): 2703-2711.
Survey of literature linking atherosclerosis and high intake of dietary fats.

934 Glueck, Charles J., and Connor, William E. "Diet-coronary heart disease relationships reconnoitered." American Journal of Clinical Nutrition 31, 5 (May 1978): 727-737.
Review of medical literature regarding relationship between diet and heart disease covers animal experiments, studies of population groups (including vegetarians), genetic factors, and influence of dietary fat, cholesterol, protein.

935 Haines, A. P.; Chakrabarti, R.; Fisher, Diana; Meade, T. W.; North, W. R. S.; and Stirling,

Yvonne. "Hemostatic variables in vegetarians and non-vegetarians." <u>Thrombosis Research</u> 19, 1-2 (1980): 139-148.

Vegetarians had lower cholesterol, diastolic blood pressure, factor II, fibrinolytic activity and antithrombin III levels than controls.

936 Hardinge, Mervyn G.; Crooks, Hulda; and Stare, Frederick J. "Nutritional studies of vegetarians. IV. Dietary fatty acids and serum cholesterol levels." <u>American Journal of Clinical Nutrition</u> 10 (June 1962): 516-524.

Study indicates 1) significant negative correlation between serum cholesterol and unsaturated fatty acids; 2) positive correlation between animal fat and serum cholesterol; 3) inverse relationship between ratio of polyunsaturated:saturated fatty acids and serum cholesterol; and in younger age groups, no significant difference between serum cholesterol levels in vegetarians and non-vegetarians.

937 Hickie, J. B., and Ruys, Jan. "Serum cholesterol and serum triglyceride levels in free-living and vegetarian Australian adolescent children." <u>Circulation</u> 52, 4 Supplement II (Oct. 1975): 4.

Abstract of paper finding that vegetarian children tested had significantly lower levels of serum cholesterol but no significant difference in serum triglyceride levels.

938 Hill, P.; Wynder, E.; Garbaczewski, L.; Garnes, H.; Walker, A. R. P.; and Helman, P. "Plasma hormones and lipids in men at different risk for coronary heart disease." <u>American Journal of Clinical Nutrition</u> 33, 5 (1980): 1010-1018.

When fed a Western diet, South African vegetarian black men exhibited increased triglyceride and cholesterol levels, decreased high-density lipoprotein levels and increased urinary excretion of testosterone, while black North American men fed a vegetarian diet had decreased plasma lipids and urinary excretion of testosterone.

939 Hur, Robin. "Hypertension can be cured." <u>Vegetarian Times</u> (May-June 1979): 50-53.

Medical evidence for value of vegetarian diet in the prevention and treatment of high blood pressure.

940 Jhatakia, K. U. "Profile of coronary artery disease in vegetarian community." Indian Heart Journal 25, 2 (Apr. 1973): 94-99.
   Retrospective analysis of 691 cases of coronary artery disease in a vegetarian Indian community.

941 Kant, A. K.; Reber, E. F.; and Milner, A. N. "Dietary influence on the serum lipid profile of oral contraceptive users." Federation Proceedings 39, 3 (1980): 649.
   Investigation of serum lipids in oral contraceptive users found no obvious differences between vegetarians and non-vegetarians.

942 Kirkeby, Knut. Blood lipids, lipoproteins, and proteins in vegetarians. Oslo, 1966. (Acta Medica Scandinavica. Supplementum 443)
   Vegetarians studied had lower serum cholesterol, phospholipids, total lipids and beta lipo-proteins than omnivore controls.

943 Kirkeby, Knut. "Plasma lipids in a moderately low-fat, high-carbohydrate diet, rich in polyunsaturated fatty acids." Acta Medica Scandinavica 180, 6 (1966): 767-776.
   Vegetarians had lower cholesterol and triglycerides than controls; no difference was observed in free fatty acids.

944 Kirkeby, Knut, and Bjerkedal, Inger. "The fatty acid composition in serum of Norwegian vegetarians." Acta Medica Scandinavica 183, 1-2 (Jan.-Feb. 1968): 143-148.
   Statistically significant differences were found in the fatty acid composition of cholesterol esters, triglycerides, and phospholipids in healthy vegetarian and non-vegetarian men 40 to 70 years of age.

945 Kritchevsky, David. "Fiber, lipids, and atherosclerosis." American Journal of Clinical Nutrition 31, 10 Supp. (Oct. 1978): 565-574.
   Review of influence of dietary fiber on lipid metabolism and atherosclerosis cites lower levels of cholesterol in vegetarians compared to omnivores.

946 Kritchevsky, David. "Nutrition and heart disease." Food Technology 33, 12 (Dec. 1979): 39-42.

Reviews role of animal fat, fiber and other factors in heart disease.

947 Lee, K. T.; Kim, K. S.; and Kim, D. L. "Chemico-pathologic studies in geographic pathology: serum lipids compared in three groups of young Koreans including 1) Buddhist priests on "pure" vegetarian diets, 2) soldiers on low-fat Korean army diet, and 3) soldiers on high-fat U. S. army diet." Federation Proceedings 20, 1 (1961): 95.
Korean Buddhist priests consuming strict vegetarian diets had serum lipids slightly lower than those on Korean army diets, but substantially lower than those consuming U. S. army diets. (Abstract only.)

948 Lee, Kyu Taik; Kim, Dong Nack; Han, Yong Sup; and Goodale, Fairfield. "Geographic studies of arteriosclerosis. The effect of a strict vegetarian diet on serum lipid and electrocardiographic patterns." Archives of Environmental Health 4, 1 (Jan. 1962): 10-16.
Strict vegetarian Korean Buddhist monks and nuns had a lower incidence of arteriosclerosis and considerably lower levels of cholesterol and other serum lipids than lacto-vegetarian Trappist monks in the U. S., and markedly lower levels than Benedictine monks and U. S. Army personnel, both of whom consumed large amounts of animal fat.

949 Levine, Allen S., and Parker, Shirley J. "Impossible to lower cholesterol." American Journal of Clinical Nutrition 32, 11 (Nov. 1979): 2168-2169.
Letter disputes claim that vegetable sources are unable to lower cholesterol intake to 300 mgs. per day and still keep protein level at 12 percent; provides sample menu.

950 McCullagh, E. Perry, and Lewis, Lena A. "A study of diet, blood lipids and vascular disease in Trappist monks." New England Journal of Medicine 263, 12 (Sept. 22, 1960): 569-574.
Trappist monks studied had diets low in animal, but not total, fat, and although exhibiting low cholesterol levels, were not entirely protected from hypertension or arteriosclerosis.

951 Malhotra, A. S., and Ganguly, A. K. "Blood pressure of military recruits. An epidemiological study."

Indian Journal of Medical Research 64, 2 (1976): 229-243.

Study of blood pressure in male Indian military recruits revealed no correlation with dietary habits (vegetarian or non-vegetarian) or height, and a positive correlation between age, body weight, alcohol consumption, and length of military service.

952　Mattson, F. H.; Erickson, B. A.; and Kligman, A. M. "Effects of dietary cholesterol on serum cholesterol in man." American Journal of Clinical Nutrition 25, 6 (June 1972): 589-594.

Consumption of cholesterol-free vegetarian diets reduced serum cholesterol, and the ingestion of cholesterol elevated serum cholesterol levels.

953　Moore, Margaret C.; Guzman, Miguel A.; Schilling, Prentiss E.; and Strong, Jack P. "Dietary-atherosclerosis study on deceased persons." American Dietetic Association. Journal 68, 3 (Mar. 1976): 216-223.

Comparisons of dietary histories and coronary artery autopsy results in 253 deceased men indicated that starch and vegetable protein were associated with lesser atherosclerotic lesion involvement, while animal protein and fat were associated with greater incidence of atherosclerosis.

954　Ornish, Dean; Gotto, A. M.; Miller, R. R.; Rochelle, D.; and McCallister, G. "Effects of a vegetarian diet and selected yoga techniques in the treatment of coronary heart disease." Clinical Research 27, 4 (1979): 720A.

Vegetarian diet and yoga techniques were found to have therapeutic benefits for patients suffering from coronary heart disease. (Abstract only.)

955　Phillips, R. L.; Lemon, F. R.; Beeson, W. L.; and Kuzma, J. W. "Coronary heart disease mortality among Seventh-day Adventists with differing dietary habits: a preliminary report." American Journal of Clinical Nutrition 31, 10 (Oct. 1978): S191-S198.

A six-year study of over 24,000 California Seventh-day Adventists age 35 and over finds that non-vegetarian males have a risk of fatal coronary heart disease three times greater than vegetarian SDA males of comparable age.

956 Ruys, J. and Hickie, J. B. "Serum cholesterol and triglyceride levels in Australian adolescent vegetarians."
British Medical Journal 2, 6027 (July 10, 1976): 87.
Brief communication describes study in which vegetarian adolescents had significantly lower mean serum
cholesterol levels but only slightly lower serum triglyceride levels than non-vegetarian adolescents.

957 Sachs, F. M.; Rosner, Bernard; and Kass, Edward H.
"Blood pressure in vegetarians." American Journal
of Epidemiology 100, 5 (1974): 390-398.
Study of 210 vegetarians found a mean blood pressure of 106/60mm. for ages 16-29, suggesting a relationship between blood pressure levels and consumption of meat.

958 Sachs, Frank; Castelli, William P.; Donner, Allen;
and Kass, Edward H. "Plasma lipids and lipoproteins in vegetarians and controls." New England
Journal of Medicine 292, 22 (May 29, 1975): 1148-
1151.
Vegetarians had lower levels of cholesterol, low-
density lipoproteins, high density lipoproteins and
triglycerides than matched meat-eating controls.

959 Simons, L. A.; Gibson, J. Corey; Paino, C.; Hosking,
M.; Bullock, J.; and Trim, J. "The influence of a
wide range of absorbed cholesterol on plasma cholesterol levels in man." American Journal of Clinical Nutrition 31, 8 (Aug. 1978): 1334-1339.
Vegetarians studied both consumed and absorbed
less cholesterol than non-vegetarians.

960 Sutton, Suzanne. "Meat-eating and diseases of the
heart and blood vessels." Vegetarian Times (Sept. -
Oct. 1977): 24-26.
How the high-fat, high-meat diet of affluent America contributes to the incidence of heart disease.

961 Taylor, C. B.; Allen, E. S.; Mikkelson, B.; and
Kang-Jy, H. "Serum cholesterol levels of Seventh-
day Adventists." Paroi Arterielle 3, 4 (Oct. 1976):
175-179.
Lacto-ovo-vegetarians had lower serum cholesterol
levels than the general U.S. population, levels which
showed no sex difference, but which increased with
age and weight. Cholesterol levels in lacto-ovo-vegetarians were higher than those of strict vegetarians.

962 Trowell, H. "Dietary fibre and coronary heart disease." Revue Europeene d'Etudes Cliniques et Biologiques 17, 4 (Apr. 1972): 345-349.
     Discussion of role of dietary fiber in prevention of heart disease cites low rates of coronary heart disease among groups of vegetarians consuming high fiber diets.

963 Turpeinen, Osmo. "Effect of cholesterol-lowering diet on mortality from coronary heart disease and other causes." Circulation 59, 1 (Jan. 1979): 1-7.
     Dietary study conducted 1959-1971 showed a substantial reduction in mortality from coronary heart disease following the nearly total replacement of saturated fats (dairy fats and meat fats) by vegetable oils.

964 Von Lossonczy, T. O.; Ruiter, A.; Bronsgeest-Schoute, H. D.; Van Gent, C. M.; and Hermus, R. J. J. "The effect of a fish diet on serum lipids in healthy human subjects." American Journal of Clinical Nutrition 31, 8 (Aug. 1978): 1340-1346.
     Lacto-ovo-vegetarian subjects had lower serum cholesterol and triglyceride levels following three weeks on a diet containing mackerel, compared to diet in which full-fat cheese replaced mackerel.

965 Walden, Richard T.; Schaefer, Louis E.; Lemon, Frank R.; Sunshine, Abraham; and Wynder, Ernest L. "Effect of environment on the serum cholesterol-triglyceride distribution among Seventh-day Adventists." American Journal of Medicine 36 (Feb. 1964): 269-276.
     Lacto-ovo-vegetarians had lower serum cholesterol and higher triglyceride levels than New York City residents, the differences becoming more pronounced following fat restriction and fat substitution diets.

966 Walker, A. R. P. "Sugar intake and coronary heart disease." Atherosclerosis 14, 2 (Sept.-Oct. 1971): 137-152.
     Reviews evidence linking excessive consumption of sugar to causation of coronary heart disease in diverse population and dietary groups, including vegetarians, and fails to find support for this hypothesis.

967 West, Raymond D., and Hayes, Olive B. "Diet and serum cholesterol levels; a comparison between vege-

tarians and nonvegetarians in a Seventh-day Adventist group." American Journal of Clinical Nutrition 21, 8 (Aug. 1968): 853-862.

Comparison of serum cholesterol levels of non-vegetarians and vegetarians matched for sex, age, height, weight, etc. showed a clear pattern that as the degree of non-vegetarianism increased, serum cholesterol levels also increased.

Cancer: General
(See also: 20, 21, 79.)

968 Armstrong, Bruce, and Doll, Richard. "Environmental factors and cancer incidence and mortality in different countries, with special reference to dietary practices." International Journal of Cancer 15, 4 (Apr. 15, 1975): 617-631.

Cancer incidence rates and mortality rates correlated with wide range of dietary and other variables resulted in strong association between meat consumption and colon cancer and fat consumption and breast and uterine cancer.

969 Capo, N. Cancer y vegetarismo practico. Barcelona, Jaime Cancer, 1968.

970 Commoner, Barry; Vithayathil, Antony J.; Dolara, Piero; Nair, Subhadra; Madyastha, Prema; and Cuca, Gregory C. "Formation of mutagens in beef and beef extract during cooking." Science 201 (Sept. 8, 1978): 913-916.

Description of potentially carcinogenic mutagens formed during ordinary cooking procedures of ground beef and beef stock.

971 Elmenhorst, H., and Dontenwill, W. "Carcinogenic hydrocarbons in the smoke from charcoal grilling." Zeitschrift für Krebsforschung 70, 2 (1967): 157-160.

Bacon grilled over fat produced a number of carcinogenic hydrocarbons from the pyrolysis of fat dropping onto the glowing charcoal. (In German.)

972 Enig, Mary G.; Munn, Robert J.; and Keeney, Mark. "Dietary fat and cancer trends--a critique." Federation Proceedings 37, 9 (July 1978): 2215-2220.

Challenges the conclusions of the McGovern report, Dietary Goals for the United States, and the theory that consumption of animal fat is associated with cancer incidence.

973 Fosbrooke, Dorothy. Many diseases, one cure: how you can help. Sowerby Bridge, W. Yorkshire, Power Publishing (U. K.) Ltd. , 1978.
Vegetarian diet as cancer therapy.

974 Gardner, Hugh. "Sowbelly blues; the links between bacon and cancer. " Esquire 86, 5 (Nov. 1976): 112-114, 140, 142, 144.
The relationship between cancer and nitrites in cured meats.

975 Gillie, Oliver. "New clues to cancer: current evidence points strongly to a dietary link. " Atlas 24 (Jan. 1977): 13-15.
Current research indicates a diet rich in animal fat and meat, especially beef, increases the risk of cancer.

976 Gonzalez, Nicholas. "Preventing cancer. " Family Health 8, 5 (May 1976): 30-33, 70, 72, 74.
Article presenting current evidence on the prevention of cancer cites the lower cancer rates of lacto-ovo-vegetarian Seventh-day Adventists.

977 Gori, Gio B. "Food as a factor in the etiology of certain human cancers. " Food Technology 33, 12 (Dec. 1979): 48-56.
Reviews epidemiologic and animal studies on cancer; identifies ten current theories of cancer and diet.

978 Graham, Saxon; Schotz, William; and Martino, Paul. "Alimentary factors in the epidemiology of gastric cancer. " Cancer 30, 4 (Oct. 1972): 927-938.
Low risk of gastric cancer was associated with the ingestion of raw vegetables, especially lettuce, tomatoes, carrots, cole slaw and red cabbage.

979 Gridley, Daila S. Effect of time and diet on the immune status of mice challenged with herpes-transformed cells. Ph. D. Loma Linda University, 1978.

Meat and high-soy protein depressed immunity and enhanced tumor development in rats. A high-fat diet was tumor-enhancing when combined with casein, but tumor inhibiting when combined with soy protein.

980 Habs, M., and Schmaehl, D. "Carcinogenic substances in food." Innere Medizin in Praxis und Klinik 6, 6 (1979): 237-249.
Review of cancer incidence associated with food consumption and food contaminants, including naturally occurring carcinogens in foods. Notes contradictory findings on the relationship between vegetarian diets and risk factors. (In German.)

981 Haenszel, William; Kurihara, Minoru; Segi, Mitsuo; and Lee, Richard K. C. "Stomach cancer among Japanese in Hawaii." U.S. National Cancer Institute. Journal 49, 4 (Oct. 1972): 969-988.
High risk foods for stomach cancer were dried salted fish and pickled vegetables; low risk foods were fresh raw vegetables, especially lettuce, and raw fish.

982 Hill, P.; Wynder, E. L.; Garbaczewski, L.; Garnes, H.; Walker, A. R. P. "Diet and urinary steroids in black and white North American men and black South African men." Cancer Research 39, 12 (1979): 5101-5105.
Urinary estrogens and androgens increased on a Western diet and decreased on a vegetarian diet.

983 Hill, Peter B., and Wynder, Ernst L. "Effect of a vegetarian diet and dexamethasone on plasma prolactin, testosterone and dehydroepiandrosterone in men and women." Cancer Letters 7, 5 (1979): 273-282.
Vegetarian diets resulted in hormonal changes, indicating diet modification may benefit patients with hormonally dependent cancers.

984 Hirayama, T. "Epidemiology of prostatic cancer with special reference to the risk lowering effect of green-yellow vegetables intake." Japanese Cancer Association. Proceedings (Aug. 1978): 280.
Ten-year followup study of 122,261 men revealed significantly lower death rate of prostate cancer for those consuming green and yellow vegetables on a daily basis.

985 Howell, M. A. "Factor analysis of international can-
     cer mortality data and per capita food consumption."
     British Journal of Cancer 29, 4 (Apr. 1974): 328-
     338.
         Analysis of international food consumption data and
     male cancer mortality rates revealed correlation be-
     tween colo-rectal cancer and beef consumption; stom-
     ach cancer and potatoes; and cancer of the larynx
     and wheat, vegetables and fruit.

986 Hunter, Beatrice Trum. "Diethyl-stilbestrol; a known
     cancer-inciting drug in meats for Americans." Con-
     sumer Bulletin 55 (Aug. 1972): 17-19.
         Potential health hazards of the growth-promoting
     hormone DES in cattle feed and as implant in cattle
     and poultry.

987 Jukes, Thomas H. "Diethylstilbestrol in beef produc-
     tion: What is the risk to consumers?" Preventive
     Medicine 5, 3 (Sept. 1976): 438-453.
         Writer finds no evidence that DES use in beef pro-
     duction causes any increased risk of cancer.

988 Jukes, Thomas H. "Out of the frying pan." Nature
     274 (July 27, 1978): 307.
         Carcinogenic substance produced in the charcoal-
     broiling of meats.

989 Karplyuk, I. A., and Gogol, A. T. "Hygienic aspects
     of using smoking preparations in the processing of
     meat products." Voprosy Pitaniia no. 5 (1978):
     16-19.
         Review of the literature regarding cancer hazards
     of smoked foods and liquid smoke preparations for
     meat. (In Russian.)

990 Leonardo, Blanche. Cancer and other diseases from
     meat consumption; here's the evidence. Santa Monica,
     CA, Leaves of Healing Publications, 1979.
         Compilation of articles from journals and newspa-
     pers on the potential hazards of meat, poultry and
     fish consumption.

991 Lijinsky, W., and Ross, A. E. "Production of car-
     cinogenic polynuclear hydrocarbons in the cooking of
     food." Food and Cosmetics Toxicology 5, 3 (Aug.
     1967): 343-347.

Carcinogenic benzo[a]pyrene and other polynuclear hydrocarbons were produced by the pyrolysis of fat from meats cooked by various methods, and varied according to the amount of fat, length of exposure to the flames, and closeness to the heat source.

992 Lijinsky, W., and Shubik, P. "Benzo[a]pyrene and other polynuclear hydrocarbons in charcoal-broiled meat." Science 145 (July 3, 1964): 53-55.

Many possibly carcinogenic polynuclear hydrocarbons were identified in charcoal-broiled steaks, most notable of which was benzo[a]pyrene occurring per steak in amounts equivalent to that in approximately 600 cigarettes.

993 McMartin, K. E.; Kennedy, K. A.; Greenspan, P.; Alam, S. N.; Greiner, P.; and Yam, J. "Diethylstilbestrol: a review of its toxicity and use as a growth promotant in food-producing animals." Journal of Environmental Pathology and Toxicology 1, 3 (Jan.-Feb. 1978): 279-313.

Review of the literature on DES: toxicology, efficacy, risks, and benefits.

994 Mohler, K. "Possibilities for the buildup of toxic, especially carcinogenic, substances in food of animal origin as the result of technological methods." Wiener Tieraertzliche Monatsschrift 57, 10 (Oct. 1970): 321-325. (In German.)

995 Navarro, Manuel E. "The role of nutrition in the control of cancer." Acta Manilana 17, 27, series A (June 1978): 3-15.

Review of literature finds that persons who eat little or no meat, but consume large amounts of vegetables, fruits and seeds are less subject to cancer.

996 Petrakis, N. L. "Historic milestones in cancer epidemiology." Seminars in Oncology 6, 4 (1979): 433-444.

Review of significant findings in cancer research notes that vegetarian diets are associated with low cancer rates, while meat consumption, especially beef, is correlated with high risk.

997 Powell, Jim. "Cancer and your diet: be prudent in what you eat, and help foil the No. 1 villain."

Science Digest 82 (Sept. 1977): 38-40.
Noting changes in U. S. dietary habits and the
significantly lower cancer rates of vegetarians,
advocates a prudent low-fat, low-caloric diet rich
in fruits, vegetables, grains and dairy products.

998 Reddy, Bandaru, S.; McCoy, G. David; and Wynder,
Ernst L. "Nutritional and environmental factors
in carcinogenesis." In: Fleisher, M. The clinical biochemistry of cancer; proceedings of the 2nd
Arnold O. Beckman Conference in Clinical Chemistry, San Antonio, TX, 1978, p. 239-264.

999 Schmaehl, D.; Danisman, A.; Habs, M.; and Diehl,
B. "Experimental investigations on the influence
upon the chemical carcinogenesis. 3rd communication: studies with 1, 2 dimethylhydrazine."
Zeitschrift für Krebsforschung 86, 1 (1976): 89-
94.
Study demonstrated that DMH is a carcinogen
of the intestine, ear duct, kidney and liver of the
rat. Rats fed a vegetarian diet had fewer liver
and kidney tumors, and had significantly prolonged
tumor induction periods.

1000 Schutz, Contreras M. "Early diagnosis of cancer."
Patologia Quirúrgica, Citologia Exfoliativa 4, 1
(1978): 3-26.
Positive correlation found between gastric cancer and smoked meat and fish consumption; negative correlation found between diet rich in wheat
products. (In Spanish.)

1001 Shamberger, Raymond J.; Shamberger, Barbara A.;
and Willis, Charles E. "Malonaldehyde content
of food." Journal of Nutrition 107, 8 (Aug. 1977)
1404-1409.
Tests for the presence of malonaldehyde, a
carcinogenic initiator and mutagen, revealed greatest amounts in beef, turkey, chicken, with small
amounts in cheeses and either minute or no
amounts in fruits and vegetables.

1002 Shamberger, Raymond J., and Willis, Charles E.
"Chemical identification of a carcinogen present
in beef and other meats." American Association
for Cancer Research. Proceedings 17 (1976): 222.

Study to chemically identify malonaldehyde observes lower cancer mortality in groups consuming little or no meat. (Abstract only.)

1003 Shamberger, Raymond J., and Willis, Charles E. "A new carcinogen is present in beef and other meats." American Association for Cancer Research. Proceedings 16 (1975): 68.
Abstract of study of malonaldehyde, a carcinogen found in meats.

1004 Smith, S.; Schultz, T.; Ross, J.; and Leklem, J. "Nutrition and cancer attitudes and knowledge of Seventh-day Adventists." Federation Proceedings 38, 3 (1979): 713.
Attitudinal questionnaire found that Seventh-day Adventists as a group feel there is a relationship between nutrition and cancer. (Abstract only.)

1005 Spingarn, Neil E., and Weisburger, John H. "Formation of mutagens in cooked foods. I. Beef." Cancer Letters 7, 5 (Sept. 1979): 259-264.
Mutagens are formed in the frying, broiling, and boiling of meat, rapidly when frying, or more slowly when broiling; hamburgers from commercial fast food franchises were frequently mutagenically active.

1006 Sutton, Suzanne. "Meat-eating and cancer." Vegetarian Times (July-Aug. 1977): 11-15.
Surveys the medical literature linking meat consumption and cancer incidence.

1007 Wahi, P. N. "The epidemiology of oral and oropharyngeal cancer. A report of the study in Mainpuri District, Uttar Pradish, India." World Health Organization. Bulletin 38, 4 (1968): 495-521.
Oral hygiene and dietary factors such as vegetarianism had no significant effect on oral cancer risk in a rural area of India.

Cancer: Breast Cancer
(See also: 968, 983.)

1008 Armstrong, B. "Epidemiology and hormonal mechanisms in breast and endometrial cancer." In:

Australian Symposium on Nutrition and Cancer. Proceedings. Adelaide, Australia, Nov. 20-24, 1978. South Australian Postgraduate Medical Education Association, Inc., 1978.
Review of dietary variables associated with incidence of cancers of the breast and endometrium. (Meeting abstract.)

1009 Gray, G. E. "Breast-cancer incidence and mortality rates in different countries in relation to known risk factors and dietary practice." British Journal of Cancer 39, 1 (1979): 1-7.
Breast cancer mortality rates in 34 countries were most highly correlated with total fat consumption, and incidence rates of breast cancer were most highly correlated with animal protein consumption.

1010 Hankin, Jean H., and Rawlings, Virginia. "Diet and breast cancer: a review." American Journal of Clinical Nutrition 31 (Nov. 1978): 2005-2016.
Review of literature describes dietary risk factors to breast cancer including body fatness, intake of fat and protein, and nutritionally related hormone levels.

1011 Hems, G. "The contributions of diet and childbearing to breast-cancer rates." British Journal of Cancer 37, 6 (1978): 974-982.
Dietary data and breast cancer mortality rates for women in 41 countries indicated that breast cancer was positively correlated with total fat, animal protein, animal calories, and consumption of refined sugar.

1012 Hill, P., and Wynder, F. "Diet and prolactin release." Lancet 2, 7989 (Oct. 9, 1974): 806-807.
Letter describes experiments in which a vegetarian diet decreased the release of prolactin, a hormone associated with higher incidence of breast cancer in women.

1013 Hill, Peter; Chan, P.; Cohen, L.; Wynder, E.; and Kuno, K. "Diet and endocrine-related cancer." Cancer 39, 4 Supplement (April 1977): 1820-1826.
Dietary factors, especially high fat diet, increase mammary tumor incidence and influence hormone profile in mammary cancer.

1014 Hill, Peter; Wynder, Ernst L.; and Helman, Percy.
      "Plasma hormone levels in pre- and post-meno-
      pausal vegetarian women fed a western diet."
      Federation Proceedings 38, 3 (1979): 865.
          Modifications of hormone levels in vegetarian
      women fed a Western meat diet, with implications
      for breast cancer incidence. (Abstract only.)

                    Cancer: Colon Cancer
          (See also: 968, 985, 1251, 1283.)

1015 Anon. "Diet, intestinal flora, and colon cancer."
      Nutrition Reviews 33, 5 (May 1975): 136-137.
          Fecal excretion of neutral sterols and bile acids
      was much higher in subjects consuming the average
      American diet than in vegetarians.

1016 Aries, V.; Crowther, J. S.; Drasar, B. S.; Hill,
      M. J.; and Williams, R. E. "Bacteria and the
      aetiology of cancer of the large bowel." Gut 10,
      5 (1969): 334-335.
          Comparison of fecal specimens from English
      and Ugandan subjects with mixed and vegetarian
      dietary habits showed wide variation in bacterial
      count, suggesting that intestinal bacteria may con-
      vert bile salts into carcinogens and that cancer of
      the large bowel may be related to diet-dependent
      variations in intestinal flora.

1017 Berg, John W., and Howell, Margaret A. "The geo-
      graphic pathology of bowel cancer." Cancer 34, 3
      Supplement (Sept. 1974): 807-814.
          International data reinforce the hypothesis that
      bowel cancer and beef consumption are closely as-
      sociated.

1018 Bishop, Jerry E. "Cancer vs. what you eat." Sci-
      ence Digest 75 (Mar. 1974): 10-14.
          Review of medical studies linking cancer of the
      colon and rectum with a high-fat, high-meat diet.

1019 Bjelke, E. "Colorectal cancer: clues from epidemi-
      ology." In: International Cancer Congress, 11th,
      Proceedings, Florence, Italy, Oct. 20-26, 1975,
      vol. 6, Tumors of Specific sites, p. 324-330.

Review of epidemiological data suggesting colo-
rectal cancer promoting factors to be fat, meats,
especially processed meats, and alcoholic beverages, and inhibiting factors to include vegetarian
diet, fiber, vitamin A active compounds and in-
ducers of microsomal enzyme synthesis.

1020   Bjelke, Erik.   "Colon cancer and blood-cholesterol."
       Lancet 1, 866 (June 1, 1974):   1116-1117.
       Letter discusses relationship between high in-
       take of processed meats, coffee consumption, and
       colon cancer.

1021   Burkitt, D. P.   "Large-bowel cancer: an epidemio-
       logic jigsaw puzzle."   U. S. National Cancer Insti-
       tute.   Journal 54, 1 (1975):   3-6.
       Review of available information on bowel cancer
       notes lower risk of bowel cancer among American
       vegetarians, suggesting that the lower consumption
       of dietary fiber, higher consumption of dietary fats
       and slower intestinal transit times of non-vege-
       tarians may be factors associated with high risk.

1022   Burkitt, Denis P.   "Colonic-rectal cancer: fiber and
       other dietary factors."   American Journal of
       Clinical Nutrition 31, 10 Supp. (Oct. 1978):   S58-
       S64.
       Reviews evidence that fiber-depleted diets are
       associated with high prevalence of colonic-rectal
       cancer in Western countries; cites lower rates for
       vegetarian Seventh-day Adventists.

1023   Correa, Pelayo.   "Epidemiology of polyps and can-
       cer."   Major Problems in Pathology 10 (1978):
       126-152.
       Survey of medical literature finds close corre-
       lation between high meat and fat consumption, low
       fiber consumption and large bowel cancer.

1024   Enstrom, J. E.   "Colorectal cancer and consumption
       of beef and fat."   British Journal of Cancer 32, 4
       (Oct. 1975):   432-439.
       Comparison of beef and fat consumption in the
       U. S. with colorectal cancer incidence and mortal-
       ity rates does not support hypothesis that beef and
       fat consumption are involved in the etiology of
       colorectal cancer.

1025 Finegold, Sydney M. , and Sutter, Vera L. "Fecal flora in different populations, with special reference to diet." American Journal of Clinical Nutrition 31, 10 Supp. (Oct. 1978): S116-S122.
Summary of various studies of fecal microbial flora in population groups, including vegetarians, with special reference to high and low risk of colon cancer.

1026 Finegold, Sydney M.; Sutter, Vera L.; Sugihara, Paul T.; Elder, Harvey A.; Lehmann, Shirley M.; and Phillips, Roland L. "Fecal microbial flora in Seventh-day Adventist populations and control subjects." American Journal of Clinical Nutrition 30, 11 (Nov. 1977): 1781-1792.
Little difference was found in fecal flora between the vegetarian and non-vegetarian SDA's although there were significant differences between groups at high risk (American/Western diet) and low risk (Adventist diet) for colon cancer.

1027 Goldberg, M. J.; Smith, J. W.; and Nichols, R. L. "Comparison of the fecal microflora of Seventh-day Adventists with individuals consuming a general diet. Implications concerning colonic carcinoma." Annals of Surgery 186, 1 (1977): 97-100.
Qualitative and quantitative study of fecal microflora found no statistically significant differences between vegetarians and non-vegetarians, indicating that animal fat and protein do not significantly alter fecal microflora.

1028 Goldin, B. "Influence of diet and age on fecal bacterial enzymes." American Journal of Clinical Nutrition 31, 10 (Oct. 1978): S136-S140.
Study of rats found that a high-beef diet increases the activity of three bacterial enzymes implicated in the etiology of colon cancer.

1029 Goldin, B. R. , and Gorbach, S. L. "Diet and its effect on enzymes linked to colon cancer." Digestion 16, 3 (1977): 240-241.
Relationship between a meat diet and increased incidence of colon cancer appeared to be related to the elevation by a meat diet of certain microbial enzymes in the intestinal flora which generate carcinogens in the bowel. (Abstract only.)

1030 Goldin, Barry R., and Gorbach, Sherwood L. "The
      relationship between diet and rat fecal bacterial
      enzymes implicated in colon cancer." U. S. Na-
      tional Cancer Institute. Journal 57, 2 (Aug. 1976):
      371-375.
           High beef diet in rats was associated with high
      risk of colon cancer, due to elevated levels of
      enzymes in the colon microflora.

1031 Gonvers, J. J. "Epidemiology and etiology of cancer
      of the colon and rectum." Praxis 68, 26 (1979):
      864-868.
           Review of the epidemiology and etiology of can-
      cer of the colon and rectum finds a positive cor-
      relation between these cancers and the amount of
      dietary animal fat consumed. Low relative fiber
      consumption also appears to be related to colorec-
      tal cancer development. Cites low colorectal can-
      cer incidence among vegetarians. (In French.)

1032 Graham, Saxon; Dayal, Hari; Swanson, Mya; Mittel-
      man, Arnold; and Wilkinson, Gregg. "Diet in the
      epidemiology of cancer of the colon and rectum."
      U. S. National Cancer Institute. Journal 61, 3
      (Sept. 1978): 709-714.
           Study of 256 colon cancer patients and 330 rec-
      tal cancer patients found no increase in cancer
      risk with high beef consumption, but found an in-
      crease in risk with decreases in the frequency of
      vegetable consumption. Decrease in risk was as-
      sociated with frequent ingestion of vegetables, es-
      pecially cabbage, brussels sprouts, and broccoli.

1033 Haenszel, William; Berg, John W.; Segi, Mitsuo;
      Kurihara, Minoru; and Locke, Frances B. "Large-
      bowel cancer in Hawaiian Japanese." U. S. Na-
      tional Cancer Institute. Journal 51, 6 (Dec. 1973):
      1765-1779.
           Study of Japanese bowel cancer patients revealed
      excess risks for individuals consuming Western-
      style meals, especially those emphasizing beef,
      string beans and starches.

1034 Hentges, David J.; Burton, Glenna C.; Flynn, Mar-
      garet A.; Franz, John M.; Gehrke, Charles W.;
      Gerhardt, Klaus O.; Maier, Bruce R.; Tsutakawa,
      Robert K.; and Wixom, Robert L. "Effect of a

high beef diet on bacterial flora and chemical
components of human feces: a summary of results." In: International Symposium on detection
and prevention of cancer, 3rd, April 26-May 1,
1976, pt. 1, p. 693-706.
High meat consumption caused some increase
in anaerobic bacteria, but no increase in either
neutral or acid steroids.

1035   Hentges, David J.; Maier, Bruce R.; Burton, Glenna
       C.; Flynn, Margaret A.; and Tsutakawa, Robert
       K. "Effect of a high-beef diet on the fecal bac-
       terial flora of humans." Cancer Research 37, 2
       (Feb. 1977): 568-571.
       Study found that animal protein consumption had
       little effect on the fecal bacterial profile in hu-
       mans, although other studies indicated that animal
       fat rather than animal protein was associated with
       the induction of colon cancer.

1036   Hepner, G. W. "Altered bile acid metabolism in
       vegetarians." American Journal of Digestive Dis-
       eases 20, 10 (Oct. 1975): 935-940.
       Study of bile acid kinetics in groups of healthy
       vegetarians and controls found that enterohepatic
       conservation of cholic acid was more efficient in
       vegetarians, with possible significance to decreased
       risk of cancer of the colon.

1037   Heyden, S., and Escher, M. "Colon and rectal can-
       cer: epidemiological considerations." Praxis 63,
       44 (1974): 1312-1315.
       Review of global epidemiology of rectal and
       colonic cancer. Lower rates were found in vege-
       tarian Seventh-day Adventists, Jewish men, and
       women of Afro-Asiatic origin. Differences in food
       preparation and consumption of fat or sucrose-rich
       foods appeared to influence relative risks. (In Ger-
       man.)

1038   Hill, Michael J. "Metabolic epidemiology of dietary
       factors in large bowel cancer." Cancer Research
       35, 11 (Nov. 1975): 3398-3402.
       Discussion of high- and low-fiber, high- and
       low-meat, and high- and low-fat diets in relation
       to colon cancer.

1039 Howell, Margaret A. "Diet as an etiological factor in the development of cancers of the colon and rectum." Journal of Chronic Diseases 28, 2 (Feb. 1975): 67-80.
      Review of relevant studies indicates strong correlation between beef consumption and colorectal cancer.

1040 Huang, Charles T. L.; Gopalakrishna, G. S.; and Nichols, Buford L. "Fiber, intestinal steroids, and colon cancer." American Journal of Clinical Nutrition 31, 3 (Mar. 1978): 516-526.
      Literature review notes lower plasma lipids, different plasma lipoprotein patterns and lower risk of colon cancer among American vegetarians.

1041 Kelsey, M. I., and Hwang, K. K. "A comparison of lithocholic acid metabolism by intestinal microflora in subjects of high- and low-risk colon cancer populations." Digestion 16, 3 (1977): 263.
      Study of metabolism of lithocholic acid, a major fecal bile acid which promotes cancer of the colon and liver in rats, found high preneoplastic activity in microflora from subjects on a high beef-fat diet, but found low or absent activity with the flora of subjects on a mixed or vegetarian diet. (Abstract only.)

1042 Kelsey, M. I.; Molina, J. E.; and Hwang, K. K. "A comparison of lithocholic acid metabolism by intestinal microflora in subjects of high- and low-risk colon cancer populations." Frontiers of Gastrointestinal Research 4 (1979): 38-50.
      Metabolic study of lithocholic acid by intestinal microflora in human subjects consuming high-beef, low-beef, or vegetarian diets.

1043 Kuhnlein, Urs; Bergstrom, Danielle; and Kuhnlein, Harriet. "Mutagens in feces from vegetarians and non-vegetarians." Mutation Research 85, 1-2 (Feb. 1981): 1-12.
      Lacto-ovo-vegetarians and strict vegetarians had significantly lower levels of fecal mutagens than non-vegetarians, with implications for risk of colon cancer.

1044 Lipkin, Martin. "Susceptibility of human population

groups to colon cancer." Advances in Cancer Research 27 (1978): 281-304.

Reviews environmental and genetic factors which distinguish high risk population groups; studies of high-fat and meat association with colon cancer summarized.

1045 MacDonald, Ian A.; Webb, G. Robert; and Mahony, David. "Fecal hydroxysteroid dehydrogenase activities in vegetarian Seventh-day Adventists, control subjects and bowel cancer patients." American Journal of Clinical Nutrition 31, 10 Suppl. (Oct. 1978): S233-S238.

Comparison of fecal anaerobic bacteria, enzyme activity, and pH values of stool in bowel cancer patients, vegetarians and controls.

1046 MacLennan, R.; Jensen, O. M.; Mosbech, J.; and Vuori, H. "Diet, transit time, stool weight, and colon cancer in two Scandinavian populations." American Journal of Clinical Nutrition 31, 10 Supp. (Oct. 1978): S239-S242.

High risk to colon cancer group consumed more white bread, meat, and beer, and less potatoes and milk than low-risk group; Protective role of dietary fiber, unrelated to transit time, is suggested.

1047 Maier, Bruce R.; Flynn, Margaret A.; Burton, Glenna C.; Tsutakawa, Robert K.; and Hentges, David J. "Effects of a high-beef diet on bowel flora: a preliminary report." American Journal of Clinical Nutrition 27, 12 (Dec. 1974): 1470-1474.

With reference to the relationship between bowel cancer and bowel flora, comparison of intestinal microflora determined that coliforms increased under meatless diet and bacteroids increased under a high beef diet.

1048 Nigro, Norman D.; Singh, Dharm V.; Campbell, Robert L.; and Pak, Myung Sok. "Effect of dietary beef fat on intestinal tumor formation by Azoxymethane." U.S. National Cancer Institute. Journal 54, 2 (Feb. 1975): 439-442.

A diet high in beef fat enhanced carcinogenesis in rats; a greater number and larger intestinal tumors were observed than in rats fed normally.

1049 Paymaster, J. C., and Gangadharan, P. "The problem of gastro-intestinal cancer in India." Indian
Practioner 24, 1 (1971): 7-15.
Review of gastro-intestinal cancer incidence and
risk factors in India notes that the low incidence
of gastric, colon and rectal cancer among Hindu
populations seems to be associated with their strict
vegetarian diet.

1050 Phillips, Roland L. "Role of life-style and dietary
habits in risk of cancer among Seventh-day Adventists." Cancer Research 35, 11, pt. 2 (Nov.
1975): 3513-3522.
Preliminary research strongly suggests that the
lacto-ovo-vegetarian diet practiced by Seventh-day
Adventists protects against colon cancer and that
meat consumption, especially beef and lamb, increases relative risks of cancer of the colon.

1051 Raicht, Robert F.; Cohen, Bertram I.; Fazzini, Eugene P.; Sarwal, Amar N.; and Takahashi, Mak-
oto. "Protective effect of plant sterols against
chemically induced colon tumors." Cancer Research 40, 2 (Feb. 1980): 403-405.
Plant sterols abundant in vegetarian diets may
serve to exert a protective effect in preventing and
retarding colon tumor formation.

1052 Reddy, Bandaru S.; Hedges, Allan; Laakso, Kristina;
and Wynder, Ernst L. "Fecal constituents of a
high-risk North American and a low-risk Finnish
population for the development of large bowel cancer." Cancer Letters 4, 4 (Apr. 1978): 217-222.
Although both groups had similar amounts of
dietary fat and protein, the low-risk Finnish group
consumed less meat, more dairy products and
more cereal fiber than the high risk New York
subjects, suggesting a possible protective effect of
these factors in colon cancer.

1053 Reddy, Bandaru S.; Mastromarino, Anthony; and Wynder, Ernst. "Diet and metabolism: large-bowel
cancer." Cancer 39, 4, Supplement (Apr. 1977):
1815-1819.
Colon cancer incidence is associated primarily
with high dietary fat consumption which influences
bile acids, neutrol sterols and intestinal microflora.

1054   Reddy, Bandaru S.; Mastromarino, Anthony; and Wyn-
         der, Ernst L.   "Further leads on metabolic epi-
         demiology of large bowel cancer."   Cancer Re-
         search 35, 11, pt. 2 (Nov. 1975):   3403-3406.
               Colon cancer was associated with high fat con-
         sumption affecting cholesterol metabolites, fecal
         bile acids and neutral sterols.

1055   Reddy, Bandaru S.; Narisawa, T.; and Weisburger,
         J. H.   "Effect of a diet with high levels of pro-
         tein and fat on colon carcinogenesis in F344 rats
         treated with 1, 2-Dimethyl-hydrazine."   U. S. Na-
         tional Cancer Institute.   Journal 57, 3 (Sept.
         1976):   567-569.
               Rats fed diets containing high levels of beef
         protein and fat or high levels of soybean protein
         and corn oil had greater incidence of colon tumors
         than rats fed normally.

1056   Reddy, Bandaru S.; Sharma, Chand; Darby, Loretta;
         Laakso, Kristina; and Wynder, Ernst L.   "Meta-
         bolic epidemiology of large bowel cancer: fecal
         mutagens in high-risk and low-risk populations for
         colon cancer: a preliminary report."   Mutation
         Research 72, 3 (1980):   511-522.
               Fecal mutagen activity was higher in subjects
         on a high-fat, high-meat diet compared to low-fat,
         low-meat and vegetarian diets.

1057   Reddy, Bandaru S.; Watanake, K.; and Weisburger,
         J. H.   "Effect of high-fat diet on colon carcino-
         genesis in F344 rats treated with 1, 2-Dimethyl-
         hydrazine, methylazoxy-methanol acetate, or
         methylnitrosourea."   Cancer Research 37, 11
         (Nov. 1977):   4156-4159.
               Rats fed a diet containing 20 percent fat had a
         higher incidence of colon tumors than rats fed a
         5 percent fat diet.

1058   Reddy, Bandaru S.; Weisburger, John H.; and Wynder,
         Ernst L.   "Effects of high risk and low risk diets
         for colon carcinogenesis on fecal microflora and
         steroids in man."   Journal of Nutrition 105, 7
         (July 1975):   878-884.
               Diets high in animal protein and fat affect the
         composition of intestinal microflora and also levels
         of certain steroids which may act as promoters,
         co-carcinogens and/or carcinogens for the colon.

1059 Reddy, Bandaru S. , and Wynder, Ernst L. "Large-bowel carcinogenesis: fecal constituents of populations with diverse incidence rates of colon cancer." U. S. National Cancer Institute. Journal 50, 6 (June 1973): 1437-1442.
Study of fecal microflora and bile activity in meat eaters and vegetarians found a strong relationship between colon cancer and bile acid and neutral sterol excretion, both of which were high in meat eaters.

1060 Schmaehl, D.; Habs, M.; Wolter S.; and Kuenstler, K. "Experimental investigation on the influence upon chemical carcinogenesis: 4th communication. Influence of different diets on colon carcinogenesis by 1, 2-dimenthylhydrazine in Sprague-Dawley rats." Zeitschrift für Krebsforschung 93, 1 (1979): 57-66.
Rats were fed four types of diets (vegetarian, high fat, high cholesterol and high carbohydrate) and were injected with a chemical carcinogen. Rats on the high carbohydrate diet had lowest incidence of tumors; rats on the vegetarian diet had the longest survival times.

1061 Winkler, R. "The colo-rectal carcinoma. Studies on epidemiology and animal experimental carcinogenesis." Fortschritte der Medizin 96, 3 (Jan. 19, 1978): 115-119. (In German.)

1062 Wynder, E. L. , and Reddy, B. S. "Dietary fat and colon cancer." U. S. National Cancer Institute. Journal 54, 1 (1975): 7-10.
Association between colon cancer and dietary animal fat is suggested. Colon cancer rates of Japanese immigrants increased significantly as they adopted American diets. Increase in colon cancer appeared to be related to intake of beef.

1063 Wynder, E. L.; Reddy, B. S.; McCoy, D.; Weisburger, J. H.; and Williams, G. M. "Diet and cancer of the gastrointestinal tract." Advances in Internal Medicine 22 (1977): 397.

1064 Wynder, Ernst L. , and Reddy, Bandaru S. "The epidemiology of cancer of the large bowel." Digestive Diseases 19, 10 (Oct. 1974): 937-946.

Review of literature relating to demography, animal studies and dietary intake suggests correlation between dietary fat intake and colon cancer; charts compare fecal sterols, bile acids in various population groups including vegetarians.

1065 Wynder, Ernst L., and Reddy, Bandaru S. "Studies of large-bowel cancer: human leads to experimental application." U.S. National Cancer Institute. Journal 50, 5 (May 1973): 1099-1106.
Editorial reviews medical literature for epidemiologic and experimental evidence relating to bowel cancer.

Digestive System
(For colon cancer, see 1015-1065.)
(See also: 177, 932, 945, 946, 962, 978, 981, 985, 1000, 1007, 1239.)

1066 Birkner, Herman J., and Kern, Fred, Jr. "In vitro adsorption of bile salts to food residues, salicylazosulfa-pyridine, and hemicellulose." Gastroenterology 67, 2 (1974): 237-244.
Investigation demonstrated the adsorption of bile salts to certain food residues (celery, corn, lettuce, potato and string beans) to be important determinant of stool mass and water content in vegetarians, and a factor in fat adsorption and bowel function in some patients.

1067 Burkitt, D. P. "The protective value of plant fibre against many modern diseases." Qualitas Plantarum--Plant Foods for Human Nutrition 29, 1-2 (July 6, 1979): 39-48.
A diet high in vegetable fiber is thought to protect against diverticular disease, appendicitis, hiatus hernia, varicose veins, hemorrhoids, colon cancer, gallstones, coronary heart disease, obesity and diabetes.

1068 Burkitt, D. P.; Walker, A. R. P.; and Painter, N. S. "Dietary fiber and disease." American Medical Association. Journal 229, 8 (Aug. 19, 1974): 1068-1074.
Authors present evidence that many chronic

diseases of Western civilization result in part
from the decrease in dietary fiber consumption in
refined diets.

1069 Burkitt, Denis. "Food fiber and disease prevention."
Comprehensive Therapy 1, 5 (Sept. 1975): 19-22.
Characteristically Western diseases, including
heart disease, cancer of colon and rectum, gallstones, diverticular disease, appendicitis, hemorrhoids, hiatus hernia, obesity, diabetes and dental
caries are linked to lack of dietary fiber; chart
illustrates intestinal transit time and stool weight
in groups consuming various refined and unrefined
diets.

1070 Crowther, J. S. "Sarcina ventriculi in human faeces."
Journal of Medical Microbiology 4, 3 (Aug. 1971):
343-350.
Sarcina intestinal flora were found in three
quarters of Ugandan or Indian vegetarians and in
only a few people eating mixed diets.

1071 Drasar, B. S.; Crowther, J. S.; Goddard, P.; Hawks-
worth, G.; Hill, M. J.; Peach, S.; Williams, R.
E.; and Renwick, A. "The relation between diet
and the gut microflora in man." Nutrition Society.
Proceedings 32, 2 (Sept. 1973): 49-52.
Description of differences in the fecal flora of
groups of people consuming various diets; change
to vegetarian diet produced no demonstrable change
in the predominant fecal flora.

1072 Gear, J. S. S.; Ware, A.; Fursdon, P.; Mann, J.
I.; Nolan, D. J.; Brodribb, A. J.; and Vessey,
M. P. "Symptomless diverticular disease and intake of dietary fibre." Lancet 1, 8115 (Mar. 10,
1979): 511-514.
Vegetarians had a significantly higher mean
fiber intake and less diverticular disease than
non-vegetarians, providing evidence for the association between low intake of cereal fiber and diverticular disease.

1073 Gear, J. S. S.; Ware, A. C.; Nolan, D. J.; Fursdon, P. S.; Brodribb, A. J. M.; and Mann, J. I.
"Dietary fibre and asymptomatic diverticular disease of the colon." Nutrition Society. Proceed-

ings 37, 1 (May 1978): 13A.
Vegetarians consumed almost twice as much
fiber as controls and had only one-third the incidence of diverticular disease.

1074 Gear, John. Epidemiological studies on the role of
dietary fibre in the etiology of disease. Ph. D.,
Oxford University, 1978.
Dissertation determined that compared to non-
vegetarians, vegetarians consumed twice as much
fiber, had faster bowel transit times, and had
one-third the incidence of diverticular disease.

1075 Goldin, Barry R.; Swenson, Linda; Dwyer, Johanna;
Sexton, Margaret; and Gorbach, Sherwood L. "Effect of diet and Lactobacillus acidophilus supplements on human fecal bacterial enzymes." U.S.
National Cancer Institute. Journal 64, 2 (Feb.
1980): 255-261.
Vegetarians studied had lower metabolic activity
of fecal microflora. The short-term elimination
of red meat from omnivorous diets did not lower
activity, although addition of L. acidophilus did have
this effect.

1076 Goldstein, Jack. Triumph over disease--by fasting
and natural diet. New York, Arco Publishing Co.,
1977.
After six years of progressively debilitating con-
ventional medical treatments, author recovered
from ulcerative colitis through the Natural Hygiene
techniques of fasting and raw-foods vegetarian diet.

1077 Guinée, P.; Uqueto, N.; and Van Leeuwen, N. "Escherichia coli with resistance factors in vegetarians, babies, and non-vegetarians." Applied Microbiology 20, 4 (Oct. 1970): 531-535.

1078 Hardinge, Mervin [sic] G. H. "Plant fibers in human
health." In: Topics in dietary fiber research.
Edited by Gene A. Spiller. New York, Plenum
Press, 1978, p. 117-126.
Review article on health and nutritional aspects
of fiber in vegetarian diets.

1079 Hardouin, J. P., and Blanc, D. "Gastric ulcer.
Clinical signs, diagnostic approach and course."

Revue du Praticien 25, 27 (1975): 2089-2094.
Medical treatment of gastric ulcer by absolute
bedrest and lacto-vegetarian diet. (In French.)

1080 Holm, C. N., and Hansen, L. P. "Vegetable fibers
and duration of gastro-intestinal passage." Ugeskrift for Laeger 137, 10 (1975): 561-565.
Vegetarians studied consumed about twice as
much fiber as non-vegetarians; daily consumption
of more than 35 mgs. fiber per kg. of body weight
appeared to insure rapid gastro-intestinal passage.
(In Danish.)

1081 Klein, M.; Baek, S. M.; and Kim, U. "A phytobe-
zoar in an adult." Mount Sinai Journal of Medicine
43, 4 (1976): 388-390.
Case of rare gastric concretion in vegetarian
adult.

1082 Miettinen, T. A., and Tarpila, S. "Fecal beta-sitosterol in patients with diverticular disease of the
colon and in vegetarians." Scandinavian Journal
of Gastroenterology 13, 5 (1978): 573-576.
Patients with diverticular disease of the colon
had subnormal excretion of beta-sitosterol, indicating a diet low in plant foods, whereas vegetarians
had high levels of beta-sitosterol. Findings agreed
with current research that diverticular disease is
associated with dietary fiber deficiency.

1083 Owen, R. L., and Brandborg, L. L. "Jejunal mor-
phologic consequences of vegetarian diet in humans." Gastroenterology 72, 5, pt. 2 (May 1977):
A88.
Intestinal villi from healthy American vegetarians demonstrated changes similar to those from
healthy individuals from underdeveloped countries.
(Abstract only.)

1084 Piscitelli, Laurie H. "Vegetarian ileostomates: mutu-
ally compatible?" ET Journal 6, 1 (Winter 1979):
12-14.
Review of difficulties encountered by strict vegetarian ileostomates.

1085 Plester, D., and Rauch, S. "Effect of vegetarian diet
on the composition of saliva in man." Archiv für

Ohren-, Nasen- und Kehlkopfheilkunde 184, 5 (July 5, 1965): 399-402. (In German.)

1086 Prasad, G. C.; Prakash, V.; Tandon, A. K.; and Deshpande, P. J. "Studies on etiopathogenesis of hemorrhoids." American Journal of Proctology 27, 3 (1976): 33-41.
    Studies of 123 patients concludes that a person is likely to develop hemorrhoids if he falls into one or more of the following categories: male over age 30; laborer or clerical worker; has an endomorphic constitution; eats a non-vegetarian diet; sits in an uncomfortable position for long periods of time; has disturbed liver function, pancreatic function and fat metabolism.

1087 Tandon, G. S.; Skukla, R. C.; Gurg, S. K.; Das, M.; and Saxena, R. C. "Study of gastric secretion in dogs with reference to Indian diet." Indian Journal of Physiology and Allied Sciences 31, 1 (1977): 27-30.
    Dogs fed vegetarian diets did not show appreciable changes in gastric secretions compared with controls.

1088 Van Berge Henegouwen, G. P.; Huijbregts, A. W.; Hectors, M.; Van Schaik, A.; and Werf, S. V. D. "Bran feeding and vegetarian diet do not alter biliary lipids and bile acid kinetics in young males." Gut 20, 10 (1979): A930.
    Brief communication presents findings that neither bran feeding nor vegetarian diet alters cholesterol saturation in young males.

1089 Verma, H. N.; Mishra, A. P.; Prasad, D. D.; and Agarwal, R. K. P. "Volvulus of the caecum." Indian Journal of Surgery 39, 5 (1977): 252-256.
    Five cases of volvulus caecum are reported; higher incidence was found in males, in the second and third decades of life, and in persons on a vegetarian diet.

Diabetes

1090 Cook, Kathleen A. "Diabetics can be vegetarians." Nursing 9, 10 (Oct. 1979): 70-73.

Survey of recent nutritional studies of diabetics
indicating that increased carbohydrates and decreased fat consumption has no ill effects, while
decreasing serum cholesterol and lipid levels.
Charts of basic exchanges, menus, combining
complementary proteins.

1091 Hur, Robin. "Diabetes." Vegetarian Times (Jan. -
Feb. 1979): 38-40.
Review of medical research indicating that a
diet high in natural, unrefined carbohydrates is
the optimal diet for controlling diabetes.

1092 Jorgensen, Caryl Dow, and Lewis, John E.   The
ABC's of diabetes. New York, Crown, 1979.
Alphabetical definitions and explanations of medical terms and concepts often encountered by the
diabetic, with considerable treatment of conven-
tional and vegetarian food exchanges.

1093 Nuttall, Frank Q., and Brunzell, John D.   "Principles
of nutrition and dietary recommendations for individuals with diabetes mellitus: 1979.   Report of
the American Diabetes Association." American
Dietetic Association. Journal 75, 5 (Nov. 1979):
527-530.
Lacto- and lacto-ovo-vegetarian diets can be
nutritionally adequate for diabetics; pure vegetarian
diets should be supplemented with vitamin B12 and
perhaps iron and calcium.

1094 Smith, Elizabeth. Vegetarian meal-planning guide for
diabetic persons; a lacto-ovo-vegetarian diet. Winnipeg, Hyperion Press, 1979.
Contains food lists, charts, and practical information on food groups, portions, meal plans, and
snacks for the lacto-ovo-vegetarian diabetic.

1095 Trowell, Hugh. "Diabetes mellitus and dietary fiber
of starchy foods." American Journal of Clinical
Nutrition 31, 10 Suppl. (Oct. 1978): S53-S57.
Study of diabetes mortality rates in England and
Wales and the rarity of diabetes in rural vegetarian
Africans suggests that high-fiber, high-carbohy-
drate diets may protect against the disease.

Skeletal System
(See also: 299, 1152, 1153, 1157, 1159,
1163, 1167, 1168, 1307, 1393, 1399.)

1096   Anon.   "Vegetarians have stronger bones."   Prevention 31, 1 (Jan. 1979): 98.
          Brief summary of study finding that elderly
vegetarian women experienced less bone mineral
loss and osteoporosis than their meat-eating counterparts.

1097   Chandra, Satish, and Chawla, T. N.   "Prevalence of
anodontia among Lucknow city school children."
Indian Dental Association.   Journal 47, 12 (Dec.
1975):   489-496.
          Study of 15,000 Indian children correlated de-
velopmental absence of teeth with socio-economic
and other factors; partial anodontia was more
prevalent among vegetarian children.

1098   Davidson, F.   "Nutrition today; the case for alternative diets."   New Zealand School Dental Service
Gazette 39, 5 (Oct. 1978):   36-37.

1099   Elias, M.   "Feasibility of dental strontium analysis
for diet-assessment of human populations."   American Journal of Physical Anthropology 53 (July
1980):   1-4.

1100   Ellis, Frey R.; Holesh, S.; and Ellis, John W.   "Incidence of osteoporosis in vegetarians and omnivores."   American Journal of Clinical Nutrition 25,
6 (June 1972):   555-558.
          Vegetarians studied had significantly greater
bone densities, and hence less osteoporosis, than
age and sex matched omnivore controls.

1101   Ellis, Frey R.; Holesh, S.; and Sanders, T. A. B.
"Osteoporosis in British vegetarians and omnivores."   American Journal of Clinical Nutrition
27, 8 (Aug. 1974):   769-770.
          Letter updates bone density data from earlier
study.

1102   Exton-Smith, A. N.   "Osteoporosis."   Nutrition 27, 2
(Apr. 1973):   116-125.

1103   Herre, Craig W., and Herwig, Robert V. "Vegetari-
       an vs. normal as causal agents in tooth decay."
       Kansas State Dental Association. Journal 61, 4
       (Oct. 1977): 12-14.
       Omnivorous diet promoted greater amounts of
       decay and produced a more acid environment than
       did the vegetarian diet.

1104   Léger, Jean. "Fasting and vegetarianism; their oral
       manifestations." Information Dentaire 47 (May 13,
       1965): 1877-1887.
       Effects of fasting and vegetarianism on the
       teeth and gums. (In French.)

1105   Léger, Jean. "Fasting and vegetarianism; their oral
       manifestations." Information Dentaire 47 (May
       20, 1965): 1999-2010.
       Further examination of the influence of diet on
       dental caries. (In French.)

1106   Marsh, A. G.; Sanchez, T. V.; Mickelsen, O.;
       Keiser, J.; and Mayor, G. "Cortical bone density
       of adult lacto-ovo-vegetarian and omnivorous wom-
       en." American Dietetic Association. Journal 76,
       2 (Feb. 1980): 148-151.
       Omnivorous women ages 50-89 had lost 35 per-
       cent bone mineral mass, whereas vegetarian wom-
       en in the same age group had lost only 18 percent.

1107   Misra, B. D. "Epiphyseal union of the long bones of
       upper limb by X-ray in Gujrat." Anatomical So-
       ciety of India. Journal 16, 1 (1967): 35.
       Study of ages of epiphyseal fusion in Indian
       vegetarian boys and girls. (Abstract only.)

1108   Sanchez, T. V.; Mickelsen, O.; Marsh, A. G.; Garn,
       S. M.; and Mayor, G. H. "Bone mineral mass
       in elderly vegetarian females." American Journal
       of Roentgenology 131, 3 (1978): 542.
       Omnivore women showed significantly more loss
       of bone mineral mass and bone width than vege-
       tarian women, especially long-term vegetarians.
       (Abstract only.)

1109   Slavkin, Harold C. "Preventive dentistry through nu-
       tritional awareness." San Fernando Valley Dental
       Society. Bulletin 6, 6 (May 1972): 16-17, 50.

Discussion of vegetarian and Zen macrobiotic diets.

Protein
(See also: 111, 120, 150, 170, 186, 229, 257, 288, 303, 909, 1188.)

1110 Ajayi, O. A., and Linkswiler, H. M. "Nitrogen retention of young adults fed mixtures of vegetable proteins." Qualitas Plantarum--Plant Foods for Human Nutrition 24, 3-4 (May 21, 1975): 317-326.
Nitrogen balance studies on subjects given four vegetable protein combinations.

1111 Allen, Hannah. The happy truth about protein. Yorktown, TX, Life Science, n. d.
Exposes myths of human protein requirements; cites dangers of high protein diets; chart of vegetable sources of amino acids.

1112 Altman, Nathaniel. "Non-meat protein." Vegetarian Times (Dec.-Jan. 1977): 21-23.
Clarification of the protein question for vegetarians.

1113 Anon. "Animal protein seen as factor in kidney disease." Food Engineering (Dec. 1975): 28, 33.
High meat diets tend to stress the kidneys due to higher urea levels than are produced by vegetarian diets.

1114 Catterton, Catherine; Abernathy, R. P.; and Korslund, Mary K. "Nitrogen balance in young women fed a lacto-vegetarian diet plus egg white or a nonspecific nitrogen source." Federation Proceedings 32, 1 (1973): 937.
Evaluation of egg white and non-specific nitrogen sources as supplements to a low-protein lacto-vegetarian diet. (Abstract only.)

1115 Cremer, H. D. "The importance of plant protein in human nutrition." Ernährungs-Umschau 23, 3 (1976): 75-82. (In German.)

1116 Doyle, Margaret D.; Morse, L. M.; Gowan, J. S.; and Parsons, M. R. "Observations on nitrogen

and energy balance in young men consuming vegetarian diets." American Journal of Clinical Nutrition 17, 6 (Dec. 1965): 367-376.
Nitrogen balance studies on eight men consuming controlled vegetarian diets.

1117 Doyle, Margaret D.; Morse, Lura M.; Gowan, Jean S.; and Parsons, Mary. "Studies on nitrogen balance in young men consuming vegetarian diets." Federation Proceedings 23, 2 (1964): 396.
Nitrogen balance studies conducted for two consecutive years in which protein was supplied entirely from vegetable sources.

1118 Hardinge, Mervyn G.; Crooks, Hulda; and Stare, Frederick J. "Nutritional studies of vegetarians. V. Proteins and essential amino acids." American Dietetic Association. Journal 48, 1 (Jan. 1966): 25-28.
Study of lacto-ovo-vegetarians, pure vegetarians, and non-vegetarians found that all subjects generously exceeded twice their minimum requirements for protein and essential amino acids.

1119 Leveille, Gilbert A. "Issues in human nutrition and their probable impact on foods of animal origin." Journal of Animal Studies 41, 2 (Aug. 1975): 723-731.
Proportion of protein derived from meat, poultry and fish increased significantly between 1909 and 1965; discusses possible relationship between cancer of the large intestine and dietary protein and/or fat; suggests that protein consumption could be safely reduced in the United States.

1120 Lin, T.; Chen, M. L.; and Chen, J. S. "Observation on dietary protein utilization in vegetarians." Chinese Journal of Physiology 21, 3 (Dec. 31, 1975): 143-149.
Study of utilization of low and high vegetable protein diets showed that vegetarians utilized the ingested vegetable protein slightly more efficiently than did the non-vegetarians.

1121 Manno, Anne. "The importance of protein in the meatless meal." Forecast for Home Economics 18 (Jan. 1973): F16-17, 40-41, 46.
Functions and sources of protein; recipes.

1122   Marsh, Alice G.; Ford, Dwain L.; and Christensen,
       Dorothy K. "Metabolic responses of adolescent
       girls to a lacto-ovo-vegetarian diet." American
       Dietetic Association. Journal 51, 5 (1967): 441-
       446.
           Measurements of metabolic response of 16 ado-
       lescent girls on a controlled lacto-ovo-vegetarian
       diet determined that consumption of eight essential
       amino acids exceeded requirements and all sub-
       jects maintained positive nitrogen balance.

1123   Null, Gary, and Null, Steve. Protein for vegetarians.
       Rev. and enlarged. New York, Pyramid Books,
       1975.
           Emphasis on high-protein diet, not on vegetari-
       anism. Menu plans contain sausage, meat loaf,
       corned beef, liver, spaghetti with meatballs, etc.

1124   Nyman, Mavis Carlotta. A nitrogen balance study on
       young college women consuming low protein vege-
       tarian diets. Ph. D., University of Minnesota,
       1963.
           Nitrogen balance study of 36 days duration in-
       volving five women consuming three vegetarian
       diets supplemented with either milk, millet or nuts.

1125   Ramos-Aliaga, Roger. "Biochemical and nutritional
       aspects of growing rats receiving proteins from
       two Peruvian Andes dietary patterns." Archivos
       Latinoamericanos de Nutricion 28, 4 (1978): 378-
       400.
           Protein quality determined for two experimental
       vegetarian diets typical of Peruvian Andes resi-
       dents. (In Spanish.)

1126   Rao, M. Narayana, and Swaminathan, M. "Plant pro-
       teins in the amelioration of protein deficient
       states." In: Bourne, Geoffrey H. World Review
       of Nutrition and Dietetics, New York, S. Karger,
       v. 11, 1969, p. 106-141.

1127   Register, U. D.; Inano, Mitsuko; Thurston, C. E.;
       Vyhmeister, Irma B.; Dysinger, P. W.; Blanken-
       ship, J. W.; and Horning, M. C. "Nitrogen bal-
       ance studies in human subjects on various diets."
       American Journal of Clinical Nutrition 20, 7 (July
       1967): 753-759.

Using the nitrogen balance method to evaluate protein quality of vegetable protein mixtures as meat substitutes, authors found no significant differences in the ability of pure vegetarian, lacto-vegetarian and non-vegetarian diets to maintain positive nitrogen balance.

1128 Robertson, W. G.; Peacock, M.; Heyburn, P. J.; Hanes, F. A.; Rutherford, A.; Clementson, E.; Swaminathan, R.; and Clark, P. B. "Should recurrent calcium oxalate stone formers become vegetarians?" British Journal of Urology 51, 6 (1979): 427-431.

Vegetarian diets which are low in animal protein are associated with low relative probability of kidney stone formation, whereas diets high in animal protein increase relative risk.

1129 Sanchez, Albert; Scharffenberg, J. A.; and Register, U. D. "Nutritive value of selected proteins and protein combinations. I. The biological value of proteins singly and in meal patterns with varying fat compositions." American Journal of Clinical Nutrition 13, 10 (Oct. 1963): 243-249.

Quality of protein in selected meals based on non-meat sources was determined.

1130 Vegetable protein in modified diets. (Sound recording) Western New York Dietetic Association, Buffalo, Communications in Learning, 1974.

Vitamin B12
(For Vitamin B12 and vegans, see 1237,
        1242, 1243, 1245, 1247, 1252, 1255,
        1262, 1263, 1271, 1276, 1277, 1278,
        1281, 1287, 1290, 1291, 1292, 1293,
        1301, 1302, 1303.)
(See also: 894, 1173, 1174, 1390.)

1131 Amin, S.; Spinks, T.; Ranicar, A.; Short, M. D.; and Hoffbrand, A. V. "Long-term clearance of (57 Co) cyanocobalamin in vegans and pernicious anemia." Clinical Science 58, 1 (Jan. 1980): 101-103.

Subjects with pernicious anemia cleared vitamin B12 more rapidly than did vegans and controls.

1132 Anon. "Contribution of the microflora of the small
        intestine to the vitamin B12 nutriture of man."
        Nutrition Reviews 38, 8 (Aug. 1980): 274-275.
            Brief review of vitamin B12 synthesis by in-
        testinal microflora in vegetarians and vegans.

1133 Anon. "Gut reactions to deficiency." SciQuest (Apr.
        1980): 3.
            Physiological aspects of vitamin B12 deficiency
        among vegetarian East Indians living in Great
        Britain.

1134 Banerjee, D. K., and Chatterjea, J. B. "Serum
        vitamin B12 in vegetarians." British Medical
        Journal 5204 (1960): 992-994.
            Indian vegetarians studied had lower serum
        vitamin B12 levels than non-vegetarians.

1135 Banerjee, D. K., and Chatterjea, J. B. "Vegetarian-
        ism and serum vitamin B12." Calcutta. School
        of Tropical Medicine. Bulletin 8, 3 (July 1960):
        115-117.
            Investigation of serum vitamin B12 in Indian
        vegetarians and non-vegetarians found significantly
        lower levels in vegetarians.

1136 Britt, R. P.; Harper, Christine; and Spray, G. H.
        "Megaloblastic anaemia among Indians in Britain."
        Quarterly Journal of Medicine 40, 160 (Oct. 1971):
        499-520.
            Cases of megaloblastic anemia and related
        deficiencies described in 25 vegetarian Indian im-
        migrants in Britain.

1137 Chatterjea, J. B. "Nutritional megaloblastic anaemia
        in tropical zones." Indian Medical Association.
        Journal 48, 2 (Jan. 16, 1967): 51-59.
            Nutritional megaloblastic anemia in developing
        countries represents folic acid and/or vitamin
        B12 deficiencies, especially in poor vegetarians.

1138 Chen, Jui-San, and Kao, Chao-Tsun. "Study of im-
        portant blood-forming components in vegetarians."
        K'o Hsueh Fa Chan Yueh K'an 4, 1 (1976): 2111-
        2116.
            Iron and vitamin B12 levels measured in vege-
        tarians and non-vegetarians. Vegetarians had

lower B12 values, but no symptoms of deficiency. (In Chinese.)

1139 Dastur, D. K.; Quadros, E. V.; Wadia, N. H.; Desai, M. M.; and Bharucha, E. P. "Effect of vegetarianism and smoking on vitamin B12, thiocyanate, and folate levels in the blood of normal subjects." British Medical Journal 3, 821 (July 29, 1972): 260-263.
Non-vegetarian non-smokers had highest B12 levels; smokers had higher levels of plasma thiocyanate; and vegetarians had significantly higher serum folate levels.

1140 Gleeson, M. H., and Graves, P. S. "Complications of dietary deficiency of vitamin B12 in young Caucasians." Postgraduate Medical Journal 50, 585 (July 1974): 462-464.
Report of two cases of vitamin B12 deficiency.

1141 Habib, G. G. "Nutritional vitamin B12 deficiency among Hindus." Tropical and Geographical Medicine 16 (Sept. 1964): 206-215.
Report of ten cases of megaloblastic anemia in vegetarian Hindus.

1142 Hoffbrand, A. V., and Lavoie, A. "Blood and neoplastic diseases: megaloblastic anaemia." British Medical Journal 2 (June 8, 1974): 550-553.
Description of methods of diagnosis and treatment of megaloblastic anemia, which sometimes occurs in vegans and those having vitamin B12 or folate deficiency.

1143 Inamdar-Deshmukh, A. B.; Jathar V. S.; Joseph, D. A.; and Satoskar, R. S. "Erythrocyte vitamin B12 activity in healthy Indian lactovegetarians." British Journal of Haematology 32, 3 (Mar. 1976): 395-401.
Plasma vitamin B12 levels, but not erythrocyte B12 levels, were lower in vegetarians than in non-vegetarians.

1144 Jathar, V. S.; Inamdar-Deshmukh, A. B.; Rege, D. V.; and Satoskar, R. S. "Vitamin B12 and vegetarianism in India." Acta Haematologica 53, 2 (1975): 90-97.

Indian lacto-vegetarians had lower serum and urinary excretion of vitamin B12, while showing no apparent symptoms of deficiency.

1145 Kappeler, R., and Gubser, M. "Megaloblastic vitamin B12 deficiency anemia with erythroleukemic blood picture." Schweizerische Medizinische Wochenschrift 108, 15 (April 15, 1978): 560-563.
       Case of severe megaloblastic anemia in a vegetarian, complicated by marked erythroleukemic blood findings and severe heart failure. (In German.)

1146 Linnell, J. C.; Hoffbrand, A. V.; Peters, T. J.; and Matthews, D. M. "Chromatographic and bio-autographic estimation of plasma cobalamins in various disturbances of vitamin B12 metabolism." Clinical Science 40, 1 (Jan. 1971): 1-16.
       Calculations of plasma cobalamins in subjects with pernicious anemia, folate deficiency or gastritis, and in vegans.

1147 Linnell, J. C.; MacKenzie, Heather M.; Wilson, J.; and Matthews, D. M. "Patterns of plasma cobalamins in control subjects and in cases of vitamin B12 deficiency." Journal of Clinical Pathology 22, 5 (Sept. 1969): 545-550.
       Method for analysis of plasma cobalamins in subjects with pernicious anemia and in vegans is described.

1148 Mehta, B. M.; Rege, D. V.; and Satoskar, R. S. "Serum vitamin B12 and folic acid activity in lactovegetarian and non-vegetarian healthy adult Indians." American Journal of Clinical Nutrition 15 (Aug. 1964): 77-84.
       Indian vegetarians had lower serum vitamin B12 and folic acid activity than non-vegetarians.

1149 Satoskar, R. S. "Further observations on serum vitamin B12 and folic acid activity in lacto-vegetarian and non-vegetarian healthy Indian adults." Indian Journal of Medical Sciences 20, 11 (1966): 876-877.
       Vegetarians had lower levels of serum vitamin B12 and folic acid, but no apparent symptoms of vitamin B12 deficiency. (Abstract only)

1150   Satyanarayana, N. S.   "Plasma vitamin B12 levels in
        vegetarians."   Indian Journal of Medical Research
        51, 2 (1963):   380-385.
            Plasma vitamin B12 levels were lower in vege-
        tarians than in non-vegetarians, but no clinical
        symptoms of deficiency were found.

1151   Schloesser, Lee L., and Schilling, Robert F.   "Vita-
        min B12 absorption studies in a vegetarian with
        megaloblastic anemia."   American Journal of
        Clinical Nutrition 12, 1 (Jan. 1963):   70-74.
            Report of successful treatment of a Hindu vege-
        tarian suffering from megaloblastic anemia as a
        result of faulty vitamin B12 absorption.

                            Vitamin D

1152   Anon.   "Vitamin D deficiency rickets, revisited."
        Nutrition Reviews 38, 3 (Mar. 1980):   116-118.
            Review of nutritional, racial, cultural and en-
        vironmental factors contributing to increase in
        rickets in Western cultures; discusses cases of
        rickets in children of Black Muslims consuming
        severely restricted diets devoid of animal-derived
        products.

1153   Bachrach, Steven, and Parks, John S.   "An outbreak
        of vitamin D deficiency rickets in a susceptible
        population."   Pediatrics 64, 6 (Dec. 1979):   871-
        877.
            Describes 24 cases of rickets in black infants
        with limited vitamin D intake, exclusion of meat
        and/or dairy products and no supplemental vita-
        mins.

1154   Brodie, M. J.; Davies, D. S.; Dollery, C. T.; Fras-
        er, H. S.; Hillyard, Carmel J.; MacIntyre, I.;
        Mucklow, J. C.; and Wilmana, P. F.   "Antipyrine
        induction and hepatic vitamin D hydroxylation in
        man."   British Journal of Clinical Pharmacology
        7, 4 (Apr. 1979):   719P.
            Brief communication describes changes in vita-
        min D levels in Asian vegetarians, non-vegetarians
        and controls following antipyrine ingestion.

1155 Chakrabarti, A. K.; Johnson, S. C.; Samantray, S.
K.; and Reddy, E. R. "Osteomalacia, myopathy
and basilar impression." Journal of the Neurological Sciences 23, 2 (1974): 227-235.
Case of bone tenderness and muscular weakness
in blind, diabetic vegetarian Indian male who was
rarely exposed to sunlight.

1156 Dent, C. E., and Gupta, M. M. "Plasma 25-hy-
droxyvitamin-D levels during pregnancy in Caucasians and in vegetarian and non-vegetarian
Asians." Lancet 2, 7944 (Nov. 29, 1975): 1057-
1060.
Although pregnant vegetarian Asians had lower
levels of 25-0. H. D, there was no clear evidence
that pregnancy increased vitamin D requirements
and therefore predisposed to osteomalacia.

1157 Dent, C. E.; Round, J. M.; Rowe, D. J. F.; and
Stamp, T. C. B. "Effect of chapattis and ultraviolet irradiation on nutritional rickets in an Indian
immigrant." Lancet 1, 815 (June 9, 1973): 1282-
1284.
Case of rickets due to deficiency of both sunlight and vitamin D in the vegetarian diet was suc-
cessfully treated with oral vitamin D and ultraviolet
irradiation of the skin.

1158 Dent, C. E., and Smith, R. "Nutritional osteomalacia." Quarterly Journal of Medicine 38, 150 (Apr.
1969): 195-209.
Osteomalacia due to vitamin D deficiency de-
scribed in number of patients, most of whom were
either strict vegetarian immigrants to Britain or
non-vegetarians who had avoided fatty foods for
many years.

1159 Dwyer, Johanna T.; Dietz, W. H., Jr.; Hass, G.;
and Suskind, R. "Risk of nutritional rickets
among vegetarian children." American Journal of
Diseases of Children 133, 2 (Feb. 1979): 134-140.
Children consuming macrobiotic diets were found
to be at greater risk of nutritional rickets. (See
also no. 1163.)

1160 Dwyer, Johanna T.; Dietz, William; Hass, Gerald; and
Suskind, Robert. "Vitamin D nutriture in vege-

tarian children." Federation Proceedings 37, 3 (1978): 333.

Adequacy of vitamin D intakes in 52 children under 6 years of age. (Abstract only.)

1161 Eastwood, J. B.; de Wardener, H. E.; Gray, R. W.; and Lemann, J. L., Jr. "Normal plasma -1, 25-(OH)2 -vitamin-D concentrations in nutritional osteomalacia." Lancet 1, 8131 (June 30, 1979): 1377-1378.

Cases of osteomalacia in three patients, two of whom were strict Indian vegetarians.

1162 Elinson, Paul; Neustadter, Lawrence M.; and Moncman, Michael G. "Nutritional osteomalacia." American Journal of Diseases of Children 134, 4 (Apr. 1980): 427.

Letter briefly describes case of osteomalacia due to inadequate vegetarian diet, lack of exposure to sunlight, and extended lactation.

1163 Finberg, Laurence. "Human choice, vegetable deficiencies and vegetarian rickets." American Journal of Diseases of Children 133, 2 (Feb. 1979): 129.

Comments upon study by Dwyer on cases of rickets in strict vegetarian children. (See also no. 1159.)

1164 Gupta, M. M.; Round, J. M.; and Stamp, T. C. B. "Spontaneous cure of vitamin D deficiency in Asians during summer in Britain." Lancet 1, 7858 (1974): 586-588.

Report of hypocalcemia in healthy Asian vegetarians living in Britain, emphasizing importance of sunlight in the maintenance of vitamin D nutrition and the prevention of rickets.

1165 Hilb, Anne. "Metabolic study on a patient with nutritional vitamin D deficiency." Journal of Human Nutrition 31, 5 (Oct. 1977): 359-361.

Case history of Indian vegetarian patient whose diet, although high in yogurt and calcium, was nearly devoid of vitamin D.

1166 Hunt, Sandra P.; O'Riordan, J. L. H.; Windo, J.; and Truswell, A. S. "Vitamin D status in differ-

174 / Recent Works

ent subgroups of British Asians." British Medical
Journal 2, 6048 (Dec. 4, 1976): 1351-1354.
Dietary intake of vitamin D and time spent out
of doors were calculated for five Ugandan religious groups with differing dietary and social cus-
toms.

1167 Rudolf, Mary; Arulanantham, Karunyan; and Green-
stein, Robert M. "Unsuspected nutritional rickets." Pediatrics 66, 1 (1980): 72-76.
Children at risk to develop rickets were those
on restricted diets, those breast-fed for an unu-
sually long time, and black children; diagnosis and
treatment of four cases of rickets in children.

1168 Scharffenberg, J. A. "Vegetarian diets." American
Journal of Diseases of Children 133, 11 (Nov.
1979): 1204.
Letter disputes assumptions and conclusions of
studies of rickets in strict vegetarian children.

1169 Wilmana, P. F.; Brodie, M. J.; Mucklow, J. C.;
Fraser, H. S.; Toverud, Else Lydia; Davies, D.
S.; Dollery, C. T.; Hillyard, Carmel J.; MacIn-
tyre, I.; and Park, B. K. "Reduction of circulat-
ing 25-hydroxyvitamin D by antipyrine." British
Journal of Clinical Pharmacology 8, 6 (1979):
523-528.
Asian vegetarians had lower vitamin D levels
and longer antipyrine half-lives than white non-
vegetarians.

Mental Health
(See also: 72, 1299.)

1170 Chyaette, Conrad; Chyaette, Clifford; and Althoff,
Dale. "Left-handedness and vegetarianism." South
African Medical Journal 56, 13 (Sept. 22, 1979):
505-506.
Letter presents Freudian interpretation to cor-
relation between left-handedness and vegetarianism.
Reprinted as Chyaette, Conrad. "Sinistrality."
Southern Medical Journal 73, 1 (Jan. 1980): 92.

1171 Etchegoyen, R. H. "A note on ideology and psychoanalytic technique." International Journal of Psy-

cho-Analysis 54, 4 (1973): 485-486.
Objectivity of the analyst must not be compromised by ideological conflicts with patient's life habits and beliefs; case of vegetarian patient is presented.

1172 Friedman, Stanley. "On vegetarianism." American Psychoanalytic Association. Journal 23, 2 (1975): 396-406.
Vegetarianism is discussed in terms of oral cannibalistic impulses and primal scene impressions.

1173 Godt, P., and Kochen, M. "Vitamin B12 deficiency due to psychotically induced malnutrition." Nervenarzt 48, 4 (1977): 225-227.
Case of vitamin B12 deficiency, megaloblastic anemia and funicular myelosis in patient who had become a strict vegetarian six years earlier in the course of a paranoid psychosis. (In German.)

1174 Jathar, V. S. "Serum vitamin B12 levels in Indian psychiatric patients." British Journal of Psychiatry 117, 541 (Dec. 1970): 699-704.
Study of 152 psychiatric patients, both vegetarian and meat eating, failed to identify psychiatric symptoms attributable to vitamin B12 deficiency.

1175 Kline, Paul, and Mohan, Jitendra. "Oral personality traits among female students in North India: a cross-cultural study." Psychological Studies 23, 1 (1978): 1-4.
No significant differences were found in oral traits between British meat-eaters and Indian vegetarians, leading authors to reject Freudian hypothesis concerning the derivation of oral personality traits from oral fixation.

1176 Lester, David. "Food fads and psychological health." Psychological Reports 44, 1 (Feb. 1979): 222.
Tests regarding food preferences and measurements of psychoticism, extraversion, and neuroticism found that undergraduate subjects with food fads such as vegetarianism or vitamin supplements did not differ in psychological health from other subjects.

1177 Marks, Isaac M.; Cameron, Paul M.; and Silberfeld, Michel. "Operant therapy for an abnormal personality." British Medical Journal 1, 5750 (Mar. 20, 1971): 647-648.
      Description of the use of operant therapy to influence the behavior of an adolescent girl.

1178 Meng, Heinrich. Leben als Begegnung. Stuttgart, Hippokrates, 1971.
      Historical account of the German psychoanalytic and related cultural movements discusses such topics as vegetarianism, dietary therapy, pacifism, socialism, Bauhaus, parapsychology, vivisection, and Christianity. (In German.)

1179 Obis, Paul Barrett. "Are vegetarians naturally left-handed?" Vegetarian Times (Mar. 1980): 10-11.
      Critique of Chyaette's study finding Freudian correlation between vegetarianism and left-handedness.

1180 Passebecq, Andre. "Dietary reform and vegetarianism. Psychological study." Action et Pensée 44, 3-4 (1968): 38-44.
      People most likely to become vegetarians are those who are influenced by writings on evolution, reincarnation, and the "massacre" of the soul; are seeking a cure; and suffer from feelings of guilt. (In French.)

1181 Weinstein, Lawrence. "The effects of certain vegetable vs. particular meat breakfasts on the magnitude of human positive contrast and self-ratings of positive emotionality." Psychonomic Society. Bulletin 15, 3 (Mar. 1980): 200-202.
      Subjects consuming vegetable diets for breakfast rated themselves to be in a significantly more positive frame of mind emotionally than did matched subjects eating meat breakfasts.

Infants, Children
(See also: 145, 190, 222, 250, 262, 937, 956, 1153, 1159, 1160, 1162, 1163, 1167, 1168.)
(For vegans, see 1238, 1255, 1258, 1262, 1269, 1280, 1282, 1284, 1294, 1296, 1297, 1301, 1304.)

1182   Anon.   "Exotic diets and the infant."   British Medical
       Journal 1, 6116 (Apr. 1, 1978):   804-805.
       Editorial expresses concern for two groups of
       children: those of the Asian immigrant community
       in the United Kingdom who may become deficient
       in vitamins D and B12, and those of the so-called
       cult diets in the United States, e. g. vegans, mem-
       bers of yogic sects, Zen macrobiotics, and
       Seventh-day Adventists.

1183   Anon.   "Growth of vegetarian children."   Nutrition
       Reviews 37, 4 (Apr. 1979):   108-109.
       Critique of methodology and conclusions of study
       on growth velocities of vegetarian children.

1184   Anon.   "Vegetarian diets for children."   Nutrition and
       the M. D. 4, 2 (Dec. 1977):   2-3.
       Brief summary of nutritional aspects of vege-
       tarian diets.

1185   Burke, Edmund C., and Huse, Diane M.   "Multiple
       nutritional deficiencies in children on vegetarian
       diets."   Mayo Clinic Proceedings 54, 8 (Aug.
       1979):   549-550.
       Editorial calls attention to health risks to chil-
       dren consuming extremely restrictive diets.

1186   Dickerson, J. W. T., and Fehily, Ann M.   "Malnu-
       trition in infants receiving cult diets."   British
       Medical Journal 1, 6164 (Mar. 10, 1979):   682.
       Responding to paper critical of vegetarian diets,
       writer points out distinctions between vegetarian,
       vegan, fruitarian and macrobiotic diets.

1187   Dillard, Robert P.   "Vegetarianism and breast-feed-
       ing."   Pediatrics 66, 1 (July 1980):   156-157.
       Letter criticizes implication in article by Shull
       and Dwyer that breast-feeding is related to inade-
       quate nutrition in vegetarians.

1188   Dumm, M. E.; Rao, B. R. H.; Benjamin, V.; and
       Pereira, S.   "Protein needs of children on vege-
       tarian diets."   Federation Proceedings 24, 2
       (1965):   173.
       Study of safe minimal protein intakes in chil-
       dren.   (Abstract only.)

1189 Dwyer, J. T. "Physical measurements of vegetarian infants and preschool children." American Journal of Clinical Nutrition 29, 4 (Apr. 1976): 477.
Abstract of paper finding vegetarian and macrobiotic children to be slightly smaller than nonvegetarian children.

1190 Dwyer, Johanna T. "Physical measurements of vegetarian infants and preschool children." Clinical Research 24, 3 (1976): 499A.
Abstract of study of physical measurements in 119 children whose parents characterized themselves as vegetarians.

1191 Dwyer, Johanna T.; Andrew, Elizabeth M.; Valadian, Isabelle; and Reed, Robert B. "Size, obesity and leanness in vegetarian preschool children." American Dietetic Association. Journal 77, 4 (Oct. 1980): 434-439.
Vegetarian and macrobiotic children studied were slightly smaller and leaner than average.

1192 Dwyer, Johanna T.; Miller, Linda G.; Arduino, Nancy L.; Andrew, Elizabeth M.; Dietz, William H., Jr.; Reed, James C.; and Reed, Homer B. C., Jr. "Mental age and I.Q. of predominantly vegetarian children." American Dietetic Association. Journal 76, 2 (Feb. 1980): 142-147.
Vegetarian and macrobiotic children had mental ages averaging a year beyond their chronological ages, and had a mean I.Q. of 116.

1193 Dwyer, Johanna T.; Palombo, Ruth; Thorne, Halorie; Valadian, Isabelle; and Reed, Robert B. "Preschoolers on alternate lifestyle diets." American Dietetic Association. Journal 72, 3 (Mar. 1978): 264-270.
Measurements of 119 vegetarian and macrobiotic children found them to be slightly smaller, lighter and leaner than non-vegetarians.

1194 Erhard, Darla. "A starved child of the new vegetarians." Nutrition Today 8, 6 (Nov.-Dec. 1973): 10.
Description of severely malnourished child of parents adhering to strict cult diet.

1195 Feeley, Ruth M.; Staton, Annie L.; and Moyer, Elsie Z. "Fat metabolism in pre-adolescent children on

all-vegetable diets." American Dietetic Association. Journal 47 (Nov. 1965): 396-400.
Fat intake, fecal fat excretion and serum lipid levels were determined in 12 seven- to nine-year-old girls fed controlled low protein diets.

1196 Fomon, Samuel J., and Strauss, Ronald G. "Nutrient deficiencies in breast-fed infants." New England Journal of Medicine 299, 7 (Aug. 17, 1978): 355-357.
Editorial recommends routine supplementation of breast-fed infants with vitamin D, iron or other nutrients; urges vitamin B12 supplementation for infants of strict vegetarian mothers.

1197 Gupta, S.; Agarwal, K. N.; Khurana, V.; and Chawla, S. L. "Protein iron and alfa amino nitrogen contents in human milk." Archives of Child Health 15, 5 (Sept. 1973): 215-219.
Measurements of protein, iron, and alfa amino protein in colostrum, transitional and mature breast milk of Indian vegetarians and non-vegetarians.

1198 Gyllenswärd, Åke. "Nutritional defects in breast fed children." Läkartidningen 75, 5 (Dec. 20, 1978): 4782-4783. (In Swedish.)

1199 Hardinge, Mervyn G., and Mann, George V. "Raising infant on vegetarian diet." American Medical Association. Journal 227, 1 (Jan. 7, 1974): 88.
Question and answer column responds that lacto-ovo-vegetarian and lacto-vegetarian diets, if reasonably chosen and skillfully managed, are adequate for all age groups, including infants.

1200 Khanduja, P. C.; Agarwal, K. N.; and Taneja, P. N. "Haematological values of school children in different socio-economic groups." Indian Pediatrics 6, 9 (Sept. 1969): 577-587.
Hematological profiles of 673 Indian children in three different socio-economic groups and with differing dietary practices.

1201 Kishore, N.; Sharma, R. V.; Saxena, S. K.; and Prasad, R. "A study on serum glycoproteins in normal Indian children with special reference to

different age groups, sex, castes and their dietary habits." Indian Pediatrics 13, 1 (Jan. 1976): 7-12.
  122 infants and children studied to determine variations in proteins according to age, sex, caste and diet.

1202 MacLean, William C., Jr., and Graham, George G. "Vegetarianism in children." American Journal of Diseases of Children 134, 5 (May 1980): 513-519.
  Review of types of vegetarian diets, health status, potential nutritional problems, and dietary management of the vegetarian child.

1203 Moran, J. Roberto, and Greene, Harry L. "The B vitamins and vitamin C in human nutrition. 1. General considerations and 'obligatory' B vitamins." American Journal of Diseases of Children 133, 2 (Feb. 1979): 192-199.
  Review of metabolism, deficiency conditions and therapeutic use of B vitamins notes that some fad diets, such as health food, Zen macrobiotic and strict vegetarian diets, may be harmful to growing children.

1204 Peter, Molly Broughton. "Nursing mothers and environmental contaminants." U.S. Environmental Protection Agency. EPA Journal 4, 10 (Nov.-Dec. 1978): 13, 39.
  EPA is preparing a follow-up to 1975 study finding lower levels of pesticide residues, but no significant differences in PCB levels, in the milk of vegetarian mothers compared to non-vegetarians.

1205 Rigsby, G. Robert. "Vegetarian diet." American Medical Association. Journal 228, 4 (Apr. 22, 1974): 460.
  Brief letter defends raising children on vegetarian diet.

1206 Roberts, I. F.; West, R. J.; Ogilvie, D.; and Dillon, M. J. "Malnutrition in infants receiving cult diets: a form of child abuse." British Medical Journal 1, 6159 (Feb. 3, 1979): 296-298.
  Case histories of four severely malnourished infants receiving fruitarian and macrobiotic diets.

1207 Robson, J. R. K.; Konlande, J. E.; Larkin, F. A.;
      O'Connor, P. A.; Liu, Hsi-Yen; and Horner, J.
      M. "Zen macrobiotic diets." Lancet 1, 815 (June
      9, 1973): 1327.
      Analysis of kokoh, a Zen macrobiotic infant
      feeding mixture.

1208 Roy, Claude C.; Bagnell, Philip C.; Chance, Graham;
      Davidson, Georges F.; Habbick, Brian F.; Jones,
      Adrian B.; Pencharz, Paul; Ste.-Marie, Micheline;
      and Spady, Donald. "Infant feeding practices re-
      visited." Canadian Medical Association. Journal
      122, 9 (1980): 987-989.

1209 Scharffenberg, John A. "Vegetarian diets in children."
      Mayo Clinic Proceedings 54, 12 (Dec. 1979): 815.
      Letter challenges views presented in editorial
      in Aug. 1979 issue.

1210 Shull, M. W., and Dwyer, J. T. "Vegetarianism and
      breast feeding--a reply." Pediatrics 66, 1 (July
      1980): 157.

1211 Shull, M. W.; Reed, Robert B.; Valadian, Isabelle;
      Palombo, Ruth; Thorne, Halorie; and Dwyer, J.
      T. "Velocities of growth in vegetarian preschool
      children." Pediatrics 60, 4 (Oct. 1977): 410-417.
      Macrobiotic and vegetarian children studied were
      slightly shorter and weighed slightly less when
      compared to norms established by Harvard growth
      study; these differences seemed to disappear between
      the ages of three and five years.

1212 Shull, M. W.; Valadian, I.; Reed, R. B.; Palombo,
      R.; Thorne, H. and Dwyer, J. "Seasonal varia-
      tions in preschool vegetarian children's growth
      velocities." American Journal of Clinical Nutrition
      31, 1 (Jan. 1978): 1-2.
      Letter notes differences in growth rates of a
      group of vegetarian children in the Boston area
      compared to other children.

1213 Toppenberg, Glenn D. "Vegetarian diet." American
      Medical Association. Journal 228, 4 (Apr. 22,
      1974): 460.
      Letter takes exception to implications in earlier
      article that raising children as vegetarians is dif-
      ficult, irresponsible and ethically incorrect.

1214 Trahms, Cristine M., and Feeney, Moira C. "Evaluation of diet and growth of vegan, vegetarian and non-vegetarian preschool children." Federation Proceedings 33, 3 (1974): 675.
Some nutritional inadequacies were identified in most of the children studied; those on vegan diets seemed especially at risk. (Abstract only.)

1215 Zed, Christine A., and Heywood, Peter F. "The nutritional status of ovo-lacto-vegetarian and non-vegetarian preschool children." Nutrition Society of Australia. Proceedings 2 (1977): 85.
Both vegetarian and non-vegetarian children were adequately nourished, the former having lower mean serum cholesterol and lower intakes of saturated fat and cholesterol.

Young Adults
(See also: 957, 1122, 1124, 1175, 1176, 1381.)

1216 Anon. "Food revisionists." British Medical Journal (May 18, 1974): 345-346.
Editorial expresses concern for youthful food faddists adopting the macrobiotic diet.

1217 Bergan, James G.; Blazar, Marc; and Massi, Leo. "Evaluation of nutritional status of new vegetarians (macrobiotics): biochemical status." Federation Proceedings 34, 3 (1975): 897.
Second part of study to assess nutritional status of macrobiotics. (Abstract only.)

1218 Bergan, James G., and Brown, Phyllis T. "Nutritional status of 'new' vegetarians." American Dietetic Association. Journal 76, 2 (Feb. 1980): 151-155.
Nutritional assessment of 76 "vegetarians," many of whom consumed fish, found them to be extremely lean and consuming acceptable diets with respect to most nutrients.

1219 Brown, P. T., and Bergan, J. G. "The dietary status of 'new' vegetarians." American Dietetic Association. Journal 67, 5 (Nov. 1975): 455-459.
Study of food habits and nutrient intakes of 60 followers of the Zen macrobiotic diet.

1220 Brown, P. T., and Bergan, J. G. "The dietary status of practicing macrobiotics: a preliminary
communication." Ecology of Food and Nutrition
4, 2 (1975): 103-107.
Inadequate intakes of energy, riboflavin, calcium, iron and niacin were found in a 10-day study
of eight individuals consuming Zen macrobiotic
diets.

1221 Dwyer, Johanna T.; Kandel, Randy F.; Mayer, Laura
D. V. H.; and Mayer, Jean. "The 'new' vegetarians; group affiliation and dietary strictures
related to attitudes and life style." American Dietetic Association. Journal 64, 4 (Apr. 1974):
376-382.
Interrelation between degree of food avoidances
and affiliation with vegetarian groups in survey of
100 young adults who called themselves vegetarians.

1222 Dwyer, Johanna T., and Mayer, Jean. "Vegetarianism in drug users." Lancet 2, 739 (Dec. 25,
1971): 1429-1430.
Letter expresses concern for "hard-core" young
adult vegetarians whose diet serves to prevent a
relapse into drug use. (See also no. 1232.)

1223 Dwyer, Johanna T.; Mayer, L.; Kandel, R.; and
Mayer, J. "The new vegetarians: food avoidances
and attitudes of 100 young vegetarians." Federation Proceedings 32, 1 (1973): 937.
Patterns of food avoidance in young adults limit-
ing consumption of animal foods. (Abstract only.)

1224 Dwyer, Johanna T.; Mayer, L. D. V. H.; Kandel,
R. F.; and Mayer, J. "The new vegetarians;
who are they?" American Dietetic Association
Journal 62, 5 (May 1973): 503-509.
Interview and questionnaire results from 100
young vegetarians not affiliated with any organized
religious group revealed diverse dietary habits,
lifestyles, and attitudes toward health professionals;
nearly 40 percent or more interviewed consumed
poultry and/or fish.

1225 Dwyer, Johanna T.; Mayer, Laura D. V. H.; Dowd,
Kathryn; Kandel, Randy Frances; and Mayer, Jean.
"The new vegetarians: the natural high?" Ameri-

can Dietetic Association. Journal 65, 5 (Nov.
1974): 529-536.
Investigation of attitudes, opinions, reasons for
dietary modifications in 100 youthful so-called
vegetarians.

1226 Erhard, Darla. "The new vegetarians. Part I.
Vegetarianism and its medical consequences."
Nutrition Today 8, 6 (Nov.-Dec. 1973): 4-9, 11-
12.
Medical and nutritional problems created by
counterculture groups practicing pseudo-religious,
extremely restrictive diets. Author characterizes
these cult members as sincere, well-educated,
self-reliant, socially mobile, having no unifying
philosophical movement or coherent doctrine, frequently malnourished, and riddled with nutrition
foibles and misinformation.

1227 Erhard, Darla. "The new vegetarians. Part II.
The Zen Macrobiotic movement and other cults
based on vegetarianism." Nutrition Today 9, 1
(Jan.-Feb. 1974): 20-25, 27.
History, philosophical precepts, and nutritional
practices of such cults as Zen Macrobiotics, Eh-
ret's Mucusless Diet Healing System, Messiah's
Crusade, and Krishna Consciousness.

1228 Erhard, Darla. "Nutrition education for the 'Now'
generation." Journal of Nutrition Education 2, 4
(Spr. 1971): 135-139.
Author's efforts to provide factual nutrition in-
formation to members of various San Francisco
Bay area counterculture groups, including Zen
Macrobiotics, One World Family Commune, Krish-
nas, and fruitarians.

1229 Frankle, Reva T., and Heussenstamm, F. K. "Food
zealotry and youth: new dilemmas for professionals." American Journal of Public Health 64, 1
(Jan. 1974): 11-18.
Description of nontraditional diet patterns, such
as vegetarianism, natural foods, macrobiotics, being adopted by American youths; stresses importance of communication between health professionals
and counterculture individuals.

1230 Jenkins, Robert R. "Health implications of vegetarian diet." American College Health Association. Journal 24, 2 (Dec. 1975): 68-71.
Guidelines, background information, health advantages of vegetarian diet.

1231 Lindamood, Diane M., and Gunning, Barbara E. "College nonvegetarians vs. vegetarians: food habits and knowledge." Journal of Nutrition Education 9, 1 (Jan.-Mar. 1977): 25.
Questionnaire finds no significant difference in nutrition knowledge between vegetarian and nonvegetarians; results indicate pronounced need for nutrition education for college age students.

1232 Mann, George V. "Vegetarianism and drug users." Lancet 1, 746 (Feb. 12, 1972): 381.
Letter cites errors; disputes methodology and conclusions of study by Dwyer and Mayer. (See also no. 1222.)

1233 Marino, Deborah Dunlap, and King, Janet C. "Nutritional concerns during adolescence." Pediatric Clinics of North America 27, 1 (1980): 125-140.

1234 Robson, John R. K. "Food faddism." Pediatric Clinics of North America 24, 1 (Feb. 1977): 189-201.
Discussion of wide range of food fads and cults, social and cultural influences, and role of physician in evaluating and counseling patients consuming alternative diets.

1235 Shimoda, Naomi. "Nutrition and life style. II. Observations of a nutritionist in a free clinic." American Dietetic Association. Journal 63, 3 (Sept. 1973): 273-275.
Relates experiences dealing with vegetarians, macrobiotics, fruitarians and organic foods advocates; stresses need for flexibility, objectivity, and thorough knowledge of nutrition.

Vegans
(For early works, see 131, 136, 137, 138,
190, 219, 222, 249, 252, 253, 263,
265, 301, 302, 305, 319.)

(For fruitarians, see 139, 140, 198, 199,
    245, 364, 873, 899, 1206.)
(For contemporary medical studies, see
    899, 904, 911, 947, 948, 1127, 1132,
    1214.)
(For general interest works, see 322, 346,
    369, 393, 397, 422, 424, 472, 486,
    490, 538, 595, 608, 610, 612, 619,
    651, 652, 653, 734, 735, 762, 768.)

1236   Anon. "Plasma apoprotein and lipoprotein lipid levels
       in vegetarians." South African Medical Journal
       54, 25 (1978): 104.
           Brief report on cholesterol levels in members
       of the Tennessee vegan community, The Farm.
       (In Dutch.)

1237   Anon. "Vegetarian diet and vitamin B12 deficiency."
       Nutrition Reviews 36, 8 (Aug. 1978): 243-244.
           Case of vitamin B12 deficiency in strict vege-
       tarian of 25 years apparently due to subtle mal-
       absorption of vitamin B12.

1238   Anon. "Vitamin B12 deficiency in the breast-fed in-
       fant of a strict vegetarian." Nutrition Reviews 37,
       5 (1979): 142-144.
           Review of case of clinical vitamin B12 deficiency
       in infant.

1239   Aries, Vivienne C.; Crowther, J. S.; Drasar, B. S.;
       Hill, M. J.; and Ellis, F. R. "Effect of a strict
       vegetarian diet on the fecal flora and fecal steroid
       concentration." Journal of Pathology 103, 1 (1971):
       54-56.
           Comparison of fecal flora and steroids in Eng-
       lish strict vegetarians and those living on a mixed
       diet revealed no gross differences in flora, but
       smaller amounts of certain steroids and total bile
       acids in the strict vegetarians.

1240   Brooks, R., and Kemm, J. R. "Vegan diet and life-
       style; a preliminary study by postal questionnaire."
       Nutrition Society. Proceedings 38, 1 (May 1,
       1979): 15A.
           Demographic study of vegan population sample.
       (Abstract only.)

1241　Burslem, John; Schonfeld, Gustav; Howald, Mary;
　　　Weidman, Stuart W.; and Miller, J. Philip.
　　　"Plasma apoprotein and lipoprotein lipid levels in
　　　vegetarians." Metabolism 27, 6 (June 1978): 711-
　　　719.
　　　　　Study indicates lower risks for the development
　　　of atherosclerosis in vegetarians consuming no
　　　animal products.

1242　Carmel, R. "Nutritional vitamin B12 deficiency.
　　　Possible contributory role of subtle vitamin B12
　　　malabsorption." Annals of Internal Medicine 88,
　　　5 (May 1978): 647-649.
　　　　　Vegan of 25 years developed severe vitamin
　　　B12 deficiency as result of both dietary restriction
　　　and subtle malabsorption.

1243　Carmel, Ralph. "Nutritional vitamin B12 deficiency:
　　　possible contributory role of subtle vitamin B12
　　　malabsorption." American Journal of Clinical
　　　Nutrition 31, 4 (1978): 706.
　　　　　Case history of vitamin B12 deficiency possibly
　　　due to malabsorption in vegan of 25 years duration.
　　　(Abstract only.)

1244　Charghi, G. "The biochemical syndrome of raw vege-
　　　tarians." Bordeaux Medical 13, 15 (1980): 711-
　　　713, 715-716.
　　　　　Raw vegetable diet produced a considerable de-
　　　crease in blood cholesterol, urea, uric acid, blood
　　　sugar and in total proteins. (In French.)

1245　Chen, J. S., and Kao, J. T. "Serum vitamin B12,
　　　iron and total iron binding capacity levels in strict
　　　vegetarians and nonvegetarians by radiosorbent
　　　assay." Clinical Chemistry 21, 7 (June 1975):
　　　1007-1008.
　　　　　Calculations of B12, iron, and total iron bind-
　　　ing capacity in vegans and non-vegetarians. (Ab-
　　　stract only.)

1246　Cotes, J. E.; Dabbs, J. M.; Hall, A. M.; McDonald,
　　　A.; Miller, D. S.; Mumford, P.; and Saunders,
　　　M. J. "Possible effect of a vegan diet upon lung
　　　function and the cardio-respiratory response to
　　　submaximal exercise in healthy women." Journal
　　　of Physiology 209 (1970): 30P-32P.

Study of vegan women and controls found no evidence for the hypothesis that lack of animal protein impairs the physiological response to exercise.

1247 Dastur, Darab K.; Santhadevi, N.; Quadros, Edward V.; Gagrot, Bomi M.; Wadia, Noshir H.; Desai, Meher M.; Singhal, Bhim S.; and Bharucha, Eddie P. "Interrelationships between the B-vitamins in B12-deficiency neuromyelopathy. A possible malabsorption-malnutrition syndrome." American Journal of Clinical Nutrition 28, 11 (Nov. 1975): 1255-1270.
    Case histories and successful treatment of five strict vegetarians in India suffering from vitamin B12 deficiency resulting from intestinal malabsorption and possible malnutrition.

1248 Dickerson, J. W. T.; Sanders, T. A. B.; and Ellis, F. R. "The effects of a vegetarian and vegan diet on plasma and erythrocyte lipids." Qualitas Plantarum--Plant Foods for Human Nutrition 29, 1-2 (July 6, 1979): 85-94.
    Vegans studied had lower serum cholesterol and triglycerides and higher short chain polyunsaturated fatty acids, especially linoleic and linolenic acids.

1249 Ellis, F. R., and Sanders, T. A. B. "Angina and vegan diet." American Heart Journal 93, 6 (June 1977): 803-805.
    Advantages of diet containing no animal products is described in case histories of four patients successfully treated for angina pectoris through the use of vegan diets.

1250 Ellis, F. R., and Sanders, T. A. B. "Angina and vegetarian diet." Lancet 1, 7970 (May 29, 1976): 1290.
    Letter describing successful treatment of angina pectoris with a diet devoid of all animal products.

1251 Ellis, Frey R., and Montegriffo, V. M. E. "The health of vegans." Plant Foods for Human Nutrition 2, 2 (1971): 93-103.
    Review article summarizes long-term effects of vegan diet: vegans tend to be lighter in weight, have lower cholesterol and blood urea levels, and

may be protected against ischemic heart disease
and colon cancer.

1252 Ellis, Frey R. , and Montegriffo, V. M. E. "Vegan-
      ism, clinical findings and investigations. " Amer-
      ican Journal of Clinical Nutrition 23, 3 (Mar.
      1970): 249-255.
          Comprehensive clinical examinations of 26 vegans
      and 24 omnivore controls determined that the veg-
      ans were lighter in weight, had lower serum B12,
      lower serum cholesterol, and higher serum folate
      levels than controls; no significant differences be-
      tween the clinical states of the two groups were
      found.

1253 Ellis, Frey R. , and Mumford, Pamela. "The nutri-
      tional status of vegans and vegetarians. " Nutrition
      Society. Proceedings 26, 2 (1967): 205-212.
          Nutritional and clinical study of vegans found
      them remarkably normal; also surveys scientific
      literature on veganism and vegetarianism.

1254 Ellis, Frey R. ; West, E. D. ; and Sanders, T. A. B.
      "The health of vegans compared with omnivores:
      assessment by health questionnaire. " Plant Foods
      for Man 2, 1-2 (1976): 43-52.
          No differences in health status were found be-
      tween vegan males and omnivore male controls;
      female vegans appeared to have better health status
      than female omnivore controls.

1255 Frader, Joel. "Vitamin B12 deficiency in strict vege-
      tarians. " New England Journal of Medicine 299,
      23 (Dec. 7, 1978): 1319.
          Letter describes case of severe vitamin B12
      deficiency and iron in infant of strict vegetarian
      mother taking no supplements.

1256 Fredericks, Carlton. "How does the vegetarian avoid
      B12 deficiency?" Prevention 31, 4 (Apr. 1979):
      47.
          Brief communication cites sources and synthesis
      of B12 by vegans.

1257 Fredericks, Carlton. "The unfortunate baby of a
      strict vegetarian. " Prevention 30, 12 (Dec. 1978):
      44-45.

Brief mention of vitamin B12 deficiency in infant of strict vegetarian.

1258 Fulton, Jean Roberts; Hutton, C. W.; and Stitt, K. R. "Preschool vegetarian children; dietary and anthropomorphic data." American Dietetic Association. Journal 76, 4 (Apr. 1980): 360-365.
Dietary and anthropomorphic data on 48 two- to five-year-old vegan children living in Summertown, Tennessee.

1259 Guggenheim, K.; Weiss, Y.; and Fostick, M. "Composition and nutritive value of diets consumed by strict vegetarians." British Journal of Nutrition 16 (1962): 467-474.
Diets of 119 strict vegetarians studied for one week were found to be inadequate in riboflavin, methionine and tryptophan.

1260 Haler, David. "Death after vegan diet." Lancet 2, 560 (July 20, 1968): 170.
Letter clarifies report of death of elderly woman consuming grossly abnormal, but not vegan, diet.

1261 Hershaft, Alex. "Vitamin B12 deficiency in strict vegetarians." New England Journal of Medicine 299, 23 (Dec. 7, 1978): 1319-1320.
Letter cites errors in report of vitamin B12 deficiency in breast-fed infant of strict vegetarian mother, and reviews health advantages of vegan diet as reported in medical literature.

1262 Higginbottom, Marilyn C.; Sweetman, L.; and Nyhan, W. L. "A syndrome of methylmalonic aciduria, homocystinuria, megaloblastic anemia and neurologic abnormalities in a vitamin B12-deficient breast-fed infant of a strict vegetarian." New England Journal of Medicine 299, 7 (Aug. 17, 1978): 317-323.
Case history and successful treatment of a six-month-old infant suffering from severe vitamin B12 deficiency and related complications; the vegan mother had eaten no foods of animal origin nor taken vitamin B12 supplements for eight years.

1263 Hines, John D. "Megaloblastic anemia in an adult vegan." American Journal of Clinical Nutrition

19, 4 (Oct. 1966): 260-268.
Case of megaloblastic anemia and vitamin B12
deficiency in forty-one-year-old male vegan.

1264 Hughes, Jane, and Sanders, T. A. B. "Riboflavin
levels in the diet and breast milk of vegans and
omnivores." Nutrition Society. Proceedings 38,
2 (1979): 95A.
Mean breast milk riboflavin concentration was
lower in vegan mothers than in omnivores. (Abstract only.)

1265 Jagenburg, R., and Svanborg, A. "Self-induced protein-calorie malnutrition in a healthy male."
Acta Medica Scandinavica 183, 1 (Jan.-Feb. 1968):
67-71.
Clinical studies of prolonged fast by 34-year-
old vegan male indicated that diets low in calories
and protein can be remarkedly well tolerated.

1266 Jensen, R. G.; Clark, R. M.; and Ferris, A. M.
"Composition of lipids in human milk: a review."
Lipids 15, 5 (May 1980): 345-355.
Literature review pertaining to composition of
human milk contains table comparing fatty acids
in vegans and omnivore controls.

1267 Kurtha, Ali N., and Ellis, Frey R. "Investigation
into the causation of the electroencephalogram ab-
normality in vegans." Plant Foods for Human
Nutrition 2, 2 (1971): 53-59.
Study of nutritional factors which could cause
abnormal EEG's in some vegans.

1268 Kurtha, Ali N., and Ellis, Frey R. "The nutritional,
clinical, and economic aspects of vegan diets."
Plant Foods for Human Nutrition 2, 1 (1970): 13-
22.
Review of two decades of research on vegans
indicates that after supplementation with vitamin
B12, the vegan diet provides adequate nutrients
for maintaining health.

1269 Lampkin, Beatrice C., and Saunders, E. F. "Nutritional vitamin B12 deficiency in an infant." Journal of Pediatrics 75, 6 (Dec. 1969): 1053-1055.
Case of megaloblastic anemia in 10-month-old
infant of a strict vegetarian.

1270 Lange, Henrik F. "Veganism and pernicious anemia."
      Nordisk Medicin 77, 5 (1967): 160. (In Norwe-
      gian.)

1271 Long, A. "Vitamin B12 for vegetarians and vegans."
      BNF Nutrition Bulletin (Jan. 1978): 222-223.
      Brief discussion of various sources of vitamin
      B12 for vegetarians and vegans.

1272 Long, Alan. "Vitamin B12 for vegans." British
      Medical Journal 2, 6080 (July 16, 1977): 192.
      Researcher for the Vegetarian Society of the
      United Kingdom takes issue with statement that
      plant sources of vitamin B12 are not available
      and offers list of vegetarian and vegan sources to
      doctors and dieticians.

1273 McKenzie, J. C. "Social and economic implications
      of minority food habits." Nutrition Society. Pro-
      ceedings 26, 2 (1967): 197-205.
      Vegan philosophy and habits discussed, in addi-
      tion to those of religious groups and immigrant
      groups.

1274 Mayer, Jean. "Can man live by vegetables alone?"
      Family Health 5 (Feb. 1973): 33, 48.
      Risks of strict vegetarian diets.

1275 Miller, Derek S., and Mumford, Pamela. "The nu-
      tritive value of western vegan diets and vegetarian
      diets." Plant Foods for Human Nutrition 2, 3-4
      (1972): 201-213.
      Analysis of British vegan and vegetarian diets.

1276 Misra, H. N., and Fallowfield, J. M. "Subacute
      combined degeneration of the spinal cord in a veg-
      an." Postgraduate Medical Journal 45, 551 (Sept.
      1971): 624-626.
      Case report and successful treatment of spinal
      cord degeneration in a 62-year-old vegan woman.

1277 Murphy, Michael F. "Vitamin B12 deficiency due to
      a low-cholesterol diet in a vegetarian." Annals
      of Internal Medicine 94, 1 (Jan. 1981): 57-58.
      After four years of vegan diet for treatment of
      angina, patient began to exhibit signs of vitamin
      B12 deficiency.

1278 Nofziger, Margaret. "B12 for complete vegetarians."
      Vegetarian Times (Mar.-Apr. 1977): 18-19.
      Nutritionist for vegan community, The Farm,
      discusses sources of vitamin B12. Advises sup-
      plementation for all strict vegetarians.

1279 Payne, R. W., and Savage, B. F. "Vitamin B12 for
      vegans." British Medical Journal 2, 6084 (Aug. 13,
      1977): 458.
      Letter discounts reports that comfrey leaves
      are a source of vitamin B12 for vegetarians or
      vegans.

1280 Purves, Rebecca, and Sanders, T. A. B. "An as-
      sessment of the nutritional health of preschool
      vegan children." Nutrition Society. Proceedings
      39, 3 (Sept. 1980): 79A.
      Study of 25 vegan children concludes that al-
      though tending to be shorter and lighter in weight,
      children can be successfully raised on a properly
      constructed vegan diet.

1281 Register, U. D.; Blankenship, J. W.; Mak, Jenny
      L.; and Zimmerman, G. J. "Effect of diet on
      serum, fecal, and urinary vitamin B12 levels of
      total vegetarians." Federation Proceedings 36, 3
      (1977): 1121.
      Studies indicate that a significant amount of vita-
      min B12 synthesized by intestinal bacteria is ab-
      sorbed in strict vegetarians. (Abstract only.)

1282 Rendle-Short, J.; Tiernan, J. R.; and Hawgood, S.
      "Vegan mothers with vitamin B12 deficiency."
      Medical Journal of Australia 2, 9 (Nov. 3, 1979):
      483.
      Letter briefly describes two cases of vitamin
      B12 deficiency in infants of vegan mothers.

1283 Sanders, T. A. B. "The health and nutritional status
      of vegans." Plant Foods for Man 2, 3-4 (1978):
      181-193.
      Review of medical studies on vegans for the
      past 25 years concludes that the vegan diet is ade-
      quate provided it is supplemented with vitamin
      B12, and that it probably protects against ischemic
      heart disease and colon cancer.

1284   Sanders, T. A. B. "How adequate are vegan diets
         for children?" Health Visit 53, 8 (Aug. 1980):
         319-322.

1285   Sanders, T. A. B. "Malnutrition in infants receiving
         cult diets." British Medical Journal 1, 6164 (Mar.
         10, 1979): 682-683.
            Letter disputes claims that vegan diet is inade-
         quate for children.

1286   Sanders, T. A. B., and Ellis, Frey R. Vegan nutri-
         tion. Surrey, England, Vegan Society, 1979.
            Booklet details guidelines for balanced vegan
         diet.

1287   Sanders, T. A. B.; Ellis, F. R.; and Dickerson, J.
         W. T. "Haematological studies on vegans."
         British Journal of Nutrition 40, 1 (July 1978): 9-
         15.
            Determinations were made of vitamin B12, fola-
         cin concentrations and blood counts in Caucasian
         vegans and omnivore controls; conclusion was that
         megaloblastic anemia is very rare in Caucasian
         vegans, and that a diet of plant foods is adequate
         for normal blood formation as long as it is varied
         and is supplemented with vitamin B12.

1288   Sanders, T. A. B.; Ellis, F. R.; and Dickerson, J.
         W. T. "Serum cholesterol and triglycerides con-
         centrations in vegans." Nutrition Society. Pro-
         ceedings 36, 1 (May 1977): 43A.
            Serum cholesterol and triglyceride levels were
         significantly lower in vegans than in omnivores,
         suggesting that the vegan diet may be the diet of
         choice in treatment of certain types of hyperlipi-
         demia. (Abstract only.)

1289   Sanders, T. A. B.; Ellis, F. R.; and Dickerson, J.
         W. T. "Studies of vegans: the fatty acid com-
         position of plasma choline phosphoglycerides, ery-
         throcytes, adipose tissue, and breast milk, and
         some indicators of susceptibility to ischemic heart
         disease in vegans and omnivore controls." Amer-
         ican Journal of Clinical Nutrition 31, 5 (May 1978):
         805-813.
            Vegans had lower weights, skinfold thickness
         measurements, vitamin B12, cholesterol and tri-

glyceride concentrations than controls. In light of
the markedly lower serum cholesterol concentrations, the authors conclude that a diet devoid of
all animal products may be the best treatment for
ischemic heart disease, angina pectoris and certain hyperlipidemias.

1290 Shun, Duk Jhe, and Kabakow, Bernard. "Nutritional
megaloblastic anemia in vegan." New York State
Journal of Medicine 72, 23 (Dec. 1, 1972): 2893-
2894.
Case of megaloblastic anemia due to vitamin
B12 deficiency in 68-year-old male vegan of sixteen years.

1291 Shurtleff, William. "Sources of vegetarian vitamin
B12." Vegetarian Times (May-June 1979): 36-37,
39-40.
Reliable non-meat sources of vitamin B12, especially in fermented soy foods, single cell proteins and sea vegetables.

1292 Smith, A. D. M. "Veganism: a clinical survey with
observations on vitamin B12 metabolism." British
Medical Journal 1 (June 16, 1962): 1655-1658.
Nine of twelve vegans investigated clinically
demonstrated complete absence of symptoms of
vitamin B12 deficiency; EEG's were normal in only
two subjects.

1293 Stewart, J. S.; Roberts, P. D.; and Hoffbrand, A. V.
"Response of dietary vitamin B12 deficiency in
physiological oral doses of cyanocobalamin."
Lancet 2, 672 (Sept. 12, 1970): 542-545.
Case of strict vegetarian Hindu with megaloblastic anemia; cites increase in vitamin B12 deficiency in areas of Britain in which the proportion
of Indian immigrants is relatively high.

1294 Sweetman, L.; Higginbottom, M.; and Nyham, W. L.
"Homocystinuria and methylmalonic aciduria: a
consequence of B12 deficiency in the breast-fed
infant of a strict vegetarian." Clinical Research
26, 2 (1978): 115A.

1295 Thomas, J.; Ellis, F. R.; and Diggory, P. L. C.
"The health of vegans during pregnancy." Nutrition

Society. Proceedings 36, 1 (May 1977): 46A.
Study finds that still-births, toxemia and anemia
were no more prevalent in vegan pregnancies than
in those of controls. (Abstract only.)

1296 Trahms, C. M.; Clements, C. L.; Knapp, B. J.;
Labbe, R. L.; and Scott, C. R. "Restriction of
growth and elevated protoporphyrin in children deprived of animal protein." Clinical Research 25, 2
(1977): 179A.
Nine vegan children were lighter and shorter
than vegetarian children. (Abstract only.)

1297 Trahms, Cristine M. "Catch-up growth in children
previously deprived of animal protein." Federation
Proceedings 36, 3 (1977): 1181.
Change from a vegan diet to a vegetarian diet
resulted in significant improvement in growth in
preschool children. (Abstract only.)

1298 Turner, R. W. D. "Vegan diet and health." British
Medical Journal 1, 6163 (Mar. 3, 1979): 613.
Letter recounts numerous health, ethical and
economic advantages of vegan diet.

1299 West, E. D. "The psychological health of vegans
compared with two other groups." Plant Foods
for Human Nutrition 2, 3-4 (Mar. 1972): 147-149.

1300 West, Eric D., and Ellis, Frey R. "The electroencephalogram in veganism, vegetarianism, vitamin
B12 deficiency and in controls." Journal of Neurology, Neurosurgery and Psychiatry 29, 5 (1966):
391-397.
The EEG's of vegans were found to be different
from those of controls, vegetarians, patients with
pernicious anemia, and patients with folic acid
deficiency.

1301 Wighton, M. C.; Manson, J. I.; Speed, I.; Robertson,
E.; and Chapman, E. "Brain damage in infancy
and dietary vitamin B12 deficiency." Medical Journal of Australia 2, 1 (July 14, 1979): 1-3.
Report of treatment of severe neurological de-
terioration due to vitamin B12 deficiency in infant
of strict vegetarian.

1302 Winawer, S. J.; Streiff, R. R.; and Zamcheck, N. "Gastric and hematological abnormalities in a vegan with nutritional vitamin B12 deficiency: effect of oral vitamin B12." Gastroenterology 53, 1 (July 1967): 130-135.
Case of nutritional vitamin B12 deficiency and megaloblastic anemia in Seventh-day Adventist vegan of 50 years.

1303 Wokes, Frank; Badenoch, J.; and Sinclair, H. M. "Human dietary deficiency of vitamin B12." American Journal of Clinical Nutrition 3, 5 (Sept. -Oct. 1955): 375-382.
Study of incidence of vitamin B12 deficiency in British vegans in relation to duration on vegan diet, symptoms presented, blood and urine analyses; compares results with those of Dutch and American vegans.

1304 Zmora, Ehud; Gorodischer, Rafael; and Bar-Ziv, Jacob. "Multiple nutritional deficiencies in infants from a strict vegetarian community." American Journal of Diseases of Children 133, 2 (Feb. 1979): 141-144.
Report of four cases of severe nutritional deficiencies in infants from strict vegetarian commune of Black Hebrews in Israel; deficiencies resulted from restrictive diets profoundly low in both calories and protein.

Miscellaneous

1305 Allen, K. G. D.; Klevay, L. M.; and Springer, H. L. "The zinc and copper content of seeds and nuts." Nutrition Reports International 16, 3 (1977): 227-230.
Determination of zinc and copper content of various seeds and nuts; emphasizes their value in diets of vegetarians.

1306 Aly, Karl-Otto, and Öckerman, Per-Arne. "Fasting and vegetarianism--a therapeutic alternative." Läkartidningen 75, 28-29 (July 12, 1978): 2619-2622. (In Swedish.)

1307   Andersson, Iris; Andersson, Sonja; Eriksson, Ragnar;
        Joost-Davidsson, Alva; Larsson, Lasse; Lind-
        ström, Folke; Lindström, Viola; and Sköldstam,
        Lars. "Treatment of rheumatoid arthritis with
        fasting and lacto-vegetarian diet." Läkartidningen
        76, 40 (Oct. 3, 1979): 3425-3427. (In Swedish.)

1308   Arora, R. B.; Saxena, K. N.; Choudhury, M. Roy;
        and Choudhury, R. R. "Sperm studies on Indian
        men." Fertility and Sterility 12, 4 (July-Aug.
        1961): 365-367.
        Semen analysis of 193 Indian males found no
        significant differences between vegetarians and non-
        vegetarians.

1309   Arunachalam, J.; Gangadharan, S.; and Yegnasubra-
        manian, S. "Elemental data on human hair sam-
        pled from Indian student population and their in-
        terpretation for studies in environmental exposure."
        In: International Symposium on Nuclear Activation
        Techniques in the Life Sciences. Proceedings.
        Vienna, 1978, p. 499-513.
        Vegetarian and non-vegetarian Indian students
        differed in mineral content of their hair.

1310   Banerjee, B., and Saha, N. "Blood uric acid level
        of Indian and Western adults and its seasonal vari-
        ation." Indian Medical Association. Journal 48,
        5 (Mar. 1, 1967): 207-210.
        Non-vegetarians had higher levels of blood uric
        acid than comparable vegetarians.

1311   Barrow, J. Gordon; Quinlan, Carroll B.; Edmands,
        Robert E.; Whitner, Virginia S.; and Goodloe,
        Mary Helen R. "Comparison by gas chromatog-
        raphy of the fatty acid content of adipose tissue
        with dietary intake of fat in vegetarian and non-
        vegetarian males." Circulation 22, 4 (1960): 720-
        721.

1312   Barua, M. J., and Bhatt, J. V. "Preliminary study
        in skinfold measurements of vegetarians and non-
        vegetarians." Indian Journal of Physiology and
        Pharmacology 22, 2 (April-June 1978): 228.
        Indian non-vegetarians had greater skin fold
        measurements than vegetarians; discussion of lipo-
        genic effect of non-vegetarian diet. (Abstract only.)

1313   Bengsch, Harold. "The nature of shellfish and eco-
       logical factors contribute to their role in food
       borne human disease." Journal of Environmental
       Health 34, 4 (Jan. -Feb. 1972): 373-378.
           Human diseases including polio, typhoid, hepa-
       titis, gastroenteritis, paralytic shellfish poisoning,
       contracted from eating infected shellfish.

1314   Bentler, W. "Residues in food of animal origin--
       avoidable or unavoidable?" Hippokrates 44, 3
       (Oct. 1973): 243-268. (In German.)

1315   Bhattacharya, R. D. "Circadian rhythm of urinary
       electrolytes from homogenous subjects with vege-
       tarian food habits." Chronobiologia 6, 2 (Apr. -
       June 1979): 79.
           Abstract of study of circadian rhythm for ex-
       creted electrolytes in fifty healthy vegetarian stu-
       dents.

1316   Bhushan, S.; Pandey, R. C.; Singh, S. P.; Pandey,
       D. N.; and Seth, P. "Some observations on hu-
       man semen analysis." Indian Journal of Physiology
       and Pharmacology 22, 4 (1978): 393-396.
           Semen analysis revealed some significantly dif-
       ferent levels in vegetarian and non-vegetarian In-
       dian medical students.

1317   Biddulph, John. "A meal of pig." Clinical Pediatrics
       12, 2 (Feb. 1973): 124.
           Brief description of enteritis necroticans, a se-
       vere inflammatory disease of the small bowel af-
       fecting New Guinea children following large meals
       of pork.

1318   Bodzy, Pamela W.; Freeland, Jeanne H.; Eppright,
       Margaret A.; and Tyree, Ann. "Zinc status in
       the vegetarian." Federation Proceedings 36, 3
       (1977): 1139.
           Vegetarians and vegans had lower levels of
       zinc than controls, suggesting that the high fiber
       and phytate content of the vegetarian diet may lead
       to a decrease in zinc status. (Abstract only.)

1319   Botez, M. I.; Cadotte, M.; Beaulieu, R.; Pichette,
       L. P.; and Pison, C. "Neurologic disorders re-
       sponsive to folic acid therapy." Canadian Medical

Association. Journal 115, 3 (Aug. 7, 1976): 217-223.
Case histories of acquired and inborn folate deficiency in six women, one of whom was a vegan.

1320 Branch, W. J.; Southgate, D. A. T.; and James, W. P. T. "Binding of calcium by dietary fibre: its relationship to unsubstituted uronic acids." Nutrition Society. Proceedings 34, 3 (Dec. 1975): 120 A.
Investigation of possible limitation of calcium absorption by high-fiber or vegetarian diets. (Abstract only.)

1321 Brodie, M. J.; Boobis, A. R.; Toverud, E. L.; Ellis, W.; Murray, S.; Dollery, C. T.; Webster, S.; and Harrison, R. "Drug metabolism in white vegetarians." British Journal of Clinical Pharmacology 9, 5 (May 1980): 523-525.
Only slight differences were found in the clearance rates of three drugs in vegetarians and non-vegetarians, indicating that daily protein consumption levels, not intake of animal fat, accounted for similarity of drug metabolism between the two groups.

1322 Brown, Ellen D.; Howard, Mary P.; and Smith, J. Cecil, Jr. "The copper content of regular, vegetarian and renal diets." Federation Proceedings 36, 3 (1977): 1122.
Copper content of three hospital diets was found to be lower than recommended. (Abstract only.)

1323 Brown, Ellen D.; McGuckin, Mary Ann; Smith, J. Cecil, Jr.; and Finkelstein, James D. "The zinc content of regular, vegetarian and renal diets." Federation Proceedings 35, 3 (1976): 360.
Regular and vegetarian hospital diets studied provided 95 percent of the RDA for zinc, whereas renal diets supplied about 50 percent of the RDA. (Abstract only.)

1324 Brown, Ellen D.; McGuckin, Mary Ann; Wilson, M.; and Smith, J. C., Jr. "Zinc in selected hospital diets." American Dietetic Association. Journal 69, 6 (Dec. 1976): 632-635.
Analysis of sample hospital meals for zinc in regular, vegetarian and renal diets.

1325 Canelas, Horacio M.; de Jorge, Francisco Bastos; and Tognola, Waldir A. "Metabolic balances of copper in patients with hepatolenticular degeneration submitted to vegetarian and mixed diets." Journal of Neurology, Neuro-Surgery and Psychiatry 30, 4 (Aug. 1967): 371-373.
    Vegetarian diets induced a marked decrease in positive copper balance in two patients with hepatolenticular degeneration.

1326 Capó, Nicolás. Medicina naturista de urgencia: trofología práctica y trofoterapia: las vitaminas, citroterapia, curación de las enfermedades por la regeneración de los órganos en distrofia. Barcelona, Spain, Instituto de Trofoterapia, 1973.

1327 Capó, Nicolás. Curación del reumatismo. Cómo curar la gripe.... Barcelona, Spain, N. Capo, 1973.

1328 Catar, G. "New aspects of toxoplasmosis transmission." Bratislavske Lekarske Listy 62, 5 (1974): 516-523.
    Meat eaters are more often infected with toxoplasmosis than vegetarians, and cats have been found to be definite hosts. (In Slovak.)

1329 Chatterjea, M. N.; Chopra, S. K.; and Grover, J. "Studies on serum amylase levels in normal Indian subjects." Medical Journal Armed Forces, India. 31, 1 (1975): 37-42.
    Serum amylase levels were found to be higher in vegetarians than in non-vegetarians.

1330 Christensen, A. "Food, life habits and health." Ugeskrift for Laeger 140, 37 (Sept. 11, 1978): 2250-2252. (In Danish.)

1331 Ciuca, A. L. "Longevity and social conditions." MMW--Münchener Medizinische Wochenschrift 107, 43 (Oct. 22, 1965): 2095-2100.
    Altitudes of 400-700 meters and diet based on vegetable and milk foods appear to favor longevity.

1332 Cole, H. H.; Gass, G. H.; Gerrits, R. J.; Hafs, H. D.; Hale, W. H.; Preston, R. L.; and Ulberg, L. C. "On the safety of estrogenic hormone resi-

dues in edible animal products." BioScience 25, 1 (Jan. 1975): 19-25.
Discussion of issues involved in determining health hazards of hormonal residues from growth promoters in meat and animal products.

1333 Cottral, G. E.; Cox, B. F.; and Baldwin, D. E. "The survival of foot-and-mouth disease virus in cured and uncured meat." American Journal of Veterinary Research (Mar. 1960): 288-297.
Study found that FMD virus could survive in certain tissues and was not inactivated by usual commercial procedure of ripening, boning, salting, and storage.

1334 Dalerup, L. M., and Visser, W. "Influence of extra sucrose, fats, protein and of cyclomate in the daily food on the life-span of rats." Experientia 27, 5 (May 15, 1971): 519-521.
Rats receiving extra meat and butter sustained more severe kidney changes and had shorter life spans than controls or animals receiving other diets.

1335 Danoff, Deborah; Lincoln, Lawrence; Thomson, D. M. P.; and Gold, Phil. "Big Mac attack." New England Journal of Medicine 298, 19 (May 11, 1978): 1095-1096.
Letter describes case of life-threatening allergic reaction to Big Mac hamburgers.

1336 Dollery, C. T.; Fraser, H. S.; Mucklow, J. C.; and Bulpitt, C. J. "Contribution of environmental factors to variability in human drug metabolism." Drug Metabolism Reviews 9, 2 (1979): 207-200.
Metabolic clearance of two drugs increased with meat, alcohol, tea, and cigarette consumption.

1337 Duke, Jim. "Vegetarian Vitachart." Quarterly Journal of Crude Drug Research 15, 2 (1977): 45-66.
Table of edible and inedible fruits, vegetables, herbs, and spices indicating relative value for 14 nutritional categories.

1338 Eddy, T. P., and Taylor, G. F. "Sublingual varicosities and vitamin C in elderly vegetarians." Age and Ageing 6, 1 (Feb. 1977): 6-13.

Elderly vegetarians had high levels of plasma vitamin C and low incidence of varicosities under the tongue.

1339 Edwards, Cecile H.; Ruffin, Minnie R.; Woolcock, Ivy M.; and Rice, Arthur W. "Efficiency of vegetarian diets as a source for growth and maintenance." Journal of Home Economics 56, 3 (Mar. 1964): 164-168.
Evaluation of growth and nitrogen balance in rats fed diet designed to simulate vegetables commonly consumed in the southeastern U.S.

1340 Fara, G. M.; del Corro, G.; Bernuzzi, S.; Bigatello, A.; di Pietro, C.; Scaglioni, S.; and Chiumello, G. "Epidemic of breast enlargement in an Italian school." Lancet 2 (Aug. 11, 1979): 295-297.
Estrogen residues in poultry and veal suspected of causing breast enlargement in school children, 3-10 years of age.

1341 Fraser, Henry S.; Mucklow, John C.; Bulpitt, Christopher J.; Khan, Clare; Mould, Geoffrey; and Dollery, Colin T. "Environmental effects on antipyrine half-life in man." Clinical Pharmacology and Therapeutics 22, 5 (Nov. 1977): 799-808.
Comparison of dietary and other environmental factors such as smoking and oral contraceptive use in vegetarians and non-vegetarians found that vegetarian diet prolonged antipyrine half-life by 50 percent.

1342 Freeland, Jeanne H.; Ebangit, M. Lavone; and Bodzy, Pamela W. "Trace mineral content of vegetarian foods: zinc and copper." Federation Proceedings 36, 3 (1977): 1124.
Analysis of 250 vegetarian foods indicated that these foods could provide adequate amounts of zinc and copper, although the availability of these minerals has yet to be determined. (Abstract only.)

1343 Freeland, Jeanne H.; Ebangit, M. Lavone; and Johnson, Pamela. "Changes in zinc absorption following a vegetarian diet." Federation Proceedings 37, 3 (1978): 253.
Vegetarian diet may reduce zinc availability. (Abstract only.)

1344 Freeland-Graves, Jeanne H.; Bodzy, Pamela W.; and Eppright, Margaret A. "Zinc status of vegetarians." American Dietetic Association. Journal 77, 6 (1980): 655-661.
Zinc intakes of lacto-ovo-vegetarian, lacto-vegetarian, and vegan men and women were measured.

1345 Freeland-Graves, Jeanne H.; Ebangit, M. Lavone; and Bodzy, Pamela W. "Zinc and copper content of foods used in vegetarian diets." American Dietetic Association. Journal 77 (Dec. 1980): 648-654.
Table and text present zinc and copper data for 74 foods commonly consumed by vegetarians.

1346 Freeland-Graves, Jeanne H.; Ebangit, M. Lavone; and Hendrikson, Pamela J. "Alterations in zinc absorption and salivary sediment zinc after a lacto-ovo-vegetarian diet." American Journal of Clinical Nutrition 33, 8 (Aug. 1980): 1757-1766.
Vegetarian diet appears to adversely affect zinc status.

1347 Ganapathy, Seetha, and Dhanda, Rita. "Protein and iron nutrition in lacto-ovo-vegetarian Indo-Aryan United States residents." Indian Journal of Nutrition and Dietetics 17, 2 (1980): 45-52.
No physical or behavior symptoms of protein-calorie malnutrition were found in Indian college students consuming lacto-ovo-vegetarian diets.

1348 Ganapathy, Seetha N., and Dhanda, Rita. "Selenium content of omnivorous and vegetarian diets." Indian Journal of Nutrition and Dietetics 17, 2 (Feb. 1980): 53-59.
Measurements of selenium in standardized omnivorous, lacto-ovo-vegetarian, and all-plant diets.

1349 Giorgio, A. J.; Cartwright, G. E.; and Wintrobe, M. M. "Pseudo-Kayser-Fleischer rings." Archives of Internal Medicine 113 (June 1964): 817-818.
Case of vegetarian whose excessive consumption of carrot juice lead to deposits of carotene in the palms and eyes, and the initial mistaken diagnosis of Wilson's disease.

1350 Gonella, M.; Barsotti, G.; Lupetti, S.; and Giovanetti, S. "Factors affecting the metabolic production of

methylguanidine." Clinical Science and Molecular Medicine 48, 5 (1975): 341-347.
Subjects on diets based on foods containing no methylguanidine (vegetarian, protein-free, and milk-egg diets) experienced a fall in the urinary output of methylguanidine as compared to the same subjects on a mixed diet.

1351 Gorman, Jeanette C., and Moore, Marian E. "Calculated and analyzed fatty acids in vegetarian diets." American Dietetic Association. Journal 50, 5 (1967): 372-375.
Comparison of calculated and analyzed values of total fat and fatty acids in two vegetarian diets of six menus each.

1352 Halpern, Seymour L. "Utilizing nutrition in quality medical care." In: Nutrition education: medical school and health care training. Edited by Myron A. Mehlman and Seymour L. Halpern. Washington, DC, Hemisphere Publishing Corporation, 1976, p. 21-32.
Article notes a number of nutritional problems frequently encountered by the physician; discusses vegetarianism as a fad diet and discounts its health claims.

1353 Heinrich, H. C.; Gabbe, E. E.; and Ičagic, F. "Nutritional iron deficiency anemia in lacto-ovo-vegetarians." Klinische Wochenschrift 57, 4 (Feb. 15, 1979): 187-193.
Cases of three lacto-ovo-vegetarians with mild to severe iron deficiency anemia.

1354 Hill, P.; Garbaczewski, L.; Helman, P.; Huskisson, J.; Sporangisa, E.; and Wynder, E. L. "Diet, lifestyle and menstrual activity." American Journal of Clinical Nutrition 33, 6 (1980): 1192-1198.
Western diet fed to vegetarian South African black women induced hormonal changes comparable to those found in women with menstrual irregularities.

1355 Hird, D. W., and Pullen, M. M. "Tape-worms, meat, and man: a brief review and update of cysticercosis caused by Taenia saginata and Taenia solium." Journal of Food Protection 42, 1 (Jan.

1979): 58-64.
Discussion of two species of tapeworm which may be transmitted to man by ingestion of contaminated meat.

1356 Holbrook, I. B.; Gross, E.; Milewski, P. J.; Shipley, K.; and Irving, M. H. "Nπ-methylhistidine excretion and myofibrillar protein breakdown in patients receiving intravenous or enteral nutrition." Clinical Science (London) 59, 3 (1980): 211-214.
Measurements of Nπ-Methylhistidine, nitrogen and creatinine in subjects on meat-free diets compared to those on I. V. or enteral nutrition.

1357 Isaksson, Björn. "Fasting and vegetarian food." Läkartidningen 75, 28-29 (July 12, 1978): 2611-2612. (In Swedish.)

1358 Isomäki, H.; von Essen, R.; and Ruutsalo, Helka-Marjatta. "Gout, particularly diuretics-induced, is on the increase in Finland." Scandinavian Journal of Rheumatology 6, 4 (1977): 213-216.
The most striking dietary peculiarity of 77 Finnish gout patients was excessive consumption of whitefish and general overconsumption of purine-rich foods; other factors were obesity and overconsumption of alcohol.

1359 Jackson, W. P. U. "Hyperglycaemia among vegetarians." South African Medical Journal 53, 22 (June 3, 1978): 880-881.
Letter describes finding that the vegetarian diet followed by Indian group does not protect against obesity or hyperglycemia.

1360 Jathar, V. S.; Hirwe, R.; Desai, S.; and Satoskar, R. S. "Dietetic habits and quality of semen in Indian subjects." Andrologia 8, 4 (1976): 355-358.

1361 Juszkiewicz, T., and Kowalski, B. "Absorption, tissue deposition and passage into eggs of N-nitrosodimethylamine in hens." International Agency for Research of Cancer. IARC Scientific Publications 19 (1978): 433-439.
Study of absorption from drinking water of DMNA into tissues and eggs of hens revealed un-

expectedly high concentrations, suggesting a potential health hazard to humans consuming poultry and eggs.

1362 Klein, Daniel Allen. Effects of exercise and a vegetarian diet on carcass composition, organ weights, and serum cholesterol and triglycerides. Ph. D. Michigan State University, 1971.
Comparison in albino rats of the effects of a strict vegetarian diet and a control diet containing animal protein under various conditions of physical activity.

1363 Kreuzer, W. "Cadmium in the kidneys of slaughtered animals; hazardous for human health?" MMW-- Münchener Medizinische Wochenschrift 120, 40 (Oct. 6, 1978): 1287-1288. (In German.)

1364 Lamm, D.; Birnbaum, M.; Fritzsch, W.; and Neumann, H. "Rare kidney diseases in pregnancy. I. Nephroticsyndrome in glomerulonephritis and pregnancy." Zentralblatt für Gynaekologie 89, 40 (Oct. 7, 1967): 1471-1476. (In German.)

1365 Lang, Virginia M.; North, Barbara B.; and Morse, Lura M. "Manganese metabolism in college men consuming vegetarian diets." Journal of Nutrition 85, 2 (1965): 132-138.
Eight subjects were found to be in positive balance for manganese.

1366 Latto, C. "Medical safaris--food for thought." International Journal of Environmental Studies 12, 1 (1978): 9-12.
Travels by a medical team to Africa and India confirm rarity of certain Western diseases, such as dental caries, appendicitis, diverticular disease, cancer of the colon, and coronary heart disease, among populations whose diets include very little sugar, little or no meat, and large quantities of fiber.

1367 Long, Alan. "Thiamine in vegetarian diets." British Medical Journal 2, 6026 (July 3, 1976): 47.
Letter discusses various aspects of thiamine biochemistry and its availability in vegetarian diets.

1368 McConnell, K. P.; Smith, J. C., Jr.; Higgins, P. J.;
Blotcky, A. J.; and Brown, E. D. "Selenium
content of different hospital diets." Federation
Proceedings 38, 3 (1979): 772.
Selenium in vegetarian hospital meals was adequate, while in regular and renal diets, it was
lower than recommended. (Abstract only.)

1369 Mannarino, Elmo. "Lipids and vegetarians." British
Medical Journal 281, 6236 (Aug. 2, 1980): 388.
Brief letter points out that lacto-ovo-vegetarian
diet is not always synonymous with a low-lipid
diet.

1370 Martin, Charles W.; Fjermestad, Jerry; Smith-Barbaro, Peggy; and Reddy, Bandaru S. "Dietary
modification of mixed function oxidases." Nutrition Reports International 22, 3 (1980): 395-407.

1371 Masur, Henry; Jones, Thomas C.; Lempert, Jeffrey
A.; and Cherubini, Thomas D. "Outbreak of toxoplasmosis in a family and documentation of acquired
retinochoroiditis." American Journal of Medicine
64, 3 (Mar. 1978): 396-402.
Toxoplasmosis infection from eating infected
lamb.

1372 Mehra, Krishna Swami. "Vitamin A and serum carotenoid in Indians." Indian Medical Association.
Journal 44 (Feb. 16, 1965): 181-182.
Serum carotenoid and vitamin A levels were
lower in Indian vegetarians than in non-vegetarians.

1373 Mehrotra, B. K.; Tandon, G. S.; and Shukla, R. C.
"Study of gastric secretion with reference to pregnancy in Indian women." Indian Journal of Physiology and Pharmacology 13, 1 (Jan. 1969): 65-72.
Gastric acid secretions decreased significantly
in pregnant women with no appreciable differences
between vegetarian and non-vegetarian pregnant
women.

1374 Mucklow, J. C.; Caraher, Marie T.; Henderson, D.
B.; and Rawlins, M. D. "The effect of individual
dietary constituents on antipyrine clearance in
Asian immigrants." British Journal of Clinical
Pharmacology 7, 4 (Apr. 1979): 416P-417P.

Brief description of study finding faster antipyrine clearance in meat-eaters than in lactovegetarians.

1375 Mucklow, J. C.; Rawlins, M. D.; Brodie, M. J.; Boobis, A. R.; and Dollery, C. T. "Drug oxidation in Asian vegetarians." Lancet 2, 8186 (July 19, 1980): 151.
Letter reports that the reduction in antipyrine oxidation in vegetarian immigrants is due to low protein intake, rather than lack of meat or animal fat.

1376 Myasnikov, S. P., and Pravosudov, V. P. "Electrocardiographic changes in dogs produced by nitrites and nitrates contained in sausages." Gigienai Sanitariia 31, 2 (Feb. 1966): 38-42.
Dogs fed sausages containing nitrites and nitrates exhibited pronounced changes in the electrocardiogram. (In Russian.)

1377 Naik, S. S.; Tanksale, K. G.; and Ganapati, R. "Study of urinary nitrogenous constituents in reactions of leprosy." Indian Journal of Medical Research 65, 2 (1977): 193-200.
Intake of nitrogen through vegetarian diets was studied in leprosy patients.

1378 Osaka, Ryoko. "A survey of the social situation of leprosy patients in JALMA leprosy Center, Agra, India: 2. Survey on the socioenvironmental aspect of inpatients." Japanese Journal of Leprosy 48, 2 (1979): 59-66.
Sociological study of leprosy patients, both vegetarian and non-vegetarian. (In Japanese.)

1379 Pal, M. N.; Bhatia, V. N.; Kotwani, B. G.; and Agarwal, D. S. "Toxoplasmosis in relation to reproductive disorders." Indian Journal of Medical Research 63, 1 (1975): 11-16.
Antibodies against toxoplasmosis were found in both vegetarians and non-vegetarians, with higher incidence associated with high age, low income groups, and contact with cats.

1380 Prakash, C., and Kumar, Anil. "Cysticercosis with Taeniasis in a vegetarian." Journal of Tropical

Medicine and Hygiene 68 (Apr. 1965): 100-103.
Rare case of cysticercosis with tapeworm in-
festation in young Indian vegetarian.

1381 Roberts, D. F.; Chinn, S.; Girija, B.; and Singh,
H. D. "A study of menarcheal age in India."
Annals of Human Biology 4, 2 (Mar. 1977): 171-
177.
Study of 1267 girls ages 9 to 18 showed no relationship between the age of onset of menstruation
and vegetarian or non-vegetarian diet.

1382 Rogowski, Bodo. "Meat in human nutrition." World
Review of Nutrition and Dietetics 34 (1980): 46-
101.
Review article on meat composition, developments in meat science, and danger of meat consumption by humans.

1383 Róiz, José. "Experiêcia com a 'Dieta Ideal'." Revista Brasileira de Medicina 26, 4 (Apr. 1969):
223-230. (In Portuguese.)

1384 Róiz, José. "Reply to: Blind passion or understanding." Revista Brasileira de Medicina 29, 5 (May
1972): 247-248. (In Portuguese.)

1385 Róiz, José. "Rum with creosote." Revista Brasileira de Medicina 25, 11 (Nov. 1968): 748-751.
(In Portuguese.)

1386 Rossander, Lena. "Iron absorption from composite
meals." Var Foeda 31, 1 (1979): 37-44.
High ascorbic acid content of vegetarian meals
favored iron absorption, whereas mixed diet with
beef inhibited absorption. (In Swedish.)

1387 Sanders, T. A. B.; Ellis, F. R.; and Dickerson, J.
W. T. "Are long-chain polyunsaturated fatty acids
necessary in the human diet?" Nutrition Society.
Proceedings 35, 3 (1976): 125A-127A.
Study of vegetarians whose diets contain no
LCPFA concludes that they are not necessary per
se in the human diet.

1388 Sanders, T. A. B.; Ellis, F. R.; and Dickerson, J.
W. T. "Polyunsaturated fatty acids and the brain."

Lancet (Apr. 2, 1977): 751-752.
Letter concludes that no dietary source of long-chain polyunsaturated fatty acids from animal fat is necessary, since those consuming diets free of animal fat are able to produce LCP's from short-chain polyunsaturates.

1389 Sangoi, J. K., and Kulkarni, B. S. "Creatinine clearance studies in normal Indian subjects." Journal of Postgraduate Medicine 18, 4 (Oct. 1972): 189-198.
No significant difference in creatinine clearance values were found between 100 normal vegetarians and non-vegetarian subjects.

1390 Satoskar, R. S.; Kulkarni, B. S.; and Rege, D. V. "Serum proteins, cholesterol, vitamin B12 and folic acid levels in lacto-vegetarians and nonvegetarians." Indian Journal of Medical Research 49, 5 (1961): 887-896.
Non-vegetarians had higher weights, and higher levels of serum cholesterol, albumin, vitamin B12 and folic acid than lacto-vegetarians.

1391 Schultz, T. D., and Leklem, J. E. "Dietary fat intake and plasma estrogen levels in premenopausal vegetarian and non-vegetarian women." Federation Proceedings 39, 3 (1980): 868.

1392 Singh, S. P.; Pandey, D. N.; Bhushan, S.; Seth, P.; and Sisodia, A. K. "Study of the intake of fluid, output and titratable acidity of urine in medical students." Indian Journal of Physiology and Pharmacology 21, 4 (Oct.-Dec. 1977): 369-373.
Non-vegetarian subjects were found to have significantly higher titratable acidity of urine than vegetarian subjects.

1393 Sköldstam, Lars; Larsson, Lasse; and Lindström, Folke O. "Effects of fasting and lactovegetarian diet on rheumatoid arthritis." Scandinavian Journal of Rheumatology 8, 4 (1979): 249-255.
Fruit and vegetable juice fasting resulted in reduced pain, stiffness, consumption of analgesics, and lower serum concentrations of orosomucoid in rheumatoid arthritis patients; nine weeks of a lacto-vegetarian diet did not result in any objective improvement.

1394   Spiro, Howard M.   "The rough and the smooth--some
        reflections on diet therapy. "   New England Journal
        of Medicine 293, 2 (July 10, 1975):   83-85.
            Essay on high-fiber and vegetarian diets in light
        of the cyclical nature of therapeutic diet theory.

1395   Sussman, Oscar.   "Does the Wholesome Meat Act of
        1967 really protect the consumer?"   Veterinary
        Medicine 63 (July 1968):   639, 642.
            Since even federally inspected meats may trans-
        mit food-borne disease, the public must not adopt
        a false sense of security in the handling, prepara-
        tion, and consumption of meats.

1396   Szabo, T.   "The present state of toxoplasmosis. "
        Mount Sinai Journal of Medicine 41, 6 (1974):
        765-773.
            Account of substantial gaps in knowledge regard-
        ing toxoplasmosis, including its occurrence in
        vegetarians.

1397   Thomas, J. A.   "Human sarcocystis. "   Journal of
        Postgraduate Medicine 22, 4 (1976):   185-190.
            Case of sarcocystis in a 54-year-old Hindu
        vegetarian female.

1398   Tizard, Ian R. ; Chauhan, S. S. ; and Lai, C. H.
        "The prevalence and epidemiology of toxoplasmosis
        in Ontario. "   Journal of Hygiene 78 (1977):   275-
        282.
            High meat consumption, especially of rare
        steaks, is probably the most significant source
        of toxoplasmosis infection in Ontario.

1399   Tobe, John H.   How to conquer arthritis.   St. Cath-
        arines, Ont. , Provoker Press, 1976.

1400   Treuherz, Joyce.   "Zinc and dietary fibre: observa-
        tions on a group of vegetarian adolescents. "   Nu-
        trition Society.   Proceedings 39, 1 (Feb. 1980):
        10A.
            Although zinc and dietary intakes were greater
        in vegetarians than in omnivores, vegetarians had
        lower levels of zinc in their hair, suggesting a
        chelation effect by dietary fiber and/or phytic acid
        on zinc.   (Abstract only.)

1401 United States. General Accounting Office. Problems in
      preventing the marketing of raw meat and poultry
      containing potentially harmful residues: report to
      the Congress. Washington, DC, General Account-
      ing Office, 1979.
          Analysis and recommendations following GAO
      report that 14 percent of meat and poultry/sam-
      pled between 1974 and 1976 contained illegal and
      potentially harmful residues of animal drugs, pesti-
      cides, or environmental contaminants. (NTIS
      technical report # PB 294 065.)

1402 Van Staveren, W. A. "Can the gap between alterna-
      tive nutrition and officially recommended nutrition
      be bridged?" Nederlands Tijdschrift voor Genee-
      skunde 123, 40 (Oct. 1979): 1747-1750. (In
      Dutch.)

1403 Vasavada, N. B., and Shah, P. B. "Serum glutamic
      oxalacetic transaminase (GOT) and pyruvic trans-
      aminase (GPT) in healthy Gujaratis." Journal of
      Postgraduate Medicine (Bombay) 10, 4 (1964):
      161-164.
          Serum GOT and GPT levels were measured in
      50 healthy Indian vegetarians.

1404 Vy, Tran. "Nutritional value of a vegetarian diet."
      American Journal of Clinical Nutrition 25, 7 (July
      1972): 647.
          Letter describes modification of excretion of
      creatine and creatinine in vegetarian Buddhist
      monks.

1405 Wadia, N. H.; Desai, M. M.; Quadros, E. V.; and
      Dastur, D. K. "Role of vegetarianism, smoking,
      and hydroxocobalamin in optic neuritis." British
      Medical Journal 3, 5821 (July 29, 1972): 264-267.
          Neither vegetarianism nor smoking played a
      significant role in the production of optic neuritis.

1406 Wadia, N. H.; Desai, M. M.; Quadros, E. V.; and
      Dastur, D. K. "Vitamin B12, thiocyanate and
      folates: II. In patients with optic neuritis."
      Neurology (Bombay) 20, 3 Supplement (1973): 433-
      441.
          Smoking, vegetarianism, and vitamin B12 played
      no role in 20 cases of optic neuritis studied.

1407   Walker, James B.   "Creatine: biosynthesis, regula-
         tion, and function."   Advances in Enzymology and
         Related Areas of Molecular Biology 50 (1979): 177-
         242.
              Comprehensive review of literature related to
         creatine contains brief section on creatinine ex-
         cretion in vegetarian diets.

1408   Whitlock, Gaylord P.   "General consumer education
         of the public on nutrition and additives."   In:
         Meat Industry Research Conference.   Proceedings.
         Arlington, VA, American Meat Institution Founda-
         tion, 1978, p. 119-129.
              Attempts to allay the doubts of consumers, vege-
         tarians and health food faddists regarding choles-
         terol, DES, food additives, and world food short-
         ages through the use of positive nutrition education
         programs.

1409   Wickramasinghe, S. N., and Saunders, J. E.   "Re-
         sults of three years' experience with the deox-
         yuridine suppression test."   Acta Haematologica
         58, 4 (1977): 193-206.
              Report of test values from 400 subjects includ-
         ing two vegans.

1410   Yamaguchi, Seiya; Matsumoto, Hisao; Kaku, Shunsuke;
         Tateishi, Miho; and Shiramizu, Michiko.   "Factors
         affecting the amount of mercury in human scalp
         hair."   American Journal of Public Health 65, 5
         (May 1975): 484-488.
              Analysis of mercury content in hair samples
         collected from several ethnic and socioeconomic
         groups and/or consuming different types of diet
         found that vegetarians had significantly less mer-
         cury than other groups.

1411   Yeary, Roger A.   "Public health significance of chem-
         ical residues in foods."   American Veterinary
         Medical Association.   Journal 149, 1 (July 15,
         1966): 145-150.
              Since approximately 275 man-made substances,
         including drugs and antibiotics, are permitted in
         the feed and water of food animals, products of
         animal origin contribute significantly to dietary
         levels of chemical and hormonal residues.

1412 Zimmerman, Walther.   "Dietetic aspects in clinical
        practice."   Zeitschrift für Allgemeinmedizin 47,
        12 (Apr. 30, 1971): 643-653.   (In German.)

APPENDIX: VEGETARIAN COOKBOOKS

THROUGH 1899

Cowen, E. M., and Beaty-Pownall, S. Fast day and vegetarian cookery. London, H. Cox, 1895.

Smith, Elizor Goodrich. Fat of the land and how to live on it; special chapters on nuts and vegetable oils, and how to use them in cooking, milk, bakeries; feeding infants and various other subjects relating to the food problem. Amherst, MA, n.p., 1896.

Vegetarian cookery. By a lady. London, F. Pitman, 186-?

1900 THROUGH 1959

Anderson, Hans Steele. Science of food and cookery. Mountain View, CA, Pacific Press Publishing Association, 1921.

Arnbrecht, Jacob. Hygienic cook book; a collection of choice recipes carefully tested. College View, NB, International Publishing Association, 1914.

Baker, Ivan. Complete vegetarian recipe book. New York, Citadel Press, 1955.

Boulder-Colorado Sanitarium. Vegetarian cook book. Boulder, CO, The Boulder-Colorado Sanitarium, 1932.

Bush, Maxine Conwell, and Fewer, Edward P. Magic recipes for the Bush & Fewer Liqua-dizer, consisting entirely of original recipes created by the authors. Mehoopany, PA, n.p., 1953.

217

Cooper, Lenna Frances, and Hall, Margaret Allen. The new cookery. Battle Creek, MI, The Modern Medicine Publishing Co. , 1929.

Drews, George Julius. Unfired foods and hygienic dietetics for prophylactic (preventative) feeding and therapeutic (remedial) feeding.... Chicago, The Author, 1909.

Finkel, Harry. Diet and cook book ... a vegetarian cook book including recipes and menus that aid in the recovery of every disease. New York, The Society for Public Health Education, 1925.

Fulton, E. G. Substitutes for flesh foods; vegetarian cook book. Oakland, CA, Pacific Press Publishing Company, 1904.

Gillmore, Marie McIlvaine. Meatless cookery, with special reference to diet for heart disease, blood pressure and autointoxication. New York, E. P. Dutton & Company, 1914.

Hamilton, Nelly Louise, and Hamilton, Edward Lee. The Havenhurst vegetarian recipe book. Sierra Madre, CA, n. p. , 1934.

Israelite House of David as reorganized by Mary Purnell. Vegetarian cook book. Benton Harbor, MI, City of David, 1956.

Jardine, Jeanne. The best vegetarian dishes I know. London, J. M. Dent & Sons, Ltd. , 1910.

Lindlahr, Anna, and Lindlahr, Henry. The nature cure cook book and A B C of natural dietetics. Chicago, The Nature Cure Publishing Co. , 1915.

Malek, Leona Alford. Meatless meals. Chicago, A. Whitman & Co. , 1943.

Partridge, Pauline Dunwell, and Conklin, Hester Martha. Wheatless and meatless days. New York, D. Appleton and Company, 1918.

Pietschman, Ann. Food for thought; over three hundred delightful recipes, mostly vegetarian. Los Angeles, Institute of Mentalphysics, 1954.

Rotondi, Pietro. Vegetarian cookery. Los Angeles, CA, Willing Publishing Company, 1942.

Rorer, Sarah Tyson. Mrs. Rorer's vegetable cookery and meat substitutes.... Philadelphia, Arnold and Company, 1909.

Schirmer, Alice Phelpe. One hundred meatless dishes. Needham, MA, The Chronicle Press, 1914.

Unity School of Christianity. Unity vegetarian cookbook; set a vege-table. Lee's Summit, MO, The School, 1955.

Vegetarian dishes; vegetable soups, entrées and savouries, salads, sweets and farinaceous foods. London, Ward, Lock & Co., Ltd., 1937.

Walker, Norman Wardhaugh. Diet and salad suggestions, for use in connection with vegetable and fruit juices. Anaheim, CA, Norwalk Laboratory, 1947.

Zerfing, Sally D. Sally's recipes. Glendale, CA, n.p., 1957.

1960 THROUGH 1980

Adams, Ruth B. Callaloo and pastelles too, plus hundreds of other delightful recipes. Mountain View, CA, Pacific Press Publishing Association, 1973.

Adler, Kief. Beyond the staff of life: the wheatless-dairy-less cookbook. Happy Camp, CA, Naturegraph, 1976.

Allen, Hannah. Homemakers' guide to foods for pleasure and health and handbook for hygienic living. Chicago, Natural Hygiene Press, 1975.

Allison, Sonia. Cooking in style. London, Elm Tree Books, 1980.

Andersen, Lynn. Rainbow Farm cookbook. New York, Harper & Row, 1973.

Andrews, Sheila. The no-cooking fruitarian recipe book. Wellingborough, England, Thorsons Publishers, 1975.

Baker, Ivan. Complete vegetarian recipe book. London, Bell & Hyman, 1978.

Baker, Ivan. Delicious vegetarian cooking. New York, Dover Publications, 1972.

Barkas, Janet. Meatless cooking: celebrity style. New York, Grove Press, 1972.

Batt, Eva. What's cooking?: a guide to good eating. Revised ed. Enfield, England, Vegan Society, 1976.

Bayramian, Mary. Around the world vegetarian cookbook. San Francisco, Troubador Press, 1976.

Berg, Sally, and Berg, Lucian. New food for all palates; great vegetarian dishes of the world; a vegetarian cook book. London, Gollancz, 1979.

Berg, Sally, and Berg, Lucian. The vegetarian gourmet; 315 international recipes for health, palate, and long happy life. New York, Herder and Herder, 1967.

Black, Patricia Hall. Vegetarian cookery. Mountain View, CA, Pacific Press Publishing Association, 1971.

Blanchard, Marjorie P. The vegetarian menu cookbook. New York, Watts, 1979.

Bloodroot Collective. The political palate; a feminist vegetarian cookbook. Bridgeport, CT, Sanguinaria Publ., 1980.

Bordow, Joan Wiener. Victory through vegetables. New York, Holt, Rinehart and Winston, 1970.

Boulding, Elise. From a monastery kitchen. New York, Harper & Row, 1976.

Bragg, Paul C., and Bragg, Patricia. Hi-protein, meatless health recipes. Desert Hot Springs, CA, Health Science, 1975.

Brooks, Karen. The complete vegetarian cookbook. New York, Pocket Books, 1976.

Brooks, Karen. The forget-about-meat cookbook. Emmaus, PA, Rodale Press, 1974.

Brown, Edith. Cooking creatively with natural foods. New York, Hawthorn Books, 1972.

Brown, Edward Espe. Tassajara cooking. Berkeley, CA, Shambhala, 1973.

Brown, Pamela. Vegetarian cooker-top cookery: delicious, wholesome, meat-free meals without using an oven. Wellingborough, England, Thorsons, 1978.

Brown, Pamela. The wholefood freezer book. Wellingborough, England, Thorsons, 1980.

Bruce, Liza. Alternative cookery. London, Tandem, 1975.

Bryant, Clare. Everyday vegetarian and food reform cooking. Shaldon, Keith Reid Ltd., 1974.

Budche, S., and Schueler, M. So a vegetarian is coming to dinner! Ventura, CA, Aazunna Pub., 1979.

Burgess, Mary Keyes. Soul to soul: a soul food vegetarian cookbook. Santa Barbara, CA, Woodbridge Press Pub. Co., 1976.

Buxbaum, Larry. The yoga food book: a guide to vegetarian eating and cooking. St. Louis, MO, Universal Great Brotherhood, 1974.

Cahill, Tilda. The best of South African vegetarian cooking: 500 choice tested recipes. Cape Town, H. A. U. M., 1977.

Cahill, Tilda. A South African vegetarian cook book. Cape Town, H. A. U. M., 1974.

Calella, John R. Cooking naturally: an evolutionary gourmet cuisine of natural foods. Berkeley, CA, And/Or Press, 1978.

Century 21 cookbook: 375 meatless recipes. Leominster, MA, Eusey Press, 1974.

Chadha, Romola. Cooking the vegetarian way. Bombay, Lalvani Pub. House, 1971.

Claire, Rosine. The French gourmet vegetarian cookbook. Millbrae, CA, Celestial Arts, 1975.

Colbin, Annemarie. The book of whole meals: a seasonal guide to assembling balanced vegetarian breakfasts, lunches and dinners. Brookline, MA, Autumn Press, 1979.

Corlett, Jim. Supernatural cookery: recipes for vegetarian gourmets. Washington, DC, Acropolis Books, 1974.

Cottrell, Edith Young. The oats, peas, beans and barley cookbook. Santa Barbara, CA, Woodbridge Press, 1974.

D'Silva, Joyce. Health eating for the new age: a vegan cookbook. London, Wildwood House, 1980.

Dinshah, Freya. XXIII World Vegetarian Congress cookbook. Malaga, NJ, North American Vegetarian Society, 1975.

Dinshah, Freya. The vegan kitchen. Malaga, NJ, American Vegan Society, 1974.

Duff, Gail. Gail Duff's vegetarian cookbook. London, Macmillan, 1978.

Easterday, Kate Cusick. The peaceable kitchen cookbook; recipes for personal and global well-being. New York, Paulist Press, 1980.

Edelstein, Naomi. The four seasons recipe book using herbs, spices, wines, liqueurs for dishes of flavour as well as aroma. London, Miss N. Edelstein, 1967.

Elliot, Rose. Beanfeast: natural foods cook book. Liss, England, White Eagle Publishing Trust, 1975.

Elliot, Rose. Not just a load of old lentils. Liss, England, White Eagle Publishing Trust, 1972.

Elliot, Rose. Simply delicious. Liss, England, White Eagle Publishing Trust, 1974.

Elliot, Rose. Thrifty fifty. Liss, England, White Eagle Publishing Trust, 1973.

Eno, David. The little brown rice book. Launceston, England, Juniper Press, 1973.

Ewald, Ellen Buchman. Recipes for a small planet; the art
and science of high protein vegetarian cookery. New
York, Ballantine Books, 1973.

Famine Foods Co-Op. Pot-luck. Winona, MN, Vision
Quest Printshop, n. d.

The Farm vegetarian cookbook. Summertown, TN, Book
Pub. Co., 1978.

Farthing, Bill. Odiyan country cookbook. Emeryville, CA,
Dharma, 1977.

Fessler, Stella Law. Chinese meatless cooking. New
York, New American Library, 1980.

Fisher, Patty. 500 recipes for vegetarian cookery. London, Hamlyn, 1969.

Fitzgerald, Pegeen. Meatless cooking; Pegeen's vegetarian
recipes. Englewood Cliffs, NJ, Prentice-Hall, 1968.

Fliess, Walter, and Fliess, Jenny. Modern vegetarian
cookery. Harmondsworth, Middlesex, Penguin Books,
1964.

Food for the soul: a guide to yogic cooking. Sumneytown,
PA, Kripalu Yoga Ashram, 1976.

Friedlander, Barbara. Earth, water, fire, air; cookbook
for the new age. New York, Macmillan, 1972.

Friedlander, Barbara. The Findhorn cookbook: an approach
to cooking with consciousness. New York, Grosset &
Dunlap, 1976.

Gephardt, Mattie L. Meatless recipes. Wheaton, IL, Theosophical Publishing House, 1975.

Gewanter, Vera. A passion for vegetables: recipes from
European kitchens. New York, Viking Press, 1980.

Goldbeck, Nikki. Cooking what comes naturally; a natural
foods cookbook featuring a month's worth of natural-
vegetarian menus. Garden City, NY, Doubleday, 1972.

Goldsmith, Maureen. The organic yenta. New York, Atheneum, 1972.

Goulart, Frances Sheridan. Bum steers: how and why to make your own delicious high protein mock meats, fake fish & dairyless deserts, and avoid useless calories, cholesterol, sodium nitrate, salmonella, trichinosis and high prices. Old Greenwich, CT, Chatham Press, 1975.

Graham, Winifred. The vegetable, fruit and nut cookbook; a vegetarian's treasure chest of culinary delights. Wellingborough, England, Thorsons, 1980.

Haddon, Joan. The Australian book of health food cookery. Sydney, Collins, 1972.

Handslip, Carole. Vegetarian cooking. London, Octopus Books, 1980.

Hannaford, Kathryn. Cosmic cookery. Berkeley, CA, Starmast Publications, 1974.

Harris, Thelma Bruner. Good food for good health; a cookbook featuring menu tips and easy-to-prepare recipes calling for the use of vegetables, fruits, grain foods, nuts, and dairy products. Nashville, TN, Southern Pub. Association, 1972.

Heindel, M. Salads and vegetarian menus. Oceanside, CA, Rosicrucian Fellowship, 1980.

Highton, N. Berry, and Highton, Rosemary B. The home book of vegetarian cookery. Boston, Faber, 1979.

Hoffman, Trudie. No oil-no fat vegetarian cookbook. Valley Center, CA, Professional Press Pub. Association, 1978.

Hon, Hazel. Three week vegetarian menu. Sydney, The Author, 1968.

Hooker, Alan. Vegetarian gourmet cookery. San Francisco, CA, 101 Productions, 1970.

Hunt, Janet. A vegetarian in the family: meatless recipes for the odd one out. Wellingborough, England, Thorsons, 1977.

Hunt, Janet. The wholefood lunch box: making the most of the midday break. Wellingborough, England, Thorsons, 1979.

Hurd, Frank J., and Hurd, Rosalie. Ten talents. College-dale, TN, College Press, 1968.

It's your world vegetarian cookbook. Glendale, CA, Seventh-day Adventist Church, 1973.

James, Isabel. Vegetarian cookery. London, Corgi, 1972.

James, Isabel. Vegetarian cuisine. Altrincham, Vegetarian Society (UK) Ltd., 1976.

Jordan, Julie. Wings of life: whole vegetarian cookery. Trumansburg, NY, Crossing Press, 1976.

Judd, Shilla A. Tried & true vegetarian recipes; first vegetarian cookbook. Berkeley, CA, Images Pr., 1971.

Kasin, Miriam. The age of enlightenment cookbook. New York, Arco, 1980.

Kaufman, William Irving. 365 meatless main dish meals. Garden City, NY, Doubleday, 1974.

Keighley, Doreen. Vegetarian cook book. Altrincham, Cheshire, Vegetarian Society (U.K.) Ltd., 1977.

Keleny, Kathleen. Quick and easy menus for using herbs for two weeks meals. Wooton-under-Edge, K. Keleny, 1969.

Kelley, Dona G. Scientific nutrition & vegetarian cookbook. Delhi, India, Ruhani Satsang, 1974.

Kendig, K. Modern vegetable protein cookery. New York, Arc, 1980.

King, Marilyn. Food for thought: a fresh food cook book. New York, Universe Books, 1976.

Kloss, Jethro. The back to Eden cookbook. Santa Barbara, CA, Lifeline Books, 1974.

Kramer, Rose. The very last cookbook; or, how to save money, stay healthy, and impress your friends. Mill-brae, CA, Celestial Arts, 1974.

Krsna Devi. The Hare Krsna cookbook: recipes for the satisfaction of the supreme personality of godhead. New York, Bhaktivedanta Book Trust, 1973.

Laden, Alice. The George Bernard Shaw vegetarian cook book; menus and recipes. London, Garnstone Press, 1972.

Lager, Mildred M. The soybean cookbook. New York, Arc Books, 1968.

Lal, Premila. Vegetable dishes. Bombay, IBH Pub. Co., 1970.

Lappé, Frances Moore, and Buchman, Ellen. Great meatless meals. New York, Ballantine Books, 1974.

Larson, Jeanne, and McLin, Ruth. The vegetable protein and vegetarian cookbook. New York, Arco, 1980.

Larson, Jeanne R., and McLin, Ruth A. 52 Sabbath menus. Nashville, TN, Southern Publishing Association, 1969.

Lay, Joan. Joan Lay's book of salads. Wellingborough, England, Thorsons, 1976.

Lee, Anna. Vegetarian cookbook. Sydney, Summit Books, 1978.

Lee, Gary. The Chinese vegetarian cook book. Concord, CA, Nitty Gritty Productions, 1972.

Lin, Florence. Florence Lin's Chinese vegetarian cookbook. New York, Hawthorn Books, 1976.

Lo, Kenneth H. C. Chinese vegetarian cooking. New York, Pantheon Books, 1974.

Loma Linda Foods. Research and Development Dept. Recipes for long life: the low cholesterol cookbook for weight conscious vegetarians. Riverside, CA, Loma Linda Foods, 1976.

Loma Linda University. School of Medicine. Alumni Association. Woman's Auxiliary. An apple a day: vegetarian cookery by doctors' wives. Los Angeles, The Association, 1967.

Louise, Mattie. Meatless recipes. Wheaton, IL, Theosophical Publishing House, 1975.

Lovejoy, Marie. International vegetarian cuisine. Wheaton, IL, Theosophical Publishing House, 1978.

Machanik, Anne. Nutritious dishes that replace meats and fishes. Cape Town, H. A. U. M., 1974.

McKinnell, Joyce. The minus meat cook book. London, Allen & Unwin, 1967.

McKinnell, Joyce. Vegetarian gourmet cookbook; nature's way to good health. Hollywood, CA, Wilshire Book Co., 1976.

MacRae, Norma M. Mushrooms 'n bean sprouts: A first step for would-be vegetarians. Seattle, Pacific Search Press, 1979.

McWilliams, Margaret. The meatless cookbook. Fullerton, CA, Plycon Press, 1973.

Manners, Ruth Ann. The quick and easy vegetarian cookbook. New York, M. Evans, 1978.

Maull, Linda. Getting it all together; the down to earth cookbook. North Hollywood, CA, Gala Books, 1971.

Max, Peter. The Peter Max new age organic vegetarian cookbook. New York, Pyramid Communications, 1971.

Meenakshi Ammal, S. Cook and see (Samaithu par); the book of South Indian vegetarian recipes. Madras, S. Meenakshi Ammal Publications, 1968.

Mehta, K. R. Vegetarian delights; a cookbook for health and happiness. New York, Exposition Press, 1966.

Michaels, Elsa. The vegetarian menu cookbook. New York, Drake Publishers, 1973.

Miller, Lindsay. The apartment vegetarian cookbook. Culver City, CA, Peace Press, 1978.

Misko, Karin. SeVa longevity cookery cookbook. Columbus, OH, Soybean Press, 1973.

Nearing, Helen Knothe. Simple food for the good life; an alternative cookbook. New York, Delacorte Press, 1980.

Null, G. New vegetarian cookbook. New York, Macmillan, 1980.

Parker, Alfred J. Our cook book for a happy and healthy life. Vancouver, Kabalarian Fraternal Organization, 1968.

Patten, Marguerite. Health food cookery. London, Hamlyn, 1972.

Patten, Marguerite. Vegetarian cooking for you. Secaucus, NJ, Chartwell Books, Inc., 1978.

Pearson, Janice. Light and life cookbook: a new age adventure in natural foods: forty days of menus and recipes for a transition to balanced vegetarian dieting. Los Angeles, Astara, 1975.

Pelton, Robert W. Meatless cooking the natural way. South Brunswick, NJ, A. S. Barnes, 1974.

Phillips, Ann Vroom. From the new world of Australia ... the soil to psyche recipe book: delightful new recipes for new age living ... plus a total plan for zestful vegetarian nutrition from the bright new world down under! Santa Barbara, CA, Woodbridge Press Pub. Co., 1977.

Quick, Vivien. Everywoman's wholefood cookbook. Wellingborough, England, Thorsons, 1974.

Richmond, Sonya. International vegetarian cookery. New York, Arco Publishing Company, 1967.

Ridgway, Judy. The vegetarian gourmet. London, Ward Lock, 1979.

Robertson, Laurel; Flinders, Carol; and Godfrey, Bronwen. Laurel's kitchen: a handbook for vegetarian cookery and nutrition. Berkeley, CA, Nilgiri Press, 1976.

Romagnoli, Margaret. The Romagnolis' meatless cookbook. Boston, Little Brown, 1976.

Rose, Carrie. The whole wheat heart of Yasha Aginsky; a vegetarian cookbook. New York, Dutton, 1971.

Rosenvold, Doris, and Rosenvold, Lloyd. Rx recipes; a guide to healthful food preparation. Montrose, CO, Rosenvold Publications, 1963.

Rosicrucian Fellowship. New Age vegetarian cookbook. Oceanside, CA, Rosicrucian Fellowship, 1975.

Ross, Shirley. The interior ecology cookbook. San Francisco, Straight Arrow, 1970.

Ruebel, Ines. World's 50 best vegetarian recipes. New York, Herder and Herder, 1971.

Ryan, Jim. The meatless meal guide for budget-minded, health conscious cooks. Los Angeles, Ryan Co., 1977.

Sacharoff, Shanta Nimbark. Flavors of India; recipes from the vegetarian Hindu cuisine. San Francisco, 101 Productions, 1972.

St. Christopher cornucopia of vegetable recipes. Letchworth, Herts. St. Christopher School, 1974.

Santa Maria, Jack. Indian vegetarian cookery. London, Rider, 1973.

Scott, David. Grains, beans, nuts. London, Rider, 1980.

Seventh-day Adventists. Food Service Improvement Committee. Dining delightfully; tested recipes from Adventist hospital chefs. Washington, DC, Review and Herald Publishing Association, 1968.

Shandler, Nina, and Shandler, Michael. How to make all the "meat" you eat from wheat. New York, Rawson, Wade Publishers, 1980.

Shepard, Sigrid M. The Thursday night feast and good plain meals cookbook: natural foods of the Eastern Hemisphere, China, Japan, Indonesia, India, the Middle East. Spokane, WA, New Age Print, 1976.

Shulman, Martha Rose. The vegetarian feast. New York, Harper & Row, 1979.

Shurtleff, William. The book of miso. Soquel, CA, Autumn Press, 1976-77.

Shurtleff, William. The book of tempeh. New York, Harper & Row, 1979.

Shurtleff, William. The book of tofu. Brookline, MA, Autumn Press, 1975.

Shyamala, Mahadevan. Vegetarian delicacies, based on the South India style of cooking. Delhi, Shri Bharat Bharati, 1973.

Sickler, Roberta. Ritual of the hearth; a cookbook of 20 menus and 117 unique vegetarian recipes in praise of life. New York, Macmillan, 1973.

Smaridge, Norah. Graymoor's treasury of meatless recipes. Peekskill, NY, Graymoor Press, 1965.

Smit, Lillian. The meatless cookbook. London, Hale, 1975.

Smith, Elizabeth Bernice. Vegetarian meal-planning guide; a lacto-ovo-vegetarian diet. Winnipeg, Hyperion Press, 1979.

Smith, Margaret Ruth. Ann Seranne's good food without meat. New York, Morrow, 1973.

Southey, Paul. Vegetarian gourmet cookbook. New York, Van Nostrand Reinhold Co., 1980.

Spencer, Colin. Gourmet cooking for vegetarians. London, Deutsch, 1978.

Supercook's super meals without meat. London, Marshall Cavendish Ltd., 1973.

Teichner, Mike. Mike and Olga's favorite recipes; fresh ideas in health food flavor. San Antonio, TX, Naylor Co., 1967.

Thomas, Anna. The vegetarian epicure. New York, Knopf, 1972.

Thurman, Jimmie Joan. Adventures in vegetarian cooking; over 200 meatless main dishes. Nashville, TN, Southern Publishing Company, 1969.

Treber, Grace Jean. Why kill to eat? New York, Source Publishers, 1972.

Unity School of Christianity. The new Unity Inn cookbook. Lee's Summit, MO, Unity Books, 1966.

Ved Kaur Khalsa. Conscious cookery: new age vegetarian cuisine. Los Angeles, Khalsa, 1977.

Vegan Society. First hand, first rate: five dozen hints, ideas and recipes for an economical diet. Leatherhead, Vegan Society, 1975.

Vezza, Veronica. Vegetarian cooking made easy. London, Clifton Books, 1970.

Vithaldas, Yogi, and Roberts, Susan. The Yogi cook book. New York, Crown Publishers, 1968.

Voltz, Jeanne. The Los Angeles Times natural foods cookbook. New York, Putnam, 1973.

Walker, Janet. Vegetarian cookery book. London, Mayflower, 1973.

Wason, Elizabeth. The art of vegetarian cookery. London, Allen & Unwin, 1969.

Whyte, Karen Cross. The original diet: raw vegetarian guide and recipe book. San Francisco, Troubador Press, 1977.

Wiley-Boyd, Patricia. Vegetables are beautiful. Lenexa, KS, Cookbook Publ. Inc., 1978.

Willett, Mo. Vegetarian gothic. Harrisburg, PA, Stackpole Books, 1975.

Wroth, Christina. Vegetarian cookbook: wholegrain recipes and honey desserts. San Francisco, Company and Sons, 1971.

Yogiji, Harbhajan Singh Khalsa. The Golden Temple vegetarian cookbook. New York, Hawthorn Books, 1978.

Yuchi Pines Institute. "Blessed art thou, o land, when ...
thy princes eat ... for strength, and not for drunken-
ness!" Seale, AL, Yuchi Pines Institute, 197?.

AUTHOR INDEX

Abbott, D. B. 186
Abernathy, R. P. 1114
Abhedânanda, Swâmi 43
Adams, Ruth 589
Adolph, William H. 44
Agarwal, D. S. 1379
Agarwal, K. N. 1197, 1200
Agarwal, R. K. P. 1089
Agee, James 45, 798
Aiken, William 784
Airola, Paavo 321
Ajayi, O. A. 1110
Alam, S. N. 993
Albertoni, P. 46
Albu, Albert 47
Alcott, William Andrus 1
Alexander, Alice 322
Allaby, Michael 796
Allaway, Gertrude E. 48
Allen, E. S. 961
Allen, Hannah 1111
Allen, K. G. D. 1305
Allison, Bertrand P. 49
Allsopp, A. H. 50
Almflet, G. A. 51
Alsdorf, Ludwig 540
Althoff, Dale 1170
Altman, Nathaniel 323,
324, 325, 326, 590, 799,
1112
Alvistur, Enrique 185
Aly, Karl-Otto 1306
American Academy of Pedi-
atrics. Committee on
Nutrition 752
American Dietetic Associ-

ation 753, 754
Amin, S. 1131
Anderson, Hans Steele 52,
53
Andersson, Iris 1307
Andersson, Sonja 1307
Anderton, R. 54
Andrew, Elizabeth M.
1191, 1192
Anholm, Anne C. 918
Aoyagi, Akiko 685, 686,
687, 688, 689, 690
Aquinas, Saint Thomas 3
Archer, Morton 202
Arduino, Nancy L. 1192
Aries, V. 1016
Aries, Vivienne C. 1239
Armstrong, B. 1008
Armstrong, Bruce 923,
924, 968
Armstrong, Bruce K. 894
Arora, R. B. 1308
Arulanantham, Karunyan
1167
Arunachalam, J. 1309
Åstrand, Per-Olof 568
Auxter, Thomas 805
Axon, Geoffrey R. 69, 70
Axon, William Edward
Armytage 541

Bachrach, Steven 1153
Bacialli, S. 351
Badenoch, J. 1303
Baek, S. M. 1081

233

Shandler, Michael 683
Shandler, Nina 683
Sharma, Chand 1056
Sharma, R. V. 1201
Shaw, C. P. 706
Shaw, George Bernard 271
Shaw, Jane 716
Sheldon, Charles M. 272
Shelley, Percy Bysshe
36, 37, 38
Shelton, Herbert McGolphin
634
Sheraton, Mimi 560
Sherman, Carl 635
Shimoda, Naomi 1235
Shipley, K. 1356
Shiramizu, Michiko 1410
Shorr, Ivy 747
Short, J. Gordon 485
Short, M. D. 1131
Shriver, Nellie 486, 873
Shubik, P. 992
Shukla, R. C. 1373
Shull, M. W. 1210, 1211,
1212
Shulman, Martha 487
Shun, Duk Jhe 1290
Shupper, Frances 273
Shurtleff, William 684,
685, 686, 687, 688,
689, 690, 1291
Siderits, M. A. 874
Silberfeld, Michel 1177
Simkowitz, Howie 748
Simons, L. A. 959
Simons, Madeleine A. 274
Simoons, Frederick J.
275, 488, 489
Simross, Lynn 490
Sims, Laura S. 491
Sinclair, H. M. 790, 1303
Sinclair, Upton 276, 277,
278
Singer, Peter 800, 853,
875, 876, 877, 878, 879
Singh, Dharm V. 1048
Singh, H. D. 1381

Singh, Kartar 691
Singh, S. P. 1316, 1392
Singhal, Bhim S. 1247
Sircar, B. C. Rai 73
Sisodia, A. K. 1392
Sköldstam, Lars 1307,
1393
Shukla, R. C. 1087
Skuratowicz, Paula 659
Slavkin, Harold C. 1109
Sloan, A. Elizabeth 680
Smith, A. D. M. 1292
Smith, Althea 492
Smith, E. B. 712
Smith, Elizabeth 1094
Smith, Elizabeth B. 636
Smith, J. C., Jr. 1324,
1368
Smith, J. Cecil, Jr.
1322, 1323
Smith, J. W. 1027
Smith, John Clark 493
Smith, Nathan 585
Smith, R. 1158
Smith, S. 1004
Smith, Scott 494
Smith, Scott S. 495
Smith, Torney 496
Smith-Barbaro, Peggy
1370
Snellman, Teo 497
Snyder, Jean 498
Soares, Ana Maria 909
Society for Animal Rights
880
Sokolov, Raymond A. 499
Sonken, Lori 500, 501,
502
Sonnenberg, L. 914
Sonnenberg, Lydia 637,
638
Sonnenberg, Lydia M. 661
Southgate, D. A. T. 1320
Spady, Donald 1208
Speed, I. 1301
Spingarn, Neil E. 1005
Spinks, T. 1131

SUBJECT INDEX

Absorption
    iron 1386
    vitamin B12 1151, 1242, 1243, 1247, 1256, 1281
Adolescents 174, 175, 353, 418, 434, 502, 937, 956, 1233;
    see also New Vegetarianism; Young Adults
Adsorption of bile acids 1066
Aesthetics 266, 305, 480
Aggression 57, 254
Aging 495; see also Elderly; Longevity
Ahimsa 108, 887, 888
Airola, Paavo 531
Albumin 17, 693, 1390
Alcoholic beverages 42, 129, 144, 243, 363, 462, 951,
    1019, 1336, 1358
Alcoholism 10, 14, 16, 160
Alcott, William Andrus 205, 558
Algae 422
Allegorical works 28, 45, 798, 800, 816
Allergies 693, 1335
Almanac, vegetarian 7
Altitude 919
American Association for the Advancement of Science
    (AAAS) 481
American Meat Institute 760
American National Cattlemen's Association 759
American Vegan Society 397
American Vegetarian Society 42
American Vegetarians 486
Amino acids 601, 1118, 1122
    production of 783
    in vegan diets 131, 185
    see also Protein
Amylase, serum 1329
Anatomy 1, 19, 27, 58, 96, 101; see also Physiology
Andes, Peruvian 1125

1366
DMH   see   1, 2 dimethyl-hydrazine
DMNA see   N-nitroso-dimethylamine
Dogfighting 856
Drug users 1222, 1232
Drugs
    residues, in animal products 477, 795, 1361, 1401,
        1411
    in livestock production 853
    see also Diethylstilbestrol
Dutch, works in 130, 136, 419, 518, 881, 1236, 1402
Dutch Vegetarian Society 89

Ecology 98, 232, 331, 347, 377, 403, 413, 440, 444, 467,
        506, 538, 762, 764, 769, 773, 774, 777, 779, 781,
        784, 786, 787, 796, 797
Economics 1, 5, 19, 22, 38, 48, 80, 90, 91, 98, 158,
        159, 204, 230, 232, 233, 236, 266, 268, 305, 314,
        347, 356, 379, 403, 409, 440, 444, 467, 480, 482,
        506, 538, 619, 673, 679, 757, 761, 762, 763, 764,
        766, 767, 769, 771, 774, 776, 777, 778, 779, 783,
        785, 787, 788, 790, 792, 793, 797, 858, 1268,
        1273, 1298
Educational materials 720, 721, 722, 723, 724, 725, 726,
        727, 728, 729, 730, 731, 732, 733, 736, 744, 745,
        749; see also Audio-visual materials
EEG   see   Electroencephalogram
Ehret's Mucusless Diet Healing System 149, 1227
Elderly 285, 524, 632, 1260
    vegetarian diets for 133, 613, 649
    studies of 174, 910, 911, 944, 1096, 1338
    see also Osteoporosis
Electrocardiograph 948, 1376
Electroencephalogram 1267, 1292, 1300
Electrolytes 1315
Eleusine coracana 206, 295
Endurance 17, 60, 102, 154, 155, 156, 190, 197, 227, 248,
        267, 313, 567-588; see also Athletics
England, vegetarian movement in 13, 24, 194, 287, 290,
        469, 476
Entertainment industry, use of animals in 856
Environment see Ecology
Epiphyseal fusion 1107
Ergographic studies, of vegetarians 154, 155, 156, 197,
        267, 313; see also Athletics
Escherichia coli 1077

Essenes 803, 882
Esters, cholesterol 944
Estrogen
plasma 1391
urinary 982
Ethics 1, 3, 4, 5, 15, 19, 22, 34, 35, 43, 54, 63, 76,
119, 126, 127, 144, 158, 164, 166, 212, 213, 218,
228, 230, 231, 236, 237, 266, 305, 312, 318, 324,
347, 369, 379, 403, 420, 428, 440, 458, 463,
467, 480, 491, 494, 509, 523, 538, 608, 743, 750,
786, 798, 800, 801, 805, 806, 807, 813, 814, 816,
817, 818, 824, 825, 827, 828, 830, 831, 832, 833,
834, 835, 836, 838, 840, 842, 843, 844, 845, 846,
850, 851, 852, 853, 854, 856, 858, 868, 869, 873,
875, 880, 889, 1298; see also Morality
Exhaustion
nervous 129
physical 154, 267
Extraversion 1176

Factor II 935
Factory farming 468, 771, 801, 802, 813, 821, 822, 823,
826, 833, 834, 839, 842, 846, 851, 852, 853, 857,
859, 860, 863, 871, 875, 884, 930, 931; see also
Livestock Production
Fad diets see Food Fads
Famine 159, 204, 772
The Farm (Summertown, Tennessee) 322, 393, 652, 1236,
1258, 1278
Fashion, use of animals in 33, 119, 743, 801
Fasting 149, 276, 277, 321, 401, 519, 634, 1104, 1105,
1265, 1306, 1307, 1357, 1393
Fat, dietary 933, 934, 1010, 1011, 1013, 1021, 1023, 1024,
1052, 1054, 1056, 1057, 1060, 1195, 1215, 1391; see
also Fatty Acids
Fat, saturated 82, 202, 217, 283, 289, 415, 912, 946,
953, 972, 975, 1027, 1031, 1044, 1048, 1055, 1058,
1062
Fatigue 154, 267
Fatty acids 944, 1266, 1311
dietary 936, 1351
esterified 925
free 943
polyunsaturated 936, 963
long-chain 1387, 1388
short-chain 1248

Hydrocarbons 971
    polynuclear 991, 992
Hydroxocobalamin 1405
Hydroxylation, vitamin D 1154
Hydroxysteroid dehydrogenase, fecal 1045
Hyperglycemia 1359
Hyperlipidemia 1288, 1289
Hyperlipoproteinemia 922
Hypertension 919, 922, 927, 939, 950
Hypocalcemia 1164

Ileostomates 1084
Immune status 979
Infants 222, 250, 262, 646, 648, 649, 650, 654, 657, 660,
    661, 662, 663, 1282-1215
    vegan 1238, 1255, 1257, 1258, 1261, 1262, 1269,
        1280, 1282, 1284, 1285, 1294, 1301, 1304, 222,
        651, 652, 653
Inflammation, serous 208
Information sources 463, 631, 651, 653, 730-751
    vegan 734, 735
Institutional food service see Food service, institutional
Intelligence quotient of vegetarian children 1192
Intemperance 10, 14, 16
Intensive farming see Factory farming
Intestinal microflora 1015, 1016, 1025, 1026, 1030, 1034,
        1035, 1041, 1042, 1047, 1053, 1058, 1059, 1070,
        1071, 1075, 1132, 1239
Intoxicants 811; see also Alcoholic beverages
I. Q. see Intelligence quotient
Iron 900, 1093, 1138, 1196, 1197, 1220, 1245, 1347, 1386
Iron binding capacity 896, 1245
Ischemic heart disease 1251, 1283, 1289; see also Cardio-
        vascular disease
Israeli Vegetarians' Association 454
Italian, works in 285, 402

Jacobs, Andrew 539
Jacobsen, Michael 760
Jainism 549
Japan 319, 788
Japanese, works in 1378
Jewish literature 196
Jewish vegetarianism 454, 804, 808, 830, 831, 883, 1304
Jogging see Running

Jones, Susan Smith   496
Jowar   295

Kansas   193, 548
Kant, Immanuel   861, 862, 865
Kayser-Fleischer rings   1349
Kellogg, John Harvey   103
Kidney stones   1128
Kidneys   1364
    and high-protein diets   150, 1113, 1128, 1334
Kokoh   1207
Kook, Yitzchak Hacohen, Rabbi   830
Koreans   947, 948
Kosher foods   863
Krishna Consciousness   1227, 1228
Kroc, Ray   465

Labeling, of foods   415, 758
Laboratory animals   501, 801, 856, 875
Lactation, extended   1162, 1167
Lactobacillus acidophilus   1075
Latto, Gordon   362
LCPFA   see   Long-chain polyunsaturated fatty acids
Leachman, Cloris   361, 362
Leanness in vegetarian children   1191, 1193, 1211; see also
    Body weight; Obesity
Left-handedness   1170, 1179
Legumes, amino acid production by   783
Length of life   see   Longevity
Leprosy   122, 1377, 1378
Lesser-developed countries   see   Economics; Food supply;
    Third World
Linoleic acid   1248
Linolenic acid   1248
Lipids   945, 950, 1266, 1369
    plasma   922, 943, 958, 1040, 1248
    serum   908, 928, 932, 941, 947, 948, 964, 1195
    structural   930, 931
Lipoproteins   922, 928, 942, 958, 1040, 1236, 1241
    alpha-beta ratio   928
    beta   942
    high-density   938, 958
    low-density   958
Literary works on vegetarian and animal rights   27, 28, 29,
    30, 31, 32, 38, 45, 158, 237, 503, 800, 820, 840

Plants, destruction of 310, 819, 837, 843, 885; see also
    Fruitarian diet
Plato 886
Poetry, vegetarian 503, 820
Polio 1313
Politics 1, 38, 159, 443, 454, 457, 467, 475, 500, 501,
    539, 758, 759, 760, 765, 789, 793, 794, 795, 852,
    853; see also Hearings, Congressional (U. S.)
Pollution 773, 777, 781, 791, 27
Polychlorinated biphenyls 1204
Polyps, intestinal 1023
Popularity of vegetarianism 55, 334, 347, 357, 365, 408,
    412, 433, 436, 440, 441, 617
Porphyry 881
Portuguese, works in 374, 445, 909, 1383, 1384, 1385
Position papers on vegetarian diet 752-756
Post, C. W. 103
Poultry production 833, 839, 875
Pregnancy 174, 175, 645, 547, 649, 652, 655, 656, 1156,
    1364, 1373
    and glycosuria 74
    and vegan diet 222, 346, 645, 1295
Primal scene 1172
Princeton University 700
Prolactin 983, 1012
Proteid see Protein
Protein 120, 131, 133, 136, 150, 186, 191, 257, 283, 303,
    383, 422, 474, 586, 589, 596, 600, 601, 606, 639,
    658, 674, 678, 680, 681, 765, 907, 911, 1110-1130,
    1197, 1201, 1390, 934, 1347
    alfa amino 1197
    animal 953, 1009, 1011, 1058, 1113, 1128, 1334
    combining see Proteins, complementary
    diets high in 111, 120, 150, 753, 1027, 1035, 1055,
    1123, 1128
    diets low in 186, 191, 283, 568, 1128, 1265
    plant 229, 257, 763, 764, 768, 780, 782, 797, 926,
    953, 1110, 1111, 1115, 1117, 1120, 1126, 1127,
    1130; see also Soybean foods; Textured vegetable pro-
    tein
    plasma 133
    in vegan diets 131, 136, 186, 1118
    requirements of 111, 120, 186, 288, 779, 1111, 1119,
    1188
    see also Nitrogen balance
Proteins, complementary 464, 534, 589, 601, 606, 614,
    639, 644, 657, 769, 779, 1090, 1129

11034

DATE			